The Yellow Duster Sisters

The Yellow Duster Sisters

A Wartime Childhood

SUSAN KENNAWAY

B L O O M S B U R Y
LONDON · BERLIN · NEW YORK · SYDNEY

First published in Great Britain 2011

Copyright © 2011 by M. St J. H. Kennaway 2011

Photographs reproduced in this book are from the author's own collection

The moral right of the author has been asserted

Bloomsbury Publishing Plc
36 Soho Square
London W1D 3QY

www.bloomsbury.com

Bloomsbury Publishing, London, Berlin, New York and Sydney

A CIP catalogue record for this book is available from the British Library

ISBN 978 1 4088 1210 5

10 9 8 7 6 5 4 3 2 1

Typeset by Hewer Text UK Ltd, Edinburgh

Printed in Great Britain by Clays Ltd, St Ives plc

Mixed Sources
Product group from well-managed
forests and other controlled sources
www.fsc.org Cert no. SGS-COC-2061
© 1996 Forest Stewardship Council
FSC

This book is dedicated to the Polish Forces in Britain during the Second World War.

For my sister Gyll (d. 1993) and her grandchildren,
Nick, Miranda, Abigail, Dominic, Tristan, Barnaby,
Charlie, Georgia, Will and Daisy, and her great
grandchildren, Tabitha, Verity and Megan.

Also for my grandchildren, Jack, Alexander,
Rose, Dylan, Ella, James, Edward and Katie,
and my great granddaughter Raphaella,
not forgetting Mavis and Puffy.

Endless thanks to Stanley, my husband, for help
with so many things (especially the computer!),
and to Roman Komorowski and Jean Singleton.

Also a big thank you to Alexandra Pringle who
found me and to her wonderfully patient and
helpful team at Bloomsbury, especially Anna
Simpson and Caroline Knight.

PROLOGUE

Our chauffeur East (I was never told his first name and never thought to ask) drove the big Humber slowly down Watford High Street. Mummy sat next to him, wearing a small felt hat with perky wings on each side, set close to her head. She looked like a lost bird about to take flight. I sat in the back seat with my sister Gyll, peering through the windows at the houses as we drove past them, the familiar buildings receding in the distance as we drove off to Liverpool Docks, where the ship awaited us.

As we passed the pond at the top of the road I asked, 'Mummy, what are those men doing?'

'Filling sandbags, darling.'

'Why?'

'To make the buildings safe.'

'Why?'

'Well, like at the Round House, when Daddy tried to stop the Thames coming in to the cottage from under the door. You remember, when it flooded.'

'But there isn't a river here. Why are they doing it here?'

She gave up at that point. I suppose she didn't want to talk about bombs. I knew about them, of course, but bombs in Watford, in the High Street? I could not understand it.

I couldn't see how sand could keep the high street safe from water and the men looked tired filling the hessian sacks. But I did love the white tape fixed to the shop windows, all criss-cross, like a sort of Christmas decoration, even though it was the summer. Still only July, it was just eight days after my tenth birthday.

Mummy did not seem to be inclined to answer any more questions, so we watched while the sand bags were hauled into neat walls outside the bank and Sainsbury's and as far as our own shop front.

In the spacious rear of the car, facing the mahogany-veneered fold-up tables that concealed a cocktail cabinet, my sister Gyll was crying yet once again. She made a frightful noise. Mummy turned her head towards her elder daughter and sighed with a hint of exasperation. Gyll did cry rather a lot anyway, but just now she had the perfect excuse. A dramatic occasion as good as this was too good to miss. Sometimes in the past, her tears had become such a waterfall that I felt that I should be part of the tragedy too, though I have to admit that at the naive age of just ten I did not always understand what exactly we were supposed to be so desolate about.

As you will shortly see, I am not a sentimental sort of person; if I had indulged in feeling sorry for myself I would have been finished long ago and, as it turned out, once we arrived in Africa no one, but no one was allowed to give in to self-pity or permitted any sign of weakness. It simply wasn't done.

With the doubtful benefits of age and the obvious help of hindsight and experience, I can write my war story blending the olive oil of a trusting, rather molly-coddled child and with the vinegar (balsamic of course, it's just that bit more refined) of adult knowledge.

I had thought that what happened to my sister and me was just something you had to get over, not dwell upon or use as an excuse for special understanding. No one wanted to be accused of being gutless or cowardly. But with the reminders of anniversaries of the beginning or ending of the War, or the bombing of Pearl Harbor, I am reminded that the War affected us at home too, that one and a half million children were taken from their homes to 'places of safety', and that these children, now grown old, will soon disappear, will die. Their stories will be as lost as the luggage labels that were tied round their necks, noting their names and to which school they went, while they clasped their gas-masks and their little attaché cases close to them. Duly processed, they climbed, bewildered and sobbing, into the trains that were to take them away from their families – and to where?

On arrival deep in the countryside away from cities at risk of bombing, each child would be paraded in village halls all over the country, like a slave in a market, to be picked over and chosen or rejected by prospective foster-parents. This lad might help on the farm, that young girl could become a maid of all work.

It was mandatory for any household with any spare space to take an evacuee; the penalty for refusing was a big fine. The foster parents were paid ten and six pence a week for each child, which today would be the equivalent of about twelve pounds. Regrettably – no, horrendously – some children were very badly treated and often brothers and sisters as young as three or four were parted from each other and sent to different homes. I was evacuated too, and to a place much further away than most evacuees travelled, but at least Gyll and I had each other.

Other, more fortunate, evacuees were cherished and some even wanted to stay on in their new homes after the war, their country families coming to love and educate them as they would their own. Who can blame those lucky children for not wanting to go back to London? They had almost forgotten their parents and having finally come to terms with one severance from all things familiar, why go through it again?

Many of the evacuees came back to their pre-war homes as strangers, and to a hungry London that had been bombed and blitzed, clutching their ration books that entitled them to one egg every week, and to two ounces of meat and butter weekly. In the country there had been chickens and eggs and hay and flowers.

What sort of people could have come up with such an ill-conceived plan as to separate children from their families like this? Well, people like my parents, I suppose, who thought safety came first. Perhaps it was to preserve a generation of children who could grow up and fight another war, for England, Home and Beauty. Many motives, many mistakes and some love.

Can anyone be in the least surprised at the people we children became? Remote, fearful of separation, suspicious of close relationships? Cautious, mistrusting and, sometimes, cold as ice? Did that really happen to us? Were we really part of the exodus? Was that really me? My sister and me? Well, yes.

BEGINNING

I

I had a sister. Her name was Gyll. She bossed me about a good deal, but as she was twenty-two months older than me she had age and size on her side. While Gyll was bright as a berry, rosy-cheeked and with dark curly hair, I resembled a milky junket. I remember Mummy's friends comparing our looks, and while they had many words of praise for Gyll, they pursed their lips unhappily when they gazed on me, sometimes with a curious sadness or despair as if I were not expected to see another summer, not that there was anything otherwise wrong with me. We had a brother, Dick, five years older than me and away at school. He didn't have much time for us girls anyway.

Gyll was very keen on acting. She normally spoke with quite a pronounced stutter, a bit like Mummy, who had learnt to overcome that problem by simply leaving out the difficult letters. She was married to my father, 'Ertram Eric, as Joan Edith 'Arbara. He was, in fact, generally called Eric by my mother and his friends, but not evidently by an ardent Mollie Clancy, who wrote him passionate love letters headed 'My darling Bertrand'. These he left, proudly and conveniently in an obvious place on a shelf in the library. You could hardly miss the antique-bound book, inside of which he had left the badly written outpourings of Mollie's heart. How awful for Mummy, we thought as we grew up, to have this old love affair thrust under her nose, but I'm not sure that she really cared because it made him look a right old fool. Perhaps she even had a bit of a laugh. I hope so.

Being a Great Actress, Gyll never stuttered when she trod the boards. She made up plays, the plots of which she had pinched from unsuitable novels, which she plucked from the bookcases and read, hidden, behind the sofa. (I remember one with the unforgettable title of *The Knife Behind the Curtain*.)

Careless of any sort of plot, she aimed with artistic abandon to include a couple of tragic deathbed scenes or good bloody murders. Mummy paled when she found the secreted books that Gyll had been reading, and confiscated them, but not before her elder daughter had discovered the joy of fiction and, evidently, of drama.

The stage was generally set in the hall that lay between the kitchen quarters and the sitting room. For two or three days before the theatrical event was to take place, Gyll would place, strategically, cardboard notices, complete with arrows, saying 'This way to the Sow'. Mummy and Daddy laughed but I didn't know why.

We had a lot of shows. Gyll always took the lead; I always played the dog's-body. Even when we had the Grand Pageant at school, in a wet field on a cold day, Gyll had been chosen to play King Alfred the Great, with fine stirring lines, while I was given the part of Boadicea, my armour made of silver-paper all squashed as we sheltered from the rain under a not-quite-large-enough oak tree, while I repeated and repeated to myself my only lines, 'Though I am but a woman, I too have done my duty'. When the moment came, I said 'butter woman', and Gyll giggled.

Now I sat beside her, clutching my big doll Joan, called after Mummy, the best person I knew. My doll had a moonish face and a very unfortunate hole in the top of her head where my older brother Dick had driven a knitting needle through the top of her poor large hairless skull. It was not his only beastly attempt to kill her. He had, on several occasions, hanged her from a branch of a silver-birch tree in the quiet corner of the garden, the noose pulled tightly round her fat neck, the knotting fixed to a branch too high for me to be able to reach and rescue her.

In that same bosky patch, under the cool earth where I used to watch Mummy planting crocus bulbs (only to be followed by the squirrels who immediately dug them up and presumably ate them), also lay my beautiful wooden sewing box. It had been a very special present from my godmother. This casket, lined so divinely with brilliant orange satin, with little compartments for thimble and thread, buttons, hooks and eyes and reels of cotton, had been commandeered by my brother on one never-to-be-forgotten morning for the burial of a dead starling that the cat had been found throwing about in the air, as if willing it, through an imitation of flight, back to life to be tortured yet once again. Such a purpose-built coffin was not likely to be overlooked, even though I tearfully suggested that a shortbread tin would serve the purpose equally well. My brother won the day then, as he always did.

Boys, it seemed to me, had a pretty good time all around. Only a couple of years previously Gyll and I had been ousted from home to spend Christmas at the Bushey Park Hotel with our governess, because Dick was in quarantine for infantile paralysis, an illness that is now usually known as polio. Mummy and Daddy also quarantined themselves, since they did not visit us even on Christmas Day. Gyll and I worried a little about that – we had always thought infantile paralysis was something that only affected children. Were they really in mortal danger or were we? We never knew.

At the outbreak of the war in September 1939, I had been packed off to join Gyll at her boarding school, Gardenhurst, at Burnham-on-Sea in Somerset. Gyll had been dispatched a term before to live by the sea. Gyll suffered from chronic catarrh, and cold, salty sea air was thought to be a good remedy. Well, it was either a choice of sea air or being hanged upside down by her feet, a novel theory suggested by the family doctor, to cure her ailment (which in the end turned out to be an allergy to dog hair. Goodbye Sally, the cocker spaniel, when this was discovered). Mummy, however, did not much like the idea of hanging Gyll, so banishment it was. Now I was to join her. I was quite looking forward to it.

We were not driven down to Burnham-on-Sea by East. In fact, my uncle Stuart, Daddy's brother, drove us and a more bizarre choice of driver could hardly have been made by our parents, who, for one reason or another, did not accompany us. Maybe Uncle Stuart had plenty of petrol, which was already in short supply; maybe he was going to visit his son who lived in Somerset. He intimidated me, because he was big and so unlike Daddy, but he treated Gyll and me as if we were adults and, some years later, charmingly took the time and trouble to explain abstract art to me. He was an inspired artist (a Royal Academician), an enthusiastic cricketer, playing for his county, and, above all, a very serious drinker.

On the way down to Burnham-on-Sea I remember feeling rather queasy after he had encouraged me to drink a second beer, which I was too scared to refuse, while pausing at one of the pubs on the way. Gyll was wobbling about a bit too. By the time we arrived at the school, I felt distinctly ill. I kept the information to myself as I did not want Gyll, or any of the other girls, to brand me as 'homesick', which I thought was a shaming sign of weakness. No one had explained to me that homesickness was an emotional, not a physical, response to being away from home. I dreaded that the other girls should think that I was being a sissy.

When I eventually threw up all over the dormitory floor, the matron, Miss Harris, was unexpectedly sympathetic. She dried my tears of humiliation and I loved her at once and went on loving her even when she had to tweeze painful splinters from my bottom after sliding on a rough wooden floor. Woollen knickers were not as tough as one might have expected. Or hoped.

That first night at school I said my prayers as I always did. I would begin with 'God Bless Mummy and Daddy' and always end with 'and please, God, don't let there be a fire in the night'.

We already knew about fire. In 1935, four years earlier, Mummy's beautiful black lace and taffeta dress had caught alight as she passed the fireplace in our dining room. As the flames engulfed her, her guests were paralysed with shock. She staggered into the hall, and laid herself on the rug and rolled over to kill the flames.

She was gone from us for two years. She was placed in the hands of the pioneering plastic surgeons Sir Archibald McIndoe and Sir Harold Gillies, as she needed a lot of skin grafts. The one extraordinary thing she had done, in those terrible moments of hell, was to cover her face with her hands while the flames leapt and licked her tender body as the material of her dress melted into her skin. The surgeons were soon to practise their plastic surgery skills on the young airmen, victims of war, burnt to the edge of death (like Mummy), as they fought the German Luftwaffe in the skies above Britain. These dauntless men were part of the Guinea Pig Club, so called as there was still much experimentation to be done in the healing and building of new faces and bodies. I think Mummy should have been asked to be an honorary member.

Of course, Gyll and I were not told of this terrible accident. We were told that she had gone to Germany to look after a sick friend and we were at once sent away to Bexhill-on-Sea, where my aunt Blanche ran a guesthouse. Our cousins Diana and Victoria were our new companions. We wondered why Mummy's sick friend took precedence over us for so many months, but we only found out the truth when we came back to Watford after a year, and met up with our school friend, Michael Gardner, with whom we shared a laurel hedge between our gardens. Sitting crouched in the gloom, amongst the dark damp roots and leaves, Michael told us of the fire. We faced Daddy with the fact that we knew what had happened, and his initial reaction was to be terribly angry with us, perhaps because, strangely, he needed to keep her pain to himself. Then he forbade us to rendezvous ever again with Michael and the worms in the hedge.

But we begged and badgered him to let us see her and he finally relented. She was by this time in a nursing home in Watford. We were totally unprepared for what we saw. Firstly there were long blankets suspended round the bed, like the curtains on a four-poster. Within, Mummy was suspended by slings round her back, her arms and legs hoisted by straps to the frame that held the curtains, unable to turn her head or to move. I learnt later that she was the first person to have survived such burns.

I can remember seeing her arm attached by stitches to her tummy in order to transfer and grow the skin from one to the other. Her arm had been fried almost to the bone but the operation worked and after a couple of years, although you could still see the differently coloured skin – tummy skin is paler than that of the arm – and although it was a different shape, she could use her arm almost normally.

When finally she came home, she was never the same. Maybe the terrible burning of her body, her poor sad body, had separated her from us, but she had never really been there before. She had always found it difficult to communicate her feelings, to touch and to hold and to cuddle, even before the fire. Now the painkillers and the sleeping pills numbed her. She had always been a quiet person; now she was pretty well absent altogether.

Our family wasn't perfect, but we were cherished and a little spoilt, especially by Alice, our pretty, cuddly nanny, who Mummy and Daddy had brought home with them from Switzerland, like a box of the most wonderfully delicious and constantly replenished chocolates.

Alice and her sister Margaret (Greta when she was at home in Switzerland) were the daughters of the hotel keeper in Wengen, where Mummy and Daddy stayed when they went skiing every winter. Gyll and I were wildly jealous when they took Dick with them, but luckily he broke his leg. We couldn't help rejoicing, just a little.

Alice had none of the aloof manners of the trained English nannies of the time. She was totally spontaneous, giggling, saying 'Eeeeeee Susie', tickling us in the ribs to make us laugh and devoted herself, with happiness, to our entire day and more. She had arrived in our household just before I made my own appearance, and was the first person to hold the squalling baby – me.

Perhaps we were more protected than our neighbours' children and probably it could be said that we were pampered, but Mummy was always so afraid for our safety, that there might be an accident (there had been) and that more disasters and unhappiness lay ahead (they did) but not in the way that she had ever imagined. Our parents were a little distant as was the way with so many families, seventy-odd years ago. None of the important decisions about our lives were ever discussed with us; we just did what we were told. We lived in an age when it simply was not done to explain things – events, the death of a sparrow, the severing of an Achilles tendon (Dick's naughty friend from his prep school in Watford, who should not have been stamping out the glass in our cucumber frame), the loss of our dog Sally – to children, or to ask them for their opinions. They may have believed that if we thought too long and too hard about the troubles ahead, our very small brains would be stressed and damaged. They believed for instance that you should never ask a child if they would like cereal or an egg for breakfast, or if they would prefer to wear a cardigan or a blazer. You ate what you were given, wore what was already planned for you, and if a grown-up strayed from this approach, they were said to be making a rod for their own backs. Consequently, we never saw any broken backs, not at that time anyway.

I remember that summer of 1939 we spent together as a family at the Round House. We were perfectly happy, perfectly innocent of what was to come, of the shadow of impending war that would force us apart and turn all of us – Daddy, Mummy, Dick, Gyll and me – into different people.

2

August 1939

It is too easy to remember that in our childhoods the summers were always hot, that it never rained, that there were jam tarts for tea every day. There were never any pebbles on the beach, just lovely silvery sands, and we never felt the cold or needed to put on a cardigan. We remember only that we had a wonderful carefree time and that we were secure in the knowledge and warmth of our parents' love.

We were on a family holiday in Gloucestershire. Actually quite a big family as we joined up with our cousins who had cottages in and around Lechlade, Fairford and Kempsford.

We were the Sarson, Thomas and Edmonds families and together made up a tribe of eighteen children. Big Desmond was the eldest, the leader, but at twenty definitely no longer a child. I admired his strong thighs, which I thought were a bit like mine. Desmond's little sister Hilary was quite a leader too. She had enviable long fair hair, long slim legs and the bluest of eyes.

Our family stayed at the Round House, which had belonged to my grandfather who had been born nearby and whose roots were firmly planted in Gloucestershire. There was a cottage built next to a solid, three-storey tower, which perched on the brink of the River Thames about half a mile up the towpath from Lechlade, or an exciting ride in the car across the water meadows. The tower was the ancient home of the lock-keepers who had looked after the entrance to the Thames Severn Canal at the highest navigable point of the river.

In another century, great horses with heavy hair-fringed hooves and massive buttocks and thighs would strain to pull the barges up to the lock and in his turn the keeper would strain and pull at the huge gates to allow the water to rush through so that there was a level stretch of canal for the boats to come to and fro from London to Bristol. Of course, I never saw the horses, they had long since gone, but I could imagine them, beautiful and slow-moving with their gypsy collars and dangling brasses.

The Round House, we were told, was built so there was no corner for the devil to hide in, since being a lock-keeper was a lonely, dangerous job. The cottage at the side was formerly the forge, where the horses would have been shod on their long journeys along the towpaths.

It was possible to lean out of the bedroom window and drop a fishing line into the greenish water that rushed round the stone foundations, not that we ever caught anything living, just weeds and twigs, which was a little disappointing. At the side of the cottage, fingers of willow swept the water and kingfishers balanced on the swaying branches. They hiccupped down their fishy catches, which wriggled less and less with each gulp, until quite vanished down their throats. The feathers on the back of the kingfishers' heads would rise in wet, spiky crests each time they swallowed.

The smooth green grass of the water meadows reached down to the very edge of the river, grazed short and clean by the cows, of which I was terrified. They lined the banks opposite the cottage, peering about themselves, mooing serenely and going down to drink where the winter flood water had dragged the grass and earth away, leaving shallow strands of sand and gravel. The cows may have seemed placid enough, but there was always the chance that they might suddenly stampede and chase us all over the fields.

In spring we would see mile upon mile of golden-yellow buttercups, which, we told each other, turned the cows' butter to the same brilliant colour. There were endless drifts of spotted snakeshead fritillaries in the fields above the cottage and hundreds and thousands (or so it seemed to us) of baby frogs, not much bigger than peas, everywhere. They were in the grass, squashed in the roads and we even found them in the house. We became used to scooping them up and releasing them into the long grass that fringed the canal.

We were never allowed to swim in the Thames as it flowed too swiftly. Instead, to cool off we jumped into the little tributary, the Coln, which joined the big river just by the Round House. Up-field, there were lovely deep clear pools where we plunged, shrieking, into the chill, fizzy water, disturbing the startled trout. The Coln was cold and sparkled like diamonds.

There was another, more sinister waterway. In the olden days, when nature conservation was of no consequence since the countryside was such an abundant paradise of wild flowers and birds, the canal had been cut, slicing through the water meadows. Now long since out of use, it had an air of menace, the water murky and treacherous, bound by reeds, strangling weeds and sludge. Huge ugly pike lurked in the shade of the stone bridge by the lock, ready to seize a finger or a toe were we to venture too close, the grown-ups warned.

But in its heyday, Daddy told us with pride, an uncle of his who owned a barge had had a dispute with the canal company. In a fit of temper he had pulled his barge, full of dry cement, into one of the many tunnels that ran the length of the canal from the river Thames down to the estuary of the River Severn. It was, I believe, in the long tunnel at Sapperton that he chose to scuttle his boat. I guess the lock-keepers had a decent few days off while the owners nursed their headaches and pondered on how best to move the blockage.

The Thames Conservancy Bridge was painted a pale grey. It joined the far side of the river from the cottage with the path that ran alongside the sitting room.

The Round House itself had very thick stone walls, through which ran an internal staircase. But devils there must have been, according to Daddy's scary stories of ghosts and lost loves, of drownings and unearthly screams, which could be heard on stormy nights echoing from the depths of the nearby lock.

In the evenings, once it had grown a bit too chilly to linger outdoors any longer, we would pile into the main room, low-beamed and with coarse wooden floors; no carpets because the cottage flooded in the winters. Even sandbags, with which we were to become familiar, did not help. We'd settle on any spare chair, or budge-up together near the fire, which gave the only light in the room until the paraffin lamps were lit, and play word games ('Some say this and some say that but I say Mr Greencap'), tell poems, stories and jokes.

Then while Mummy and our aunts prepared supper next door, and the men sipped their cocktails in the twilight outside, Daddy would pull up a chair to the chimney, prop his feet against the stone hearth, a drink in one hand and a cigarette in the other, and start to entertain us.

'Uncle Eric, tell us the story about the lock-keeper and his dog.'

'No, no, Daddy, the one about the bottomless well, please, please.'

'Oh, can't we have the one about the drownings?'

'The drownings, shall it be then?' he'd say, smiling rakishly at us.

And a dozen voices would yell, 'Oh, oh yes please.'

'Well,' Daddy would say, menacingly, lowering further his lazy eye, and taking a long considered pull at his cigarette. We would wriggle in uncontainable excitement. It was a familiar tale told and retold, embellished and adapted for each occasion. Our favourite was about the grizzled lock-keeper, and his comely, youthful son and a beautiful girl with whom the lad had fallen fatefully in love. Rapt, we could listen to this story time and time again.

The tale began with the lock-keeper's son helping a beautiful maiden when her boat became stuck in the reeds. He jumped in beside her and skilfully rowed her boat to the bank. There they gazed into each other's eyes and of course instantly fell in love. Then the girl would row up the river each day at sunset for a secret tryst with her lover but she would never tell him her name or where she came from. You could guess that something scary was about to happen, because he decided to follow her on foot along the towpath. But every time he did, she just vanished into the mists that hung low on the water. She disappeared from view just like that.

There would be a long pause from Daddy.

'Was it a dream, children?'

'No, no, not a dream,' we all screamed. 'Please go on.'

My father would look at his watch.

'Oh, whatever happened next? Oh, Uncle Eric, please finish the story,' one of my cousins would pipe up.

'What happened next,' my father would say with a

mischievous glint in his eye, 'was that it was time for supper.'

'Oh, please, please,' we chorused.

'Well, maybe just for five minutes,' he'd acquiesce, because I believe that even he wanted to know how it ended.

'Well, what actually happened next,' he would say slowly as he worked things out in his head, 'was what you might have expected. Well, wouldn't you have expected something really terrible to happen?

'It was a terrible stormy night and her lover was not waiting for her, as the young man always did, at their usual meeting place. She climbed out of the boat and began to search for him. All at once, the magically lovely ghostly girl appears on the hump-backed bridge and looking over the parapet sees her darling young love fighting to save the life of his old father who had stumbled and fallen into the devilish waters of the canal. She sees too that her young lover is losing the fight to save the helpless old man and is himself also drowning. She clasps her hands over her breasts and gazes up at the angry sky for a message, but, alas, there is none. She climbs to the top of the stone wall which runs the length of the bridge, and balancing for one second she tumbles into the eerie waters. As she falls you can hear her cry, "Darling, I love you. I love you for ever." '

'She jumped into the canal?' someone gulped.

'She *threw* herself in, to be with him in death as she had never been in life, to be in his deadly embrace,' Daddy was being his most dramatic.

'Oh Eric,' my mother would protest.

But he had never finished.

'And as she tumbled headlong after her lover she screamed a terrible scream, a terrible scream like the wind

21

and the rain and all the most dreadful things you ever heard. You can hear it to this very day if you go out on a dark night.'

'Eric, dear,' Mummy would intervene again, this time more firmly. 'Enough is enough.' She looked round at our frightened faces as we pleaded for more.

'Please finish the story,' we begged.

'You didn't say if they were drowned.'

'Were they?'

'Were there any . . . bodies?'

My father would look at his watch. This time he said, drily and slyly, 'Well actually not, because the boy and the old man didn't drown after all and no one ever found the girl, but that's another story.'

He would stand up.

We were always thunderstruck. Of course, we should have known better. That it wasn't really the end of the story, but then he never really finished any stories.

In the mornings, that summer in the country, we used to take a couple of flat-bottomed boats up the Coln. It was the greatest fun. We splashed in and out of the punts, jumping about the shallows where the cows came to drink. We pulled the boats upstream against the swift currents, ducking and diving from under the over-hanging bushes, some of which were very prickly, and where shadowy speckled trout flashed away, disturbed from basking in the cool, away from the bright sunlight.

At lunchtime our families would drive over the sun-dried water meadows, in a regal parade. They'd bring orange squash and both Marmite and jam sandwiches, apples and custard cream biscuits, which we would eat sitting around on the grass, giggling and joking and pushing each other about as if we were drunk. We messed about in the mud at the edge of the river, looking for snails and crayfish and other signs of watery life.

My brother Dick, together with Desmond and David, and the other older boy cousins, would stroll upstream to a shady spot to try their hand at fly-fishing for trout. No worms were allowed.

Daddy used to make his own dry flies with which he hoped to attract a hungry trout looking for a meal. The home-made flies darted across the water just like real ones, we thought.

On one particularly hot August day, Daddy came up with an ingenious method to catch a trout. He had caught a wasp that was buzzing around the picnic and had put it into a Bryant and May matchbox. By sliding the lid, just a little, enough for the wasp to begin to crawl out, Daddy was able to tie his fishing line round its middle. The wasp then flew off, a very tasty morsel for a passing fish. Alas, as Daddy cast the line across the water, the wasp battled its way back, flew round his head a couple of times as it could not get away and stung him on his nose. He looked angrily around at us, as we pointed and laughed.

'Look, just look what the wasp has done.'

Daddy did not laugh, especially as he guessed, quite rightly, that he had got what he deserved.

Even my mother laughed, albeit somewhat guiltily; I suspect that she too was a bit scared of him.

Daddy said, 'Time to be getting back anyway. Time for the news.'

We sighed. The grown-ups were always listening to the news on the wireless set.

'Come along, children, hop on,' which meant that it was time to go.

Gyll, Hilary, Anne and I, being 'only' girls and also the youngest of the bunch, had to leave the others, so that they could make their own way back downstream, dashing away in the punts, borne by the plunging, tumbling, current. Their yells of excitement echoed over the meadows.

Still, I did not really mind leaving them as we were allowed to ride on the massive mudguards and wide running boards of the lumbering black Humber. We would cling on like limpets, jumping off quickly so that we could be first to open or close the wide five-barred gates. We loved it.

Later in the afternoon Daddy took the car out several times, to drop our cousins off at Kempsford, Lechlade and Fairford.

'Oh Daddy, stop, p- please stop. Look in the field there.'

Gyll pointed to where the corn was being harvested, all gold and yellow and ripe. We clambered on to the low Cotswold-stone wall and pulled off our white cotton sun-hats to wave encouragement to some poor rabbits, who were trapped in the corn that still remained standing in a square in the middle of the field. The mechanical reaper gradually ate away at their hiding-place. As the harvester cut closer the rabbits would make a desperate bid to escape, while the farmer's son took pot shots with his gun.

> 'Run rabbit, run rabbit, run, run, run,
> Don't give the farmer his fun, fun, fun,
> He'll get by without his rabbit pie,
> So run rabbit, run rabbit, run, run, run.'

Then someone added, 'Don't give Herr Hitler his gun, gun, gun,' though I didn't quite know what was meant by that.

In the late afternoon we watched the midges and the

homeward-bound bees mingling with the flecks of corn that fluttered in the dusty shafts of sunlight. Everything around us buzzed and hummed with life. It was heaven. It was an idyllic childhood.

But even as we played, there was something a little uneasy in the air that wonderful summer. The grown-ups lingered by the wireless but, with smiling faces, would turn the sound down or completely off when we came tumbling into the cottage sitting room. There was definitely something odd going on, but we were not so interested; we were having such a jolly good time, the families all entwined together. What could be better? We didn't care about the wireless or the outside world. This was our universe.

It was the end of summer but the weather was still fine. Our parents made us a picnic to carry up the fields, but said that we must be back at three o'clock, and that we mustn't be late.

'Who has a watch?'

'I do,' one of us said.

'Well then, be good. See you at three, remember!'

So off we went while they went back into the cottage to listen to the endless news.

We crossed to the corner of the field, jumped over the stile and made our way, laughing and chatting and knocking about, until we all felt hungry and decided to have our picnic a bit early. After we had finished up all the crumbs, we decided to explore a bit further and then a bit further still. Eventually Dick asked, 'I say, what's the time?'

'Oh cripes, it's a quarter to three.'

'Blimey, we'll never get back in time.'

Swift turn, fast run, we weaved in and out of the

broken walls and straggly paths as if we were being hunted by savages. I had scratched my legs on the brambles and had a beastly stitch in my side. Hilary had a livid-looking blister on her foot as she was wearing her new plimsolls without socks.

'Golly gosh, I'm done for,' said Gyll, completely out of breath.

At last we could see the tall poplars that surrounded the cottage and then we saw our distraught parents. As we fell higgledy-piggledy over the stile, legs flying in all directions, we were all, without exception, given a good wallop on the bottom, even the eldest of us. As most of us had never been smacked before, we realised that something pretty awful was up. The girls were sobbing and the boys looked embarrassed. We had never seen our parents so cross. We were deeply ashamed.

'Where for God's sake have you *been*?' Uncle Harry bellowed. 'We have been waiting for you for hours. Where have you been?'

We stood around looking very contrite and trying to apologise but our parents wouldn't hear of it, they were all terribly, terribly angry,

'I simply can't trust you again,' said Daddy, with venom in his throat. We fidgeted about, scratching our legs and brushing off stray insects. None of us could understand just why they were so upset, but we did notice that the cars were, unexpectedly, loaded with our cases, ready for take-off.

Of course, they knew what we didn't; they had been tuning in again, to the wireless – and we had not. We did not know that *our* Prime Minister, Neville Chamberlain, had demanded that Germany should withdraw her troops from Poland, a country we had never heard of, and that since Herr Hitler had not commanded his troops to leave, that by 11.00 a.m. that morning, Britain had declared war on Germany. We did not know, in other words, that it was 3 September 1939, and that our world would never be the same again.

3

Once back in Watford, we restarted our lives just where we had left off before the holiday. But it wasn't quite the same. Once again, in the early evening, Daddy mixed Martini cocktails in the hall for Mummy, and I came down from the nursery to carry the tray to her. I was not able to resist dipping my finger into the frosted glass to give a twist to the little curl of lemon peel, although when I licked it, it always tasted quite disgusting. I couldn't imagine why she looked so pleased when I brought it to her, sitting there quietly waiting, surrounded by her knitting wools or the occasional book, smoking her endless Craven 'A' cigarettes, with the little black cat on the packet, with the slogan, 'So good for your throat'. (How could they?)

No matter how hard Mummy and Daddy tried to keep our lives on an even keel they had to consider how to follow the Government's stern warning that children in danger zones should be removed to places of safety. Gyll gleaned, using her brilliant latest detective technique – namely putting her ear to the door – that they had discussed sending us to our aunt in South Africa, which we could not believe to be true, especially as we had never met her. But if they had had plans, they had been thrown into disarray by the sinking of the *Athenia* and now their erstwhile muted voices rose as they tried to decide what to do. I was longing to hear what was being said but Gyll waved me away with dismissive hand signals.

When we went to bed that night we talked in whispers

about what might happen next. We decided to ask East, as neither Alice nor Margaret seemed right for the job. We did not usually speak to East, but this was important. Gyll went up to him, putting on an act of being coy and shy.

'Um, I s'pose you wouldn't know anything about something called the *Athenia*?'

'The *Athenia*? Whatever for? Why do you want to know about the *Athenia*, for goodness' sake, little girls like you? Why don't you go and ask your mummy?'

'Well we did, but she didn't know,' lied Gyll, with ease.

'Well, I wouldn't go botherin' with that sort of thing just now,' he said crossly. He gave us a 'goodbye-and-off-you-go' sort of smile, and carried on with his work.

Finally, Gyll made me go into the garden room and ask Mummy.

'The *Athenia*? Oh dear. What have you been hearing? You haven't been talking to that boy next door again? You know I don't like that.'

'No, no, Mummy, really. We just want to know . . .' Gyll ended uncertainly, because she could see that Mummy was beginning to cry.

At that moment, Alice put her head round the door to call us up for bedtime. We kissed Mummy and she said that she would come upstairs and tuck us in, as she always did. Upstairs in the night nursery, Daddy sat on my bed and told us yet another story of derring-do until Mummy appeared at the door. Her cigarette glowed in the dark and as she bent to kiss us goodnight we could smell her beautiful, expensive scent.

'Time to go now, Eric,' she would say. 'Goodnight Gylly-Flower, goodnight Susie-Pops. Sleep tight.'

'Goodnight, Mummy and Daddy, see you in the morning,' we chorused, and usually we would snuggle down to sleep. But not on this night. Gyll came over and climbed into my bed. We pulled the blankets over our heads so that our whispered conversations could not be heard.

'Do you think that there were refugees?' I asked Gyll. 'Because I heard Alice say that hundreds and thousands of children were drowned, but I didn't think it was about that boat.'

'Don't be stupid. There aren't hundreds and thousands of children in the whole world,' she replied with authority.

Actually, one hundred and twelve passengers and crew on the *Athenia* were drowned that day, among them children who were being evacuated to the United States.

'You know,' said Gyll, 'I don't think that they would ever send us away.'

Nothing more was said for quite a while, and soon Gyll and I forgot all about it.

It was Dick, home from school for the holiday, who took pleasure in telling us, finally, that we were to be sent away – for a jolly long time, he hoped. He too had been listening at doors.

It was the totally unexpected failure of the British Expeditionary Forces in Europe and the subsequent evacuation of the troops at Dunkirk that had sealed our fate. Mummy and Daddy were at last shocked into action. But although Mummy and Daddy were still not completely decided, Daddy at last explained to us that the Government thought it would be better if we left England for a little while, just until the war was over.

'Go away?' Gyll cried. 'What, really go away? Like Dick said? It's not fair!' And she started to cry.

Mummy intervened. 'Look darlings, I will be coming with you.' She did not of course add that she would not be staying long, but coming back to England and to Daddy and to Dick. Why didn't he have to go too? He was just a boy, not even fifteen yet, though his birthday would come soon.

'We already have places booked on a ship and if you don't go to Africa now, it might soon be too late,' Daddy said.

'But why?' Gyll asked.

'Look, it won't be for very long,' they reassured us, because the hateful Hun would be conquered in no time and then we could come home – and wouldn't that be lovely?

Dick gave a boyish little snigger in the background, because this was what he'd always wanted, no sisters.

'And what about Dick? Why doesn't he have to come? It isn't fair.'

Nobody explained why Dick should not be included.

Gyll's cry about the unfairness of it all had quite a lot to do with missing all that exciting raping and pillaging, though I had not the slightest idea what that actually meant. Dick, at the time, had looked at us scornfully and later, in a seemingly careless way, had left open one of his school books showing drawings of a battle between heavily bearded men in flowing capes and wielding frightening-looking knives, chopped limbs lying around, inert and bloodless on the sand. Did I detect the wobbly pen of my brother? Was this the place to which we were being sent?

The book lay open on the day-nursery table, and in a lofty way Dick explained to us that the illustrations depicted the Saxons and the Vikings, centuries before now, and the dreadful things they had done to the women and children, the sort of thing, he said, that the Hun would do to us if they invaded England – not that we understood what on earth he was talking about. Of course, the men, it was explained to me, by my superior brother, had sensibly escaped earlier, to form an army and fight the invaders.

Mummy said that she and Daddy had thought that Burnham-on-Sea was far enough from London to be safe, but that there were ports up the Bristol Channel which were perfect targets for the Germans. Almost everywhere that they had thought might be safe would not in fact be right for one reason or another, and so in the end they had decided that Africa was the best place for us to be. And that was that.

'Africa? Why Africa?' Gyll set up an unexpected howl, with tears streaming down her face. 'Why haven't you said so before? I don't even know where it is!'

'I don't want to go. I won't go,' I said, but nobody seemed to hear me. Did they hear us?

We were told we would only be away for six months, just until the war was over, and that we would be staying with Mummy's sister and that the sun would shine every day. We had very mixed feelings. An adventure? Yes. An escape? No.

We wept over our suitcases, which were not even big enough to take our favourite things. There was no room for our toys or books or the little things we loved, but I refused absolutely to be parted from my doll. She was to come too — and her luggage — or I wouldn't go myself.

As it was, the arrangements were a bit of a disappointment to me and more especially to Gyll, who longed to spend her nights battened down in our Anderson air-raid shelter while the bombs fell around us. She spent a good deal of time describing to me just how terrible it would be to leave Mummy and Daddy and telling me just how unfair it was that Dick, just because he was a boy, should be allowed to stay at home. She drew vivid pictures of what he would do to our toys and books and how he would receive all the favours. But, you know, he was at Public School and surely a young gentleman's education could not be interrupted just because of Herr Hitler, could it?

The plan was that Mummy should accompany us to Southern Rhodesia, where our spinster aunt Geraldine, eighteen years older than Mummy, lived with the family Marsh in Bulawayo. We had never met her and Mummy had not seen her since before her accident. After a brief sojourn, to see us safely settled, Mummy was to return home to look after the men of the family. In fact, that was not how things worked out, but for the moment that was what had been decided, without, quite clearly, the subject, namely us, being given a great deal of thought.

So that you can understand what a mistake it was to send us off to the care of my mother's sister Geraldine, you should know our aunt's story.

In 1892, not long after my mother was born, her youngest sister Blanche arrived in the family, the last of twelve babies born to my grandmother, of whom three were to die in infancy. My aunt Geraldine, the eldest child, was twenty at the time, and was expected to care for yet another baby. In fact, throughout her life she always cared for other people's children, but never her own, which made her into the kind of aunt she was to become to Gyll and me.

My grandfather was a worthless layabout who was only able to live in his house, called Compton Lodge, due to the generosity of his wealthy and aristocratic uncle, who provided him with an adequate stipend. It would have been sufficient had he not made my grandmother pregnant almost every year. He was a vain man, lazy, and selfish, who did not marry my grandmother until she had already produced three children, and then only after his family had finally agreed to the legal union. My grandmother was not considered 'good' enough for him, though she came from a very respectable family – albeit in trade, like Daddy, though in her case her father was a butcher.

My grandfather had been brought up at Chatsworth, and believed the world – or his uncle, the Duke – owed him a living. He never had a job, except briefly in the army, but expected my grandmother to economise on household matters as much as possible, hence the lack of staff to help with the children.

At her birth, Geraldine, the eldest of her parents' three children to be born out of wedlock, was farmed out with a needy family near Lincoln for three years – clearly a case of out of sight, out of mind. When she was old enough but still very young, she was brought back home to look after the stream of children that her parents produced.

When she decided that she could no longer be an unpaid nursemaid, she bravely applied for a post as governess to a family living in Sevenoaks in Kent. She had little option except to find this sort of work other than perhaps as a companion to some elderly and lonely lady. Marriage was out of the question, owing to the fact that she could not provide an acceptable birth certificate, not one of the sort required for marriage to the kind of man that my grandfather might have considered suitable to be his son-in-law. Oh the shame, the shame of illegitimacy! The same went for my next aunt, Ethel, but she had her revenge on her Papa by turning to the Roman Catholic Church and becoming a lay-sister at the convent at Arundel Castle, where the 'other' Howards lived. It nearly polished off the old man.

Illegitimacy also affected my eldest uncle Rupert. At the beginning of the First World War he was rejected on this account by the British Army and went instead to enlist as an officer in the Canadian Army. It is ironic that he died for his British King and Country having been refused permission to join a British regiment.

His next brother Alfred had already abandoned England and his bullying father, and had joined the Royal Canadian Mounted Police, and was never seen again except in a photograph that Geraldine had by her bed, wearing his splendid Mounties' hat, along with one of Rupert, the frame of which held a faded poppy.

My grandfather was furious at Geraldine's decision to leave home, and forbade her to enter what he termed 'service', though heaven only knows what he thought she had been doing for her own family. When he saw that she was adamant, he demanded that she should change her name. Needless to say she did not and went to Kent and the family at Sevenoaks as Geraldine Howard.

Mr and Mrs Bloom had a little girl called Iris, the same age as my mother. My mother used to go and stay at Sevenoaks occasionally, and became friendly with Iris.

In time Iris grew up and fell in love and became engaged to a South African Army major. Edward Marsh had won the Military Cross for bravery, and also Iris's heart. He was a handsome and charming man, but after the announcement of their forthcoming marriage and the giving and wearing of the engagement ring, it nevertheless took Iris seven years to name the day for the wedding, and agree to the subsequent journey to join Edward in Southern Rhodesia. But to be on the safe side she took my aunt Geraldine as a companion. Just 'in case', you know. But she also took her parents, the wealthy Mr and Mrs Bloom.

Illegitimacy was always with Geraldine and it affected every aspect of her life and consequently those of Gyll's and mine. I have seen photographs of her when she was young, wearing pleated muslin bodices and wide-brimmed hats decorated with an abundance of flowers. She had a straight sharp nose and an equally straight back. She had rich dark brown hair; she was almost very beautiful. What a waste.

But she hid her shameful secret under a veneer of an exacting adherence to the manners and habits of those people she wished to consider her equals, the duchesses, and the ladies that she did not know, had never met. Every T was crossed, every P and Q minded. Her little life was ruled by the importance of using correct language; middle not centre; begin not commence; looking-glass not mirror; frock not dress and one had to say 'valet' with a hard T, because otherwise it might sound as if one was copying French words and this was not considered '*comme il faut*' (how dare I?) for a very English lady, who, like her counterparts, had not forgotten Napoleon.

Our parents did not bother much with these things, since my mother wished to forget the very relations that my aunt wished to remember. My mother could not forgive them for treating her own mother so unkindly, at first for not allowing her father to marry her mother – a respectable girl from an untitled but decent family – and then, once they were married, inviting her father back to Chatsworth, but never with his wife. He was useful for house parties on account of his skills on the dance floor. While he swept about with pretty ladies in lovely ball gowns and expensive and beautiful jewellery, my grandmother was left at home to cope on her own. My own mother was firmly on her mother's side and against her foppish Papa. She wished to ignore him and his whole other family. She did not even bother to tell me, in 1945, that he had died. All of which, in a way, accounts for why Geraldine was the way she was and why Mummy was the way she was.

But Geraldine clung desperately to these niceties. Sadly for her, these rich relations were unable to make her into a true lady, but there was certainly about her an air of genteel refinement, quaintly noble and not a little high-born.

When Iris Marsh had her first baby, a boy called Alfred, Geraldine had charge of him. When he was old enough for lessons, she started a small school with half a dozen carefully selected little boys living locally in Bulawayo, whose families still referred to England as Home.

Six years later Mavis was born, just four months after me. That coincidental birth and the subsequent convenient age of Mavis was probably a contributory reason for dispatching Gyll and me to Africa.

So there we were, Gyll and I, about to set out on this great adventure to Auntie Geraldine and Africa, a country that we had no idea was so far away, since no one had bothered to show us the great cornet-shaped country that nearly dominated the globe that stood in our sitting room. Our parents finally put their plans into place, booked the tickets to send us to Bulawayo, and our fate was sealed.

4

The luggage was in the boot of the car as we sailed down Watford High Street, heading for Liverpool. Daddy stood outside his empire, a draper's store of some significance in the right part of town. He jumped to attention and saluted smartly like a soldier as we drove past, but he was not in any uniform other than his black jacket and striped trousers, as befitted a fairly well-heeled shopkeeper. Anyway he was too old to be called up for active service this time round, though he had fought in the First World War and I have a photograph of him crouched in a trench, wearing breeches and leather boots and smoking a pipe, not unlike Ernest Hemingway. His moustache, in 1916, was thick, black and swagger, and his hair dark, as it still was as we passed him that day. He was forty-four. It was 27 July 1940.

Now Mummy took my doll and I took Mummy's beautiful Persian Lamb coat, a rather surprising addition to her luggage as I had imagined that we were heading for a hot land, filled with burning sun and desert-like sand dunes, adorned with stiff palm trees and camels, which we had heard about in stories – and we had pored over illustrations in the books, pictures of little black sambos with fuzzy hair and spears, drawn from an imagination even more vivid than my own. To me, all Africa had to be much the same, hot and dry. I did not know much about jungles but thought that on the whole they were probably in another part of the world, perhaps South America, which also looked quite big on the twirling globe, but not coloured so red.

Liverpool docks seemed to be a mass of huge sheds, through which we were shepherded by harassed port officials. They thought, with only a glance, that Mummy was not only lumbered with two little girls, but also with a baby. They soon ordered us to the front of the line of straggling and impatient passengers. I was absolutely thrilled to bits and very proud of this timely intervention and nudged Gyll and we both giggled at their mistake.

'Look, he thinks Joan is a real baby,' I said with pride.

'Don't be silly of course he doesn't.'

I guessed that Gyll was a bit jealous. 'He did.'

'He didn't.'

'Now you two, don't be naughty. Just stand in line and be quiet. People are looking at us,' but Mummy nevertheless concealed my doll's face and became our accomplice. She said later that it would have been impolite to embarrass the officials by explaining that the 'baby' was a mere doll, but I think she also hoped that they had picked us out because they might see that she was pretty, tired and unhappy.

Up to this point Mummy had never undertaken anything so independent in her life, certainly not an adventure such as this, without the commanding support of Daddy. He always organised everything, in a dashing sort of way, and she made few big decisions, only being involved in domestic matters.

About the only unaided thing she did for herself was to ask East to drive her to Harrods, where she would lunch with my father's cousin, Margery, who was probably her only real friend. She would buy fine flowered silk shantung for Margery's sewing lady to make into identical frocks for Gyll and me, all smocked in beautiful and intricate patterns. Most of the other people in her life were Daddy's business acquaintances and their wives but she loved preparing for dinner parties, having been taught to cook quite excellently in Switzerland, where her father had taken his family to live as the education there was cheaper than in England. We had a perfectly good cook whose only job, it seemed, was to prepare the vegetables and to wash the pans and the kitchen floor each day. Mummy insisted too on making all our meals, even breakfast, though she would retire back to bed after that with half a grapefruit and black coffee, allowing Alice to attend to us for the remainder of the morning. Cooking was the only way she knew to show she cared – and she also found it a great deal less stressful than looking after us.

Mummy would panic dreadfully when Alice was to have her afternoon off. She would bribe her to stay in, with offers of supper for her boyfriend Eddie – in the kitchen, of course. Normally, Alice would work until her bedtime, knitting, sewing our clothes and doing the household mending; she never had much time to herself but she didn't seem to mind too much. When she said she wanted to marry Eddie but to continue looking after us, Daddy gave her the sack. Sadly, she never had any children of her own but she went on loving us for ever.

Alice was so much part of our little lives, so that in many ways we knew her better than Mummy; loved her as much; needed her more. By the time we left for Africa Alice was married and her sister Margaret had moved in to take her place. This was a commitment that lasted much of Margaret's life, but we no longer needed a nanny as such and she became the housekeeper, until she herself married, but continued to look after me, for love.

Maybe because of our obvious affection towards these two women, Mummy lost even more confidence in herself. But for all her distance, she was still our mother and we never questioned that she loved us, neither do I do so now. She simply could not express her feelings in hugs and cuddles and songs and stories the way that Alice did.

Now this timid woman, who had no experience of financial matters whatsoever, was left alone in sole care of two children. She was about to embark on a journey that would change all our lives for ever.

It was not until we emerged on to the wharf itself that we saw the great pinky-grey, towering wall that turned out to be the side of the Union Line ship that was to take us to Africa, the *Cape Town Castle*. I couldn't understand how such a massive piece of metal could float on the sea. It appeared to be immovable.

We duly handed in our ration books. Then we were expected to take off our gasmasks, not from our faces, of course, but from round our shoulders where they were suspended by a strap close to the body. Now this seemed a very naughty thing to do, because we had been admonished time and again never to be separated from them and here was this stranger with his hand held out, impatiently, and, I thought, in a very demanding way. Seeing that Gyll and Mummy were quite happily pulling the straps over their heads and dropping their masks into the huge boxes, I finally, reluctantly, followed suit while Mummy got anxious as I slowly disentangled myself.

'Come on, slow coach,' Gyll couldn't resist saying to impress the officer.

He smiled at last and said, 'It'll be all right, my dear, there on the ship without them. You'll have something else to carry instead, won't you?'

I didn't know what that could possibly be, until Gyll said, in a big-sister sort of way, 'Look, we're only swapping our gasmasks for life jackets.' And what were they? I wondered.

I remembered again hearing Mummy and Daddy talking in their bedroom upstairs. Mummy had said, 'But look, Eric, that ship had only civilians on it, evacuees, women and children, hundreds of them, all left to drown. We can't, we really can't . . .' – and then the door had slammed shut again.

'Do you think that we are in DANGER?' I asked.

'Of course,' Gyll said with a smile. I was not quite so sure myself; I did not have an imagination in the same way that she had. And the War had hardly begun.

Mummy bravely led the way up the gangplank and we were directed to the first-class passengers' accommodation, where Daddy had booked two cabins for us. Gyll and I were completely crushed to find that we had beds when we had looked forward to hammocks or, at the very least, bunks. At once we wanted to travel steerage so that we could experience a real sailor's life at sea, but alas the strict rules of the ship forbade us to enter the other classes on the boat, so we never did find out how the others lived, slept and ate. But we would have been far too shy to attempt any serious exploration and, anyway, Mummy, even while we were still in dock, would not allow us out of her sight, in case we were torpedoed, there and then in Liverpool.

When the time came to detach ourselves from dry land we hung over the ship's rails, waving goodbye to nobody we knew. Someone threw a forlorn paper streamer but there was none of the general air of celebration that was usually associated with the departure of a great liner. The band, assembled on deck for the occasion, bravely played *Finlandia*, music by Sibelius much played at this time.

We were impressed, but we were far too excited to cry; the emotions of the grown-ups around us went largely unnoticed. I thought that Mummy looked worried and so sad, perhaps thinking of the *Athenia* and wondering whether she and Daddy had made a terrible mistake. She may have thought about the children in the water, drowning, because the accompanying convoy could not turn back in order to pluck them from the sea. In fact thirteen ships from the Castle Line alone were sunk by the Germans during the War.

We had a real naval escort for the first part of the voyage, as we turned north out of Liverpool and westwards over the top of Ireland, from there heading out into the Atlantic and eventually south. It was a frightening and gloomy day when the two grey destroyers hooted their sirens and departed. We were on our own in an unending heaving, dark-grey sea. We could not even let ourselves think about what lay beneath.

That first night I was sick. The stewardess cleared it up. I went on being sick and then Gyll succumbed and we lay in our beds swathed in bath towels and surrounded by bowls. Not being allowed to open the portholes made it even worse. Oh for a breath of fresh air.

Even when we began to feel a bit better, it was impossible to go down into the airless dining room; the rolling felt far worse the lower down you went into the heavy bowels of the ship, where surprisingly they had fitted in the dining room. It was generally empty of guests. It was not helped by having the ship zig-zag every ten minutes, which pitched and tossed us about like a cork. This was said to be because it would take twelve minutes for a shadowy shark of a German submarine to adjust its sights on us in order to fire a torpedo. As the ship lurched from zig to zag, so did the contents of our last meal. Of course, in those times there was no such thing as an anti-seasickness pill, as indeed the young soldiers found to their cost, when, once embarked in their boats for the D-Day landings some years later, they waited in the bucking sea for the signal to set sail.

For the first part of our voyage the dining room was virtually deserted. It was not so bad on deck when we could breathe the salty air and after a time we even began to look forward to the mid-morning cup of Bovril that the stewards brought to us as we lay limply, cosseted in blankets, on our regimented deckchairs.

We had frequent boat drills and were shown where to assemble in an emergency, which some of us were beginning to feel was rather more likely to happen than not. Mummy looked haggard as she suffered from the withdrawal symptoms of eschewing her sleeping pills, phenobarbitone (to which she had become accustomed after the fire), for the duration of the voyage, in case there was a night raid, and consequently she hardly slept at all either, except for nodding off during the day for brief cat-naps. There were always plenty of other families willing to keep an eye on us.

We, for our part, kept our eyes on the grey sea, looking for the periscopes of German U-boats.

Once we began to feel better, we played deck-quoits in the sunshine and at night watched the fluorescent waves splashing against the hull, as the ship sliced her way through the endlessly deep and dark waters, south and further south.

Then, dressed in our pretty matching shantung frocks, with their smocked bodices, we would join Mummy in the incredibly luxurious saloon, hung about with velvets and mirrors and lit by sparkling chandeliers, where we would find her reading and sipping cocktails.

'Look, Mummy, look, that lady has green fingernails.'

Mummy gazed with distaste at the fancy lady in her finery,

on her way to an island off the east African coast where her husband was to take up a post as a minor ambassador.

'Yes, darling,' she said quietly, 'but don't stare.'

There were so many glamorous people with long cigarette holders and Eugene-waved hair who we wanted to look at. We were fascinated.

One day at teatime there was the most tremendous thump, which sent the trolley with all the sugar bowls and cucumber sandwiches and cakes hurtling across the floor. Teacups crashed from the tables, teapots spilt hot water everywhere. A gasp went up and everyone grabbed for his or her ever-present life jacket.

There was a surge for the door, most of the men first (well, every man for himself), but the purser appeared as if by magic and taking a loudhailer, told us all that there was no panic; that the ship had hit a whale. True? Your guess is as good as mine, but Mummy was convinced that we had hit something far worse, or that we had been struck, but not fatally, by the enemy. She would not, could not settle until the purser, personally, gave her his assurance that we were safe.

Still, it gave everyone a nasty surprise and reminded the grown-ups of the constant danger that we were in, just as they were beginning to relax and let down their guard and enjoy a very social life. For Gyll and me, we didn't really care about the bump as we couldn't imagine not being alive.

The orchestra played 'A Nightingale Sang in Berkeley Square', and when I hear it now I am, at once, again in that great saloon, with Mummy and Gyll, being entranced with all the glitter of the riches around us. Most of the other passengers, generally to be seen in evening dress, looked as if they were simply enjoying a summer cruise but I guess the laughter was not as light-hearted as it might otherwise have been.

The next day when we gathered for the Sunday service on deck, we sang 'Eternal Father, Strong to Save, whose arm doth bind the restless wave' and really meant it, as we copied the others, turning anxiously to scan the sea for any sight of an approaching enemy.

We had been promised a stop at Cape Verde, which even my limited understanding would have led me to think might actually have been green, but it wasn't, just a dull rock, so far as I could see.

We had been at sea for over three weeks and nearing the furthest tip of Africa when the sea decided to play us one more awful trick. As we approached the Cape, huge rollers attacked the ship and made us forget that we ever thought we had become sailors with secure sea legs. Oh no. We hadn't.

But as we entered Table Bay and saw Table Mountain and the verdant hills rising in the distance, the awful truth dawned upon us that we had finally arrived at the land that was to be our new home.

5

At Cape Town we transferred from ship to railway. It was a strange feeling to be once again on terra firma, even if it was only just for the small amount of time that it took to travel from the docks to the railway station. We felt as if we were still rolling on the big waves, and walked very unsteadily, our heads spinning.

We found our compartment. The porter stowed our small cases away for us. The trunks were packed into the luggage van to give us enough room to move around. And then we were off and away to Southern Rhodesia, on a journey that would take several days and nights through the high veldt. Can you imagine the mixture of fearful anticipation and excitement? It was splendid to be on a train and yet we still didn't know anything about our destination. I don't think that Mummy had the slightest idea herself. If she had, I hope that things might have been different.

Gyll and I examined the compartment that we were to share; Mummy had the one next to ours, with a communicating door, all decorated in lovely, shiny veneered wood. There were real bunk beds for sleeping, complete with fresh cotton sheets and solid pillows, all hitched up and tucked away so that they looked like ordinary velour-covered bench-seats in an everyday but very small sitting room. There was a basin and looking-glass fitted neatly into a cupboard in the corner, with a potty underneath, which we were supposed to use at night rather than dash down the corridor to the lavatories in our pyjamas. The black attendant, wearing a smart cap and white gloves, asked if there was anything we might need and Mummy said 'no', then searched awkwardly in her handbag for her purse to give him a tip. I don't think she knew much about the local currency but she must have been very generous as he smiled and nodded effusively, looking very pleased indeed. Gyll and I wanted to ask him questions about the journey ahead, but Mummy slid the door closed and put the bolt and chain firmly in place.

'How long now?' Gyll asked.

'A long time, darling, this is just the beginning.'

To start with the countryside was quite interesting, but as it changed, we just sat and watched without talking, there was nothing to say. In one way it was an exciting experience to be in a new country, and indeed it was fun to wobble down the corridors to the dining salon. It was not unlike an Agatha Christie film, except that there were no murders, which was a bit of a shame, but the initial excitement began to wear off as we gazed with increasing desperation at the high veldt and semi-desert of the great Karoo, or over the sparse grasslands, which were endlessly dull and seemed to stretch for ever. Was all of Africa like this? Rhodesia too? There were so few people and hardly any cattle. Was this really where we were going to live for the 'duration'? How long is a 'duration'? As far as we could see to the horizon and then further? For ever?

The train stopped from time to time to take on water or coal, but otherwise the journey was monotonous; luckily we did not know just how closely our next few years would echo this flat landscape.

We arrived at Kimberley. The platform was long and shaded as the carriages finally stopped jogging and jerking and we were able to climb down to stretch our legs and take a breath of different air. Black railroad workers, with skinny legs and crooked backs, ran the length of the train, nearly bent double, banging each wheel with a heavy hammer to ensure that they rang true, that there were no fissures in the hot heavy metal that might cause a fracture: if the wheel suddenly split an almighty derailment would follow. It would be a deadly accident, we speculated, in which we would very likely lose our lives. But, we decided, it was not quite as dangerous as being at sea.

There was a swarm of silent, black beggars holding out their pink-palmed hands for a few tikkis, the smallest unit of currency. None of the white ladies in their pretty summer frocks so much as cast a glance in their direction or at the pathetic little ornaments that were being offered for sale. Still, Mummy bravely bought a carved wooden Kampala deer for Dick without bargaining, which caused a stir of consternation and disapproval from the other passengers.

However, the atmosphere of generally self-satisfied lassitude suddenly changed. From the far end of the platform we heard the unmistakable sound of marching boots, feet marching hard to an organised beat. Then all at once the platform thronged with strong bronzed men, wearing black shirts, breeches and knee boots. They formed up neatly facing the train, shoulder to shoulder, arms held closely to their sides, at attention. Then, at a given signal, a stocky, uniformed figure stepped from the train. He must have been waiting in the corridor for the right moment to descend.

There was a fringe of ginger-blond hair showing from beneath the rim of his cap at the back. At the front the peak was surmounted by an emblem, which looked like a large bird. His face was pockmarked and darkened by the sun, while his nose and chin were flattened, as if he had walked into a wall. His eyes were the very bluest of sharp blue. He did not take off his cap, but held his arm forwards and up. The ranked men facing him returned the salute in the same fashion. It was then that I noticed the swastikas on their armbands, just like the ones I had seen on the pictures at home.

'Look, Mummy, look, German soldiers,' I breathed. We were very close. I could have touched the gingery man.

'Na-a-a-a-zis,' said Gyll, imitating Mr Churchill as we had heard him on the wireless.

Mummy looked as if she was about to faint. Perhaps she was asking herself what sort of terrible mistake she had made. With unusual strength she dragged us towards her and pushed us up the steep train steps even though we were enthralled and wanted to stay and watch. Once in the compartment she bolted the door and snapped down the blinds, sitting upright with her knees together, shaking in a way that we had never seen before. It was as if she was waiting for the men to come and seek her out and arrest her, a newly arrived English woman. An enemy. The train began to shunt a bit back, a bit forwards and then we were off again, steaming on our great journey north.

How do I remember this in such fine detail? I haven't thought of it for years, but the sequence of events comes back to me even as I write. It was the deadly precision I remember, the sort of snap you hear in a film when someone cocks a gun, the click like a hundred synchronised clocks as the men squared-up in formation. Discipline.

Much later I learnt about why some South Africans, Afrikaners mostly, chose to support the German fascists. After all, during the Boer War in 1889, when the Afrikaners, a people of mainly Dutch descent, added to by a little French and German blood, fought for total independence from the British in the Transvaal and the Orange Free States, there had been bitter bloodshed. The British, in order to get the Boers to succumb to their rule, introduced the first concentration camps, where women and children too were kept in the most appalling conditions.

No wonder, then, that some fifty years later, memories of the carnage, which eventually led to the formation of the Union of South Africa, were still a subject in the minds of many Afrikaners, who would rather have fought against Britain than for her. But they did not, in fact, get very far, since General Smuts, leader of the government, supported the British. He sent his young South African army to fight in Europe and North Africa; countless numbers of young South African soldiers gave their lives in the war against Hitler.

The determined and continuous movement of the heavy iron wheels seemed to help relax Mummy. After a time she lifted the blinds and we gazed again at the endless empty bright distances, at places that the war would never touch.

After a while she slid back the compartment door and went to stand in the corridor, where the flow of cool air was refreshing. She was joined there by a lady travelling alone in the adjoining compartment. She was a tall whey-faced woman to whom we all nodded when passing in the corridors. She and Mummy chatted together for some time and our own thoughts turned to the very thing we did not wish to contemplate, our destination. But Mummy returned to the compartment with an expression of relief on her face. She allowed herself one of her crooked, pretty little smiles.

'Just a private army,' she said, 'just a small one.'

Which did not mean a lot to us but if the idea made her happy, we would willingly go along with it. But we still didn't understand what was going on; and of course she would never have dreamed of explaining her fearful panic. Perhaps she did not want to admit it to herself. We could tell that she felt a million miles away from the Dance Studio of the Women's' League of Health and Beauty in Clarendon Road, Watford. There she had worn silky shorts and bright red tap-dancing shoes that had taffeta bows over the instep. She was quite good at tap-dancing, which was all the rage in those days. She sometimes practised at home to records on her gramophone, tapping away on the parquet floor when she thought no one could see her. She had left all that security behind to take us to Africa, to a place of safety, but at the moment of seeing those soldiers for her the threat must have seemed to be very much alive.

It was at Plumtree, on the border between Southern Rhodesia (now Zimbabwe) and The Union of South Africa (as it was then called), that we had our passports checked and our luggage inspected.

At Plumtree Station, while the immigration formalities were dealt with by Mummy, we ran up and down beside the train, sending up clouds of dust, filling our sandals with grit. It was a very basic platform, rather like one out of a Western film. The sun was hot, the air dry and bright.

What an adventure, but we knew that it would not last for too long, that Mummy and Daddy would soon send for us and that then we could leave this land that was becoming more and more frightening as we were nearing our final destination.

'How long now?' asked Gyll for the umpteenth time.

If sighs could kill, Mummy would have died long ago on this journey.

'Soon, darling, soon.'

'But how soon?'

Hours, days, weeks, months, years? Mummy didn't know how soon we'd arrive, or when our sojourn in the place would come to an end.

Mummy closed her eyes, accepting defeat. Gyll and I looked at each other guiltily, pulled long faces and abandoned any further questions. What we wanted to ask most of all was if, when we arrived, we would be welcomed, liked, loved?

If we really believed that we might be, how wrong we were.

MIDDLE

6

What a change it was to steam slowly into the shadowy station at Bulawayo, the town that was to be our home. After a lot of shuddering and jerking, the train slowly came to a halt. Straight away, we could hear the railway workers start their banging on the wheels. There was a lot of other noise that we could hear even with our windows closed. Most of our fellow passengers had opened theirs and were leaning out, waving frantically and happily to all and sundry. Not us. We were frozen still.

The crowded platform was buzzing with the clamour of people shouting for the help of the scrawny, dishevelled porters who dashed about eagerly hoping to pick up work. The bi-weekly arrival of the train from the south was a big event. To Gyll and me it seemed like the traditional welcome afforded to stagecoach travellers in the far west of America – we had seen a Western film during our one and only visit to the cinema in Watford. Mummy would not normally let us go as she was afraid that we would fall prey to some illness caught from other children in the audience, but once when she was away my godmother took Gyll and me. It was magic, real magic.

Mummy seemed reluctant to move; indeed, she looked as if she was glued to her seat. Maybe she was thinking, like us, that if we stayed on the train long enough it would take us back to our real home. Perhaps she was afraid that her sister might not be there to meet us, or that she would not recognise her after all these years; maybe she was asking herself once again if she and Daddy had made the right decision to abandon us in Africa in the care of virtual strangers. She did not know her sister any more, the deserts and the oceans had separated them for too long; her own life had spiralled in one direction, marriage and children; Geraldine's in another, nurse and governess to children not her own.

As Mummy fiddled with her hat, putting it on and taking it off again, it seemed that she was simply not going to move. Gyll and I eventually coaxed her up, as if she were an invalid. We were most reluctant to leave the train ourselves but it seemed wrong and dangerous to stay on board when everyone else was getting off. After all, the train might take off imminently for a destination northwards. Mummy made her way slowly down the corridor, carrying her beautiful black fur coat to the door and down the steep steps to the platform. Gyll and I moved closely behind, peering round her to see if there was anyone waiting to greet us.

They stood together, a motionless group, warily observing the disembarking passengers. We hesitated, uncertain about meeting this new family that we were to live with for however long it took for the war to end.

'Come on now, children,' Mummy said at last, taking a deep breath. 'Best foot forward.'

'Shouldn't we take the luggage?' Gyll asked, hoping to delay matters.

'No, dear, the natives will do that.'

'Natives?' I asked.

'Well, the black people, you know. They do things like that.'

Mummy traced her way unwillingly down the platform towards the waiting family.

Mrs Marsh, Iris, a tall big-boned woman, was the first to move towards us. She had a sensible haircut that rode up the back of her neck and she had lines between her nose and mouth. She had big, pale blue eyes. Her sleeveless blouse emphasised her strong arms and she wore a long linen skirt, longer anyway than Mummy's. Her shoes had heels shaped like the pedestal of a lavatory (rather ugly) and cross bars over the instep. We shall see these shoes again. She made Mummy look fragile.

'Joan,' Mrs Marsh cried, 'Joan, we are here!' as if we didn't know.

'Iris, dear.' They embraced, carefully, not actually touching each other to any great degree.

'And this must be Gyll and Susie.' She held us at arm's length, surveying her evacuees.

'How do you do, Mrs Marsh?' Gyll blushed.

I fear I was rather more pudding-faced. I echoed Gyll's greeting and then wondered if I should curtsey as we had been taught when the Duchess of York had come to visit Watford Peace Memorial Hospital. But Gyll did not, so neither did I.

'Oh my dear, dear sister Joan' came from the rear of the gathering. A small figure appeared, fluttering hesitantly, stepping forward shyly.

'Geraldine.'

Mummy pushed us forward, towards her sister, our aunt. They didn't look very alike. Mummy brushed her sister's thin face lightly and then it was our turn. She pecked me gingerly on the cheek, her nose cold even in the warmth of that sunny morning.

'Welcome,' she said in a little voice, 'welcome to God's own country.'

Aunty Geraldine, we soon discovered, was a great fan of Cecil Rhodes, and spoke of him as if he were almost a god. But did Cecil Rhodes, an English-born businessman, who on coming to Southern Africa had discovered the mineral wealth under the sun-baked earth, genuinely think that God himself meant him to exploit and swindle the local tribesmen? Or did he think he himself was God? Did he really not want to know or understand how the indigenous people had lived before the white men arrived with their mining equipment, having seen the vast swathes of fertile land, rich with milk and honey, ready for exploitation?

Initially, Rhodes made most of his money in the Kimberley and de Beers diamond-mining companies. He was a rich man and fancied himself as a politician. But that was not enough for this greedy soul. In 1888 he tricked the local tribal chief of the land that is now called Zimbabwe into giving him mining concessions over the lands of the Mashona and Matabele tribes, the native people amongst whom we actually lived – they in hardship, the whites in comfort. He must have been amazed that such a fruitful country was just there for the tricking and the picking.

Of course, that is what we expect of colonialism, but it amazes me still that he did it in God's name, and that at that time, good people like the Marshes and Aunty Geraldine actually believed him, whilst appreciating the temperate climate and effortless life, served by a multitude of displaced, dispossessed, disenfranchised people. But that is history – and today the price is being paid by both black and white Zimbabweans.

Poor Aunty Geraldine was someone who took very much second place in this family; she was, in fact, for all her much vaunted breeding, only a glorified servant. She was so very thin; I'm sure she had what we would today call anorexia nervosa. She used to say, quite often, that some people lived to eat but that she only ate to live. The trouble was that she didn't eat enough to keep a mouse alive.

Geraldine had short, thin, waved hair and she concealed her frail, angular body in much-mended, droopy clothes. She wore steel-rimmed spectacles on her beaky nose and the skin around her caved-in mouth was drawn and puckered, a consequence, we were told later by Mavis, of having all her teeth extracted some years before. It would have been quite possible for her to have had a set of truly comfortable and well-fitting dentures made, but she opted to give the money required to the Church instead.

Her movements were sharp and birdlike. She leant forward awkwardly as she walked, bent from the waist, and I could easily see the curved ridge of her spine. The crookedness of her back was the result of carrying too many of her siblings on her left hip, so many, many years ago. She gave off an impression of thwarted energy.

Aunty Geraldine spoke little, conveying her messages by way of meaningful looks, many of them either warning or reproachful. Sometimes she smiled, when her crinkled face took on a look of childish anticipation and even of gratitude for being included in the fun. Then her glasses would glint as she shook her head in genteel laughter, her hand held delicately before her lips so as to conceal those hideous false teeth. Her shoulders would wiggle back and forth in her eagerness to be part of the joke.

This person, then, was to be our new 'mother'.

Mrs Marsh said, 'Now then, you two, you can call her Dor-Dor. That's what Alfred used to call her, after his teddy bear.'

Gyll's eyes opened wide. After a toy bear?

'Because Dor-Dor is much easier to say than Geraldine,' Mrs Marsh continued. 'Isn't it?'

It seemed very odd, as if Mrs Marsh was trying to name a strawberry instead of a gooseberry. Not as sweet as it seemed.

'And now then, this is Mr Marsh,' Mrs Marsh continued with energy. 'You can say hello,' as if we were babies.

Mr Marsh was tall and handsome in a regular sort of way, wore a smart khaki bush shirt and shorts that fell in neat creases almost to the tops of his tidy knee socks. He was carrying a khaki solar topee, criss-crossed with cream tape and a thin leather strap across the front of the brim, complete with a small leather buckle and with a button on top of the crown. This, we were to discover, was the uniform he wore to the office each day, where he worked for a subsidiary of ICI, and they were also the clothes that he wore for most other occasions as well.

'And last but not least, here is Mavis.'

The moment we had been waiting for. She came forward a little. We stood dumbly, sharing a moment of intense curiosity, jealousy, suspicion, competition, anxiety and helplessness.

'Hello,' she said.

'Hello,' we repeated, but we had both recognised her different, Rhodesian accent in just that one little word.

'Come on, Mavis,' shouted Mrs Marsh, gamely. 'Shake hands.' We did.

'And now then Edward,' she directed her husband, 'we will need to get the luggage off.'

As a boy Mr Marsh had been in the siege of Mafeking and, when he knew us better, told us riveting stories of hunger and privation during the Boer War against the British, who wanted to add the whole of South Africa to the list of her colonies. On one occasion, when Mr Marsh was close to starvation, he had been given a plate of boiled turnips and told us that it was the best meal he had ever had. He was that sort of man. He also had a glass eye, the result of a car accident some years before. On Sunday after-noons, when he took a siesta on the veranda, or stoep, as local people called it (but not our new family, of course, because it was a word considered to be far too Afrikaans, and the ban on such words was part of the rather sad pursuit of clinging to the ways of the old country), he would take it out, revealing the wet, pink socket behind the glass ball. He would put it in a prominent position on the low wall facing the garden, so that the boys, he told us, thinking themselves to be observed by magic means, would continue their work with vigour, believing that B'wana was watch-ing even while he slept.

For the moment, though, Mr Marsh organised the trunks and the suitcases with the help of a multitude of brown bare-footed porters, who, in a fever of energy, dashed ahead of us.

'Yes, B'wana,' they cried happily, overloaded with our bits and pieces so that they could hardly move.

Mavis continued to stare at us and we stared back. She

was looking at Joan with a slightly contemptuous expression. Dolls! I felt so embarrassed. For the first time I wondered if I was too big to play with dolls, and so, disloyally, I let her dangle clumsily, held only by her wrist, as I pretended that she was a toy of no particular importance.

Mavis was a short, roundish girl, with sturdy arms and legs tanned by the sun. Next to her Gyll and I must have looked like pale slugs that had crawled out from under a damp stone. Mavis had very thick brown hair that matched the colour of her eyes and was held back in an Alice band, so that the ends curled forwards to frame her cheeks. She was as wary of us as we were of her but we had little chance at that moment to start any sort of a relationship. As soon as we emerged into the harsh sunlight of the street outside, Mavis climbed into her parents' car, which moved off into the lead, slow and stately, while we, Mummy, Gyll and I, together with Aunt Geraldine (or Dor-Dor, if you prefer), followed in a taxi.

We proceeded through the town. The buildings, low and whitewashed (bearing little resemblance to red-brick Watford), were strung out along the wide sandy streets. Aunty Geraldine told us with pride that Mr Cecil Rhodes himself had designed the town and decreed that all the main roads should be wide enough for two ox-drawn carts to turn simultaneously, not that there was evidence of many ox-drawn carts that day. The spacious, empty streets gave an impression of heat and light and dust; as we moved further from the centre of the town, the roads became more suburban. We drove past neat bungalows fronted by small gardens.

Auntie Geraldine said to Mummy, 'It's a pity that you've missed the jacarandas in flower. Blue. The trees grow all along the streets, and they give a lovely scent and lots of shade.' She smiled nervously as if she was interrupting something more important, which was something she did often, even though there was rarely anything important at all. Just now, though, our eyes were glued on the car ahead, not on the trees at all.

Driving closely behind the dependable Dodge motorcar (the Marshes also had an old Austin), we turned into the drive of 12, Bryant Road. Like the other houses we had passed, it was a solidly built, symmetrical, one-storey building, with a corrugated roof and a huge water tank on the corner to catch the rain off the roof.

'Why . . .' began Gyll, but Auntie Geraldine had the courage to anticipate her question.

'It doesn't rain very often,' she explained, and we could see that, because everything that should have been green was dry as matchsticks. There was a lot of dust too.

'When the rains come,' she said with a hint of excitement, 'just during the short rainy season, the water drains into the tank to use later. After such a long time of dry weather, you can smell it coming, you can see it coming.' And that was about the only thing that Auntie Geraldine explained to us. We later learnt, when the first rains of our visit came, that you could see the huge drops of tropical water landing with a thud on the sun baked earth, spattering drops the size of the biggest coins, and you could hear them as they bounced off the tin roofs and hitting the ground, sent up little spirals of dust.

'I expect everyone is very happy then,' Mummy said, in an exhausted voice.

'The natives all cheer and laugh,' said Auntie Geraldine, 'because they know that they will be able to grow their corn for another year. That's what they eat – corn.'

We had never heard of corn, but our aunt did not feel inclined to elaborate further. But we learnt, after the rains came, that the veldt would be covered with a thin sea of green almost overnight, and that the air would be cooler.

We went up the flight of wide steps into the middle of the house, where there was a deep veranda.

The veranda was the place where the family lived during the day, Dor-Dor occupying one small corner with her sewing boxes and her Singer treadle sewing machine. Mrs Marsh had a chaise-longue where she took her daily rest, her feet propped up on a cushion, sipping homemade lemon barley water poured from a tall glass jug which was protected from flies by a crocheted and beaded cover made by my aunt. She made lots of them. I still have two. Mrs Marsh did not seem to enjoy happy health, especially during the very hot weather, though it was really rather warm all the year round.

At night the lamps were put out early on the veranda so as not to attract an invasion of insects. On certain evenings, the flying ants could be quite spectacular, drawn by the light to fulfil their mating rituals. They would flutter in their thousands around the bare electric light bulbs, sometimes singeing their wings a little, and when their mad dance was over they dropped to the floor, in preparation to abandon their fine gauzy wings in order to wriggle off together, in pairs, under the floorboards, to consummate their unions and then to munch their way, wingless, through the woodwork, where vulnerable patches might have accidentally been missed by the ever-ready Cuprinol.

We were shown our new bedroom. Actually it was Alfred's room, but he was away in Cape Town at university. Later he joined the South African Army, fighting the hated Hun and Hitler. I suppose we had been given Alfred's little kingdom on a temporary basis, a stop-gap arrangement that somehow turned out to be rather permanent. We thought it to be awful that when Alfred came home on university holidays, or later, on leave from the army, he had to be boarded out with neighbours, since Gyll and I had stolen his space. I cannot think that anyone was thrilled by this arrangement created by these cuckoos in their nest, but then I suppose that most baby cuckoos do not have much choice either as into which nest they will be foisted.

It was a spartan room (as was most of the house) with twin iron bedsteads, each crowned with a knot of mosquito netting, which was untied and pulled down to tuck-in under the rim of the mattresses at night. There was also a metal mosquito net at the window.

Between the narrow beds hung a large and very harrowing etching, depicting a cavalry officer of the First World War kneeling beside his mortally wounded mount. The young soldier held a gun pressed to the head of the dying horse. It was entitled 'Goodbye Old Man'. I had a morbid curiosity about the picture and quite wanted to examine the details, but I simply could not bring myself to do so without fears and tears. Mummy took one look and turned away, speechless.

Mavis's room was next door to ours and her bed lay under the window. Aunty Geraldine had a small screened-off area in this same room, with pictures of Jesus, and some others of a religious nature, saints and so on with their big round orbs of eyes turned heavenwards, their halos screening off the static clouds, hung around her bed. Her photograph of Rupert was arranged on her tidy bedside table.

Mr and Mrs Marsh had a big bedroom at the back of the house, beyond Mavis's, but the best bedroom was allotted to the grandparents, Mr and Mrs Bloom from Sevenoaks, who also had a pretty, sunny, chintzy sitting room to themselves. The Marshes' sitting room, by contrast, was dark and rather gloomy, because it led off the veranda and little light filtered through.

Fortunately, the Blooms were away on holiday in Cape Town when we arrived, so Mummy was given their room, but the very fact that it would shortly be required again by the returning travellers was an indication that her visit could not be prolonged, even if she wished it might be.

Shortly after our cases had been put into our severe little room and before we had a chance to unpack, we were called to the front of the house. On the drive were assembled the staff of 12, Bryant Road. They stood in line and looked solemn, all black faces and white cotton garments, except for the garden boy who wore khaki shorts and shirt. All were bare-footed.

When they saw us they smiled happily. The first to be introduced was the tall, heavily built cook. He was called Williams, but it wasn't his real name. It so happened that Mrs Bloom's maiden name was Williams, and I cannot, in retrospect, believe that the cook's name would be the same as hers – I think it was a bit like us calling Alice, on grand occasions, Nannie Edmonds. Gyll naturally went up to Williams and proffered her hand in greeting. He hesitated.

'No,' Mrs Marsh said in a tense voice. 'We do not do that.'

Gyll turned, puzzled, red and embarrassed.

'We never, never touch the boys, the servants,' she added sharply.

Aunty Geraldine echoed, 'No, never touch the natives, dear', as if the assembled boys were not there. She added, 'They will only take advantage of you.'

Mrs Marsh nodded agreement.

But the boys continued to smile and did not seem to mind what was being said about them.

Williams cooked all the meals for the household but took his own food into the yard at the back of the house, on the servants' stoep, together with the other boys, dipping his hand, like them, into the big pot of mealy meal that rested on the ground between them. They sometimes added a piece of meat or, more usually, some vegetables, but on the whole they seemed to be very content with just the maize.

Then we were introduced to M'Kusa, the head house-boy. He was a man of medium build, who organised the housework and waited at table, always wearing rather well-worn but very clean white cotton gloves. Before each meal he was expected to take a shower in the primitive outdoor shed where they all washed themselves once a day. M'Kusa washed thrice because otherwise, my aunt explained care-fully, when he served at table he would smell 'not quite nice'. His grin was infectious, but that was never allowed to be seen in the dining room. At 12, Bryant Road, dining was a serious, even solemn, affair.

Then there was Amos, the quiet, reserved, reliable second houseboy, who did the rough cleaning jobs, and who usually wore Mr Marsh's old khaki shorts and shirts, which were far too big for him, but for this special day he had borrowed one of M'Kusa's white cotton jackets.

Last but not least there was Tikki, the garden boy, named after the smallest Rhodesian coin available, a bit like calling someone Tuppence. He was cheerful and unassuming, with big gaps in his front teeth, and he was probably not much more than fourteen years old. All the boys slept in the Kraal at the bottom of the garden in fairly crude circumstances but we were absolutely forbidden to look inside, even when Mr Marsh carried out his weekly duty of disinfecting their quarters with Jeyes Fluid at the same time as he cleaned the drains around the house. (I speak of these two events in one breath because there was little distinction made within the family between the two jobs.)

The black people were called 'kaffirs' and apparently had little intelligence and no feelings, according to the white bosses. We were the little white 'missies' and behaved accordingly when anyone was watching. In private we talked to M'Kusa about England and home and our family and he seemed to understand our homesickness, but was as nervous as we were about being caught conversing together.

After we were introduced to the staff, we were handed over to Mavis for a guided tour of the garden. It was large and tidy, with sparse flowering shrubs and trees amongst the well-weeded brown earth. There were lemon and orange trees and a small, coarse lawn, filled with Matabele ants (named after one of the more warrior-like tribes of the district) that strung out in a long trail as they marched across the garden, carrying their fat white eggs and chewing up any debris in their path. They had vicious stings and it was as well to keep out of their way, though Mavis showed us how to rout them by thumping down large stones in their trail. She searched around for a toad to put in the middle of the out column but, thankfully, failed, as it would have been stung to death and then consumed in rapid time, she said.

Seeing we were so feeble, she took great pleasure in telling us really frightful things.

'I tell you, man, there are these huge snakes up most of the trees so be careful not to stand too close or they will get you, and be careful of the button spiders. They're small, but deadly. They like to sit under the edge of the lavatory seat and bite you on the bottom. You could die, man, really.'

And then she added, just to complete this horrendous list, 'Yeah, man, they lurk at the bottom of your bed too.'

As a consequence I didn't go to the lavvy until I was absolutely desperate and was constipated for days, and Gyll and I both slept with our feet curled under our pillows, too scared to reach our toes down into the sheets.

As we explored more of the garden Mavis found a thick, black ribbed centipede, which she called a chongololo, as thick and fat as my big fountain pen. She poked it with a stick and it rolled up into a ball and then she popped it into the water butt. Fascinated, we watched it until it drowned.

In bed that night Gyll and I discussed our new 'sister'.

'Do you think we will ever be best friends?' Gyll asked quietly, so that no one else should hear.

'Who, us and Mavis?'

'Hm.'

'Well, they certainly like her the best. Even Dor-Dor,' I said, self-consciously using Aunty Geraldine's strange nickname for the first time. It was just getting dark, because we had been sent to bed rather early. Gyll sat up and turned towards me, her elbow on the bed by her pillow, her head resting on her hand. She stared at me for a moment.

'Well,' she considered, 'she's certainly cleverer than you and she does seem to win a lot of prizes at school.'

'Yes, Dor-Dor showed me the books that she had won.' I sighed. 'And she can do press-ups and underarm swing-ups on the bar.'

There was a parallel bar in the garden and a thick rope hanging from a tree for climbing. We had never encountered anything like it in our lives. I had tried to copy Mavis but had hung like a sack of potatoes. Gyll laughed at me. I was furious. It was not as if I wasn't trying very hard.

'She's like a monkey,' I added, by way of an excuse.

'Gosh, Susie, you'd better not let them hear you say that.'

The fact that Mavis was the apple of the family's eye was hardly surprising. With Alfred away she was like an only child, and Dor-Dor had looked after her since she was a baby, just like a surrogate parent, only without any influence on the big decisions of her life.

'Well, I'm jolly well going to try and climb that rope,' Gyll said stoutly. 'Maybe they will like us more if we can do boys' things.'

But of course, she never did get the hang of rope climbing either. All she could manage was to get about three feet above the ground, at which point she would fall back, landing on the chunky knot and pivot wildly round and round; it made me feel quite giddy to watch her.

Mavis, apart from being clever at school, played the piano remarkably well, with an accomplishment that made me very jealous. She'd perform with confidence and sensitivity as her admiring family sat around the piano. I longed to have lessons myself but at least she taught me a few brilliant variations of Chopsticks, though these renditions were not received with the applause I had hoped for. Very disappointing.

As our first few weeks in Africa coincided with school holiday time we were sent to play in the garden most mornings. There Gyll and I messed about disconsolately, terrified of the lurking poisonous beasties and waiting for the moment when we would be called in and allowed to find Mummy. In the afternoons various activities were arranged for us, sewing or walking, so there was little time to spare to be with her.

Even so, with only a few precious days left of her stay, she was taken by Mrs Marsh up to the Victoria Falls for a few nights; everyone said it was something she should not miss.

The weekend before her departure an excursion was arranged to the Matopos Hills, Malindidzuma, the grand spot where Cecil Rhodes was to be buried, looking over 'the view of the world', as he called it.

Gyll pouted.

'I don't want to go and see a grave,' she said crossly, looking at Mummy for help. 'It's nearly Mummy's last day. Can't they go and leave us with Mummy? We could read together or something.'

Mummy shrugged her shoulders helplessly and said, 'I think we should go. It's all arranged,' and she added, 'it's supposed to be very special.'

Reluctantly we climbed into the two cars, the children and Dor-Dor in one and Mummy and the Marshes in the other.

We had been gazing hopelessly at the flat-topped trees and scrubby bush for more than a couple of hours when we spied something just a little different. The horizon was bobbled with what seemed to be giant, solid grey clouds, perched one on the other, at any moment about to move and tumble and roll over.

The Matopos Hills are made of a massive pile of granite boulders, seemingly carelessly dropped by giant hands from the deep blue sky. They were so precariously balanced that they could easily fall and crush everything round about, but they had survived thus for millions of years. A miracle of nature.

Heaving and straining, gun carriages, ox wagons, sweating black servants with the thickest ropes, hauled Rhodes' coffin to the summit of one of the highest rocks, which had a flatish top. There were just one or two smaller stones up there for company. Here a hole was pierced in the granite for the coffin, two more slabs of granite placed on top and then a plaque with Rhodes' name. His gentleman friend Leander Star Jameson was eventually interred at his side. From here the rich land stretched away, the land that was to be the 'white man's paradise', the country to which Rhodes had given his name.

'God's own Country' we kept on hearing.

'Well, was it worth it after all?' Mrs Marsh asked Gyll.

'No.' And everyone laughed.

We three children scrambled energetically amongst the smooth monolithic rocks, Gyll and I wary that we would find ourselves faced by some nameless wild and lethal creature. The massive boulders were solid as a monster in deep sleep, as immobile as the land itself, baked hard by a dependable sun and washed smooth with the rains of millennia.

In all the excitement, Gyll got pushed into a prickly thorn bush, the long sharp needles piercing her shorts and tender flesh. Mrs Marsh, experienced at dealing with such calamities, put on her spectacles and removed what she could, a painful ordeal that lasted for days as, once back at 12, Bryant Road, Gyll lay on her tummy in the bedroom submitting to the needle, tweezers and stinging antiseptic.

Back on the Matopos Hills, Mavis discovered a tick in her ear but that had to wait for attention until we got home. She seemed relatively unconcerned, but then she couldn't see, as we could, the fat swelling body growing round and dark with her blood. We were appalled. What a frightful country. Couldn't we please go home back to England, Home and Beauty?

After that we sat carefully in the shade of an umbrella-shaped tree and soberly ate our hard-boiled eggs and sandwiches. Mummy sat close by in her elegant London clothes, as pretty as a picture and almost as distant. Perhaps her impending departure had already opened new landscapes to her, the pictures in her mind more real than what lay before her.

I often wonder what was going through our mother's mind before her return to England. She could hardly have failed to notice the favouritism meted out to her friends' daughter, nor the demanding regime built especially for us that was beginning to take shape in the household, a regime that Gyll and I had to follow to the letter. Perhaps she thought that everything would in some magic way sort itself out once the family got to know us better and Mavis had got over her perfectly understandable problem of having her private kingdom invaded by two strangers.

Mummy, strangely, played no part in the organization of our new daily routine, nor said anything while she observed us being remodelled to fit within the tight shape of our new life. She had not protested when we were admonished for doing something wrong that at home would have entirely escaped her notice; she had not complained or stuck up for us when we were criticised for some minor infringement of family rules, behaviour that would have been considered perfectly acceptable in Watford. We wondered why she did not champion us or explain or remonstrate on our behalf. She agreed that we should go to bed at six o'clock, that we should not read in bed, that we should either stay in our bedroom or be in the garden unless invited anywhere else in the house, and that we should be seen but not heard. None of this seems too awful, and other evacuees had a far worse time than we did, but at the time we were such mice; we were overwhelmed by the fear of their cold or angry disapproval. We were never sure what it was that annoyed them so much. We were so wary of doing the wrong thing.

Mummy seemed quite helpless in the face of the fundamental changes in our lives and did not interfere. She was silent. She looked away and left us.

We cried when we said goodbye, not only because she represented all that we had left behind in England – the house, the family, the love, the care and comfort of home – but because we loved her and thought we might never see her again. She could be drowned at sea on the way home, she could be bombed in Watford, or, worst of all, she might never come back to take us home so that we could all be together again.

Mrs Marsh thought it better that we should not go to the station to wave her goodbye, so Mummy left us there in the sunny garden, turning at the last moment to call to Gyll not to pick her toenails. Perhaps it was thought we would be best left alone, to get over our tears and the ugly pangs of parting. It is possible that they could not bring themselves to witness our despair and regrettable display of emotion. Maybe they had simply forgotten that we were standing there, looking for Mummy long after she had gone.

'The Absence of My Mother'

When you went away,
I cried and cried all day,
Next day I cheered up though,
And began to knit and sew.

I thought of you next day
In the old Karoo so dusty
A jogging along in the old puff-puff
In the old puff-puff so dusty.

I thought of you next day,
A leanin' o'er the rail,
Or creeping quietly round the deck,
As slow as a creeping snail.

Gyll Edmonds, aged 11

★ ★ ★

Once Mummy had departed, it began to dawn on us that our lives would never be the same again. We had to learn a new way of living and we had to learn to live in the family's way. No more holidays at the Round House or stories with Daddy at bedtime, no more holidays at all, just time off from school.

It is easy to see with hindsight why things happened the way they did, why we found ourselves to be in Africa, why the Marshes were the way they were and why they felt about us as they did. But at the time we understood little and knew nothing. We were unhappy, hopelessly miserable, but as we eventually came to realise, there is no monopoly on sadness. We are all sad at some point in our lives and it is all relative. You might lose your mother and I might lose my pet mouse. We both might feel it is the end of the world, but we learn, we learn.

7

There must have been any number of households in Bulawayo that had sprung from British beginnings but none more so than 12, Bryant Road, where the Blooms, their daughter Iris, her husband and their daughter's companion, my aunt, seemed only to be marking time before they could all go 'home' again. They did not appear to be having a very good time. I don't think they liked this part of Africa very much, except, of course, Mr Marsh, who perhaps felt, rather poignantly, a little left out of the general overly British way of running his establishment and home.

At that time expatriate society was flourishing further north in Happy Valley, where the British were hopping in and out of friends' and neighbours' beds, smacking into delicious dry martini sundowners at four in the afternoon and shooting the occasional adulterer. The Marshes in contrast appeared aloof, to have few friends but their family, while resolutely disapproving of the dissipated English aristocrats or millionaires whiling away the war in comfort in Africa and making unpleasant headlines in the local newspapers.

But there had to be a happy medium. I mean, there must have been other people, other families, living good lives, working hard, enjoying the sunshine and making Rhodesia their real home. As it was, the family that we had joined was caught in a time warp, with lives ruled and regulated to reproduce and preserve all that they had loved and admired so much about the old country. They spoke openly and frequently about their yearnings for England and the mild climate of Sevenoaks. The trouble was that what they were dreaming of was the England they remembered after the end of the First World War, after 1918. To hammer home their point, to make sure no one ever forgot it, every English custom was magnified and even the smaller details of that strict post-First-World-War regime was maintained with meticulous care. Add to this delicate brew the aged grandparents, who may have held the purse-strings, together with my aunt, a mere sixty years old and yet even more set in her ways than the Blooms, and you will see that not only had we exchanged modern for ancient but also freedom for confinement. We were sent back to the nursery days, swaddled tightly in the minutia of trivial (but obsessive) standards; you will understand why we were puzzled. I don't mean to be unkind about their love of the past; why ever should they not run their household as they preferred? It was, after all, their home and not ours, and we were quite clearly becoming a nuisance with no obvious end in sight to the invasion into their lives of the evacuees foisted upon them.

I think perhaps they did not quite know what to do with us. Mavis had had her routines and was used to that, but for us, who were used to being both seen and heard, we made many mistakes. We eventually became mute indeed.

It cannot have been easy for Mavis either but I think the starting point in our friendship was when she confessed to wanting to hold my beloved doll Joan. I graciously gave her permission. It just shows how first impressions can be so wrong.

★ ★ ★

Daddy had been a reasonably eccentric man all his life, even though a large part of it was spent as a shopkeeper. His father had forced him to abandon his chosen careers of journalism and then advertising (he opened the first Erwin, Wasey and Company Ltd office in Paris on the Boulevard Malesherbes, where he lived with my mother after their marriage) to join the lucrative family drapery business, in Watford, for which he did actually have a certain flair for increasing the profits and dividends. But he bore a grudge that he could not have been allowed a more artistic and challenging occupation than, as he said boldly, 'Selling knickers in the High Street in Watford'. Luckily for him, fortune favoured the draper and he moved on eventually to bigger and better things. Once the babies started arriving his father commanded that he should leave Paris and join him in Watford at the store. He did, however, make up for his disappointment by still casting himself as an artist when walking the floor of the shop and greeting, provocatively, with his rather wolfish, raffish smile, all his loyal lady customers.

He tended to embarrass his less open-minded acquaintances with his occasionally bizarre behaviour; he took both *The Times* newspaper and the *Daily Worker*, claimed to be a communist at the same time that he was obviously a capitalist, and would switch sides in an argument at the drop of a hat to get a good conversation going about anything from art to politics, education to wine-growing. He was a keen and excellent photographer, but he was not a very good painter. However, that did not deter him from hanging his pictures all over every inch of wall in the house. In later years he went so far as to dress like an artist, espousing a Winston Churchill hat and a large floppy bow in lieu of a tie. Old ladies loved his daring; young ladies admired his fine moustache, twinkling eyes and brash humour.

He built a swimming pool in our garden in which he insisted we should all splash about stark naked, even Mummy and Alice, and he always, always encouraged people to voice their opinions. He made us stand on a stool in the sitting room after lunch on Sundays, and talk for two minutes, with no 'ahs' 'ums' or 'ands' on any subject of his choice, that is to say, anything from dolls' houses to health foods. He had once met Doctor Allinson of the dreaded brown bread and was a forerunner of the present fashion for whole foods, insisting that we ate a piece of horribly dry, stale brown bread before starting on any white bread. If we couldn't manage the brown, then there were no biscuits nor occasional slice of cake.

He was a master of bluff and counter-bluff, covering his tracks with commanding innocence, a tactic he employed in all areas of his life; but he had a terrible temper and would fly into ungovernable rages with inanimate objects like a flat tyre (frequent in those days) or his film projector, which inevitably coiled and spilled miles of unreeled footage around the floor under the projection table, while we were sitting happily (until the fatal discovery) enjoying his home-made films in the dark or watching *Felix the Cat* and *Emil the Detective*. To be fair, even our neighbours in Watford thought our family a bit bizarre, especially when they were shown Daddy's home-made films of Mummy, Alice, Dick, Gyll and me bathing naked in our pool. Gyll and I, in our embarrassment, hid our head under the nearest cushions, while Daddy just laughed.

So you can see that all this was very different from members of the family Marsh, who clearly thought that conformity was a desirable goal and who obviously hoped that Mavis would grow up to be a perfect replica of an English miss – all, in fact, that which Daddy most despised.

Inadvertently, we put our feet right through their dreams of bringing up a perfectly 'English' daughter. The moment we set foot on Rhodesian soil, with our clear piping English accents, they noticed for the first time just how South African their own accents had become. Well, obviously not Aunty Geraldine's or the other grown-ups in the family, but Mavis had, willy-nilly, absorbed the local lilt, the short syllables and hint of Dutch harshness. 'Ach-ma-an,' she would say, and we loved it, innocently mimicking the colonial tongue.

Our own accents were the envy of all the 'nice' mothers in the neighbourhood, which was lucky as they prompted many an invitation to tea from mothers who, mistakenly I am sorry to say, hoped that their children might pick up the way we spoke. But, as luck would have it, we only wanted to speak like them, and very soon we did.

Of course, apart from our voices, we were invited for other reasons too – 'Refugees, my dear, so awful for them, poor little things, and so, so . . . English.'

All this was opening doors for Mavis too; before our arrival the family had been very selective about her friends, and with whom she should be allowed to mix. Dor-Dor and Mrs Marsh, egged on by the fastidious Mrs Bloom, had studiously avoided anyone whom they considered to be NOCD (Not Our Class Dear), but these new acquaintances were Mavis's school friends and she wanted to join in like everyone else. Now when we were invited, Mavis came too. We didn't pick up any terrible habits and nasty manners. We had cakes and jam and ice cream for tea, and listened to gramophone records and talked harmlessly about the sort of boy we would like to meet, or maybe just to whom to write letters; pen pals were all the fashion then.

But we three stood out like sore thumbs amongst the dinky little Rhodesians, Mavis, Gyll and I. Our clothes were dreadful. Whilst our friends wore dainty cotton frocks with pants to match, our own pretty clothes were stored away for special occasions that did not seem to happen. Instead we were forced into serviceable boys' khaki shorts and aertex shirts (we kind of guessed that they might be Alfred's cast-offs), durable and dreary brown ankle socks and ugly brown sandals, whereas our friends wore white socks and shiny patent pumps. You only have to look at the photographs of us miserable big dumplings in brown to realise how very out of kilter we were. If, on a rare occasion we were allowed to wear a frock, Dor-Dor would insist on brown school knickers that showed through the flimsy material. She ignored our childish embarrassment, scolding us that it was wicked in the sight of her God to take pride in one's appearance. She skimped like hell on our clothes, making whatever she could herself from the cast-off grown-ups' clothing, cutting down, hemming up, and saving all the buttons and tapes to spare for another day. I mean, I do myself find it impossible to throw away old envelopes and string and plastic bags, but I never try to make anyone else use them and neither should she have. It wasn't as if Daddy was not sending money every month to pay for our board and lodging, something that we were never told. We thought of ourselves as charity children who should be grateful to the family financially, as well as for everything else. In fact, children at that time were rarely included in discussions about money, heaven forbid, but it would have helped our self-esteem and confidence enormously if we had only known.

Dor-Dor used to wash any new material before making it up, to avoid shrinkage at a later date. M'Kusa was not very good at using the flat iron, and even our boring white linen confirmation dresses looked second-hand. I don't suppose the 'Arch' would have minded, but *we* did! Dor-Dor dyed them after the service, a nice suitable blue for going to church.

She refused Gyll's perfectly reasonable request to buy a Kestos brassiere, which was becoming, with each month, more of a matter of necessity than mere adolescent whim. Dor-Dor herself wore an old fashioned bust-bodice, though I am not sure why she needed one at all since I thought her breasts were more reminiscent of a spaniel's ears than anything else – not that I had had the chance to see them except once, by accident, when her dressing gown fell open. Her bodice, which made her chest seem even flatter, was an extraordinary garment that she had, of course, made herself. It was a mass of ribbed tape, which dangled down to hold her stocking suspenders, and strips of encased whale-bone further to mortify her body, like a sort of hair shirt I suppose.

Dismissing the notion of a brassiere as both precocious and provocative, Mrs Bloom and Aunt Geraldine had the lunatic idea of dressing Gyll up in one of Mrs Bloom's old corsets. It was sagging and grey, and just how Gyll let them put it anywhere near her I just couldn't think. It had suspenders too, which were so long they rattled against Gyll's knees.

It was the sort of garment that needed lacing. Gyll, who had skimmed through Mummy's copy of *Gone With the Wind* while crouched behind the sofa in the sitting room at Shalford Cottage, shortly before we left England, believed that if you couldn't have a bra then a Scarlett O'Hara corset would do instead.

She had read how Scarlett hung on to the bedpost to be laced in so tightly that she had achieved about the smallest waist in the county. What Gyll had not bargained for was the very active support she would have from Mrs Bloom and Dor-Dor in her quest for a fine figure. Just what pictures the two elderly ladies carried in their heads goodness only knows, but they took it in turns to pull the laces so tight that Gyll, initially filled with pride, suddenly keeled over.

Just at that moment, Mrs Marsh walked into the room. 'What are you doing to that child?' she cried in fear and horror. Gyll did indeed look very pale as she lay lifeless on the floor (but not so lifeless that she could not, secretly, send me a wink while the grown-ups dashed round looking for cold towels and water).

Mrs Marsh, with nimble fingers, unlaced the garment and held it aloft. 'It's disgusting!' she cried. 'Horrible. Take it away at once.'

She kneeled on the floor beside Gyll, who did an excellent imitation of a fair damsel recovering from an unfortunate faint. She had in fact really fainted, but for only as long as it took her to hit the floor. Once awake, she was of a mind to listen in to the panic and to extract the most sympathy possible.

After a time, Mrs Marsh helped her to sit up and she looked around her, as if in surprise.

'What happened?' she asked, in an innocent sort of way.

'You just fainted dear. Now take this glass of water and be very careful.'

Mrs Marsh turned on her mother and said quietly, 'We will discuss this later.'

Dor-Dor flapped about a bit, tidying up and taking Gyll's clothes back to our own bedroom. No more was said. But Gyll and I saw the maid from next door wearing the corset outside her yellow-and-red frock, flaunting herself as she swung down the street. But we didn't tell anyone.

On the rare occasions that we moaned about our drab, horrible clothes, seldom in public but often in private, we were condemned as being spoilt. If only. Perhaps we were. Perhaps our little outings to Harrods had spoilt us, but we thought that Mavis was dreadfully spoilt in lots of ways. It was hardly her fault, but Gyll and I did begin to identify with the story of *The Little Princess*. 'Only,' Gyll said with sadness, 'there are two of us.' As if it made it all doubly awful.

'Yes, but we don't have to clean the house for the cruel headmistress or have to sleep in a cold attic.'

Gyll tossed her head, looking for all the horrid things in our lives to compare to the miserable lot of the little Princess, but she couldn't quite find them.

'I'll tell you what,' she said after a moment's thought, 'we could always run away.'

'Run away?' I was shocked but intrigued. 'How?'

'Oh, you know, we could save up a bit of pocket money and get on a train.'

'Ha!' I laughed. 'What pocket money? I've only got sixpence.'

'Well, it might take a bit of time.'

'A bit of time? The war will be over before we can save enough. And anyway, where would the train go?'

'The war could go on for ever.'

I saw a tear beginning to roll down her cheek. She brushed it away angrily.

'Oh, I know, I know. I just thought . . .'

I had a feeling that she thought that my lack of enthusiasm had let her down.

'Well,' she said at last, keen to squeeze the last drop of anguish from any situation, 'nobody loved her. Her father was supposed to be dead and she didn't have any money and she was very unhappy.'

'But Daddy isn't dead and, and anyway, you've got me.'

'Fat lot of use you are,' she snapped angrily. That really hurt. 'And Daddy is not here. He doesn't know what is happening to us. It's just the same.'

'No, it's not,' I said stubbornly, but I ended up by agreeing that she was probably right. It was what she wanted to hear and I couldn't see how I could argue my side with my limited debating abilities. I always had to agree with her whether I thought she was right or wrong; my sister did not have to be particularly clever to get the better of me – I simply went along with everything she said, eventually.

We continued to revel in the Princess's plight.

'Do you think we were spoilt?' she asked then, 'I mean, like the Princess was before her father disappeared?'

'No, but the way they go on—'

'We went to boarding school, didn't we? That's not being spoilt.'

'And we were always jolly good. Mummy never had to get cross with us for being naughty.'

No, though in fact what actually happened, if by chance we made a mistake and did something wrong, she was never cross, just terribly, terribly sad.

About the naughtiest thing I ever did I can still see in my mind's eye as I write today. I see myself creeping along the bright green prickly leaves of the raspberry canes that flourished just outside the kitchen windows at Shalford Cottage, Watford. I could hear Mummy calling me but my mouth was full of lovely pinky red fruit which we were not supposed to take, and my fingers stained the most beautiful colour.

Gyll sighed. Home, Watford, Dick, Sally the dog, the

garden and Michael, the boy next door who we met so secretly in the laurel hedge even after prohibition, Alice, Margaret, Mummy and Daddy, all of whom assumed a miraculous beauty, a longed-for never-never land, an unreal and distant fantasy in which we were touched, tickled and kissed and our hands held when we crossed the roads. Here, the family were afraid of touching. I cannot remember a time when anyone so much as put a hand on my shoulder. Oh for the arm around me. But then there was always my sister.

We were so stunningly unprepared for life in Africa, for the rapid transition from affection to isolation. It was like being a flourishing flower, uprooted and replanted in difficult, dry soil and never watered. The attempt does not often succeed. I can tell you from experience.

Of course we had to be well behaved at home in Watford too. But when Mummy was burnt we never wanted to hurt her feelings and made special efforts not to upset her. We were used to being good and if I picked the occasional pansy to treasure its moonlight colours and pussy-cat whiskery face I did not consider that to be too naughty and still don't. One look at my pansy-filled garden now would even make you laugh. We lived pretty ordinary lives and had a fairly strict up-bringing.

Mummy had read a book by a veal farmer from New Zealand called Truby King, a vet I believe, who posed as a doctor. He claimed that he knew how to bring up babies and believe me, the man must have been as insane as the mothers who listened to him and took his advice. Never pick up your baby when it is crying, having checked first that a nappy pin has not pinioned itself to the baby's tummy button. Never feed a baby except every four hours, even if, like Gyll, she screamed with hunger while Mummy put her head under her own pillow, occasionally popping up to look at the clock to watch how many minutes longer she would have to wait before picking up her baby. Never touch your baby unless strictly necessary, in order to prevent the danger of infection. In my view, he was crackers. Thank God Mummy began to lose interest in his views as we grew older and anyway, eventually, it was much easier to give in to what she really wanted to do with us and to follow her own instincts.

So you see that we had not been brought up entirely without discipline, but in Bulawayo, ours seemed like a lifestyle designed uniquely by the dreaded calf farmer. It was six o'clock bed time, a great indignity as any child who has ever stayed up until seven will tell you, especially as at home in Watford we had reached the prestigious hour of seven thirty in the winter and eight in the summer, when we could still hear the local children shouting and whooping outside in their gardens. Now we had to be bathed and pyjama-ed by six and then, funnily enough, came the best part of the day. We were allowed into the aged grandparents' sitting room for supper, I guess to keep us out of the way, and the suppers themselves were always jolly good. We had fresh white bread and butter with sliced radishes, or lettuce and dripping (from a proper Sunday roast), or corn on the cob, which was a huge novelty to us and positively delicious.

Then Dor-Dor would ring a little hand bell and M'Kusa would come and collect the plates. We three settled down, still at the table, with our heads resting on our hands. Dor-Dor started her reading with a prayer and a passage from the Bible, but then we got down to *Jock of the Bushveldt*, *Swallows and Amazons* or *The Scarlet Pimpernel*. We cruised through shortened editions of Dickens and the best of Kipling. Marvellous – the best moment of the day, even for Mavis I thought.

After supper Gyll and I would go to bed to read until Dor-Dor popped her head round the door, said 'Lights out' and turned the switch off. Not much by way of wishing one another 'Goodnight', or even a brief smile or a wave of the hand. I don't know but perhaps she was afraid of us, of getting too close or perhaps of being rejected? Or maybe that was just the way she was.

Mavis, on the other hand, was given the chance to get to see her parents on her own, which we thought was outrageous, but was perfectly understandable if you thought about it at all. But we didn't and were consumed with jealousy.

'It's terribly unfair,' Gyll moaned. 'She's even having a second dinner with them.'

If we left our bedroom and courageously made our way across the veranda (danger of discovery at every corner), we could see through the glass doors into the lighted dining-room. We watched what was going on but they couldn't see us, like at the theatre.

Mr Bloom, he of the creeping hands, would use them for a welcome change to play the piano marvellously well. Such beautiful music. He played by ear with romantic verve. Mrs Bloom would clap her hands at the end of each piece and exclaim, 'Oh, Augustus!' as if he had suddenly produced a new and entirely unexpected talent, time after time. If only she knew what he did with us, but more of that later.

To say that our life was spartan would be an understatement. To say that we were persecuted internally as well as externally would be somewhere nearer the truth. Such weird attention was paid to the workings of our bowels that on reflection I have to question the whys and where-fores of their obsession with inner cleanliness. I am aware that cleanliness is supposed to be next to godliness, but here were we, helpless victims of more than one sort of evacuation.

At Gardenhurst, the little school at the sea, the joint headmistresses, the sisters Haines, Miss Rose and Miss Violet, insisted that we should all sit on our potties every morning after breakfast, while they kept a watchful eye on us and the contents of the pot. That seemed to be about enough. But here, at 12, Bryant Road, it was poor Mr Marsh's duty, no, not to look into the pot, but to take the grown-ups a cup of tea each morning when the household woke. Presumably it was considered 'not on' for the black servants to enter bedrooms while any of the family was in a state of undress. Mr Marsh would put on his dressing gown and slippers and 'do the rounds'. But we didn't get tea. We got a tikki's worth of Epsom salts in boiling water. Absolutely disgusting. Just what Mr Marsh thought of this barbaric practice, or any of the other more hateful customs of the household, we never knew. But he did seem to be a little apologetic as he sneaked a look round the door to make sure that we were awake, and plonked the vile laxative on the bedside table that stood between our beds, next to the water jug and our glasses.

'Drink it while it is hot,' he would say kindly, each day. 'Better for you.'

One day Gyll sat up in bed and in a very bold way asked Mr Marsh, 'Do *you* drink it?'

Mr Marsh paused a moment, the empty tray still in one hand, while with the other he held open the door, ready to leave.

'Well now,' he said, 'I have a cup of tea, but I am older

than you,' and his face betrayed pity for us. 'Go on, drink it up. It really is good for little girls.'

Gyll pulled a face and he allowed himself a big smile. With that he left the bedroom and closed the door behind him.

As we struggled out of the mosquito nets and faced the steaming cups, we were mesmerised by the awfulness of everything. We held our noses and got it down somehow, but we could only sip because it was too hot, which dragged out the torture. After a time we rebelled. The obvious solution was to tip the laxative into the water jug, that sat on our table, neatly covered by one of Dor-Dor's crocheted and beaded covers. We thought we were very clever.

Unfortunately, M'Kusa didn't know what we were doing.

One perfectly frightful day, when we were reading our library books on the veranda, Mrs Bloom suddenly appeared, flushed and taut with anger. She had been checking up on M'Kusa's work and had discovered something unforgivable.

She beckoned to Mrs Marsh.

'Come,' she said, in a Lady Bracknell sort of voice. 'And you can come too,' she called to Dor-Dor over her shoulder, as an afterthought. Dor-Dor set her sewing aside and scrambled to her feet obediently. The air was electric. Something awful was brewing and in the ominous silence Gyll and I looked at each other nervously. What could it be this time?

We had not long to wait. The mosquito-netted door flew open and Mrs Bloom re-entered, with M'Kusa in tow. He looked pretty worried too.

'What is this?' Mrs Bloom cried, holding our water-jug aloft. She ripped off the cover.

Even then the awful truth did not dawn on us.

'M'Kusa has been lazy. He has not been giving you fresh water every day. He will be punished later.'

M'Kusa cringed and dropped his head, in much the same way that he had dropped us into trouble.

'Look.'

Mrs Bloom proffered us the jug. We edged forward gingerly, not knowing quite what to expect. There, inside rim, was a delightful circle of crystals, distilled from the salts, winking prettily in the sunlight.

Gyll went crimson, guilt written all over her face.

'That's very dishonest,' Mrs Bloom cried.

'Wicked,' added Dor-Dor. 'Wicked girls.'

'Foolish,' said Mrs Marsh, a little more reasonably, but Mrs Bloom was in no mood to be reasonable.

Foolish? Yes. But we had never done science at school. We did not know how crystals were made.

'You gels,' said Mrs Bloom, 'are not trustworthy.'

'We'll see you drink your salts,' chimed in Dor-Dor. 'I'm ashamed of you. What would Mummy think?'

We didn't say anything but we were both fairly sure that Mummy wouldn't give the subject a moment's thought and that she most certainly would not have made us drink anything as disgusting as Epsom Salts.

'Go to your room for the rest of the day to think it over. No books.' M'Kusa did not lift his head as we passed.

We crept off the veranda and Gyll took my hand as we cried, together.

We got into hot water quite a lot, but they had difficulty in finding ways to deal with us to mete out our just deserts. They couldn't stop our pocket money because we were only given just enough to put something into the Church collection plate or buy a poppy on Armistice Day, and anyway what else would we have bought? If we needed a new pencil, or some paints or paper, we had to ask Dor-Dor, who, having satisfied herself that the need was genuine, would buy them for us herself. Luckily, we were sometimes sent or given some cash for birthdays so that we had a tiny reserve of our own to buy some gobstoppers or sherbet fountains off one of the girls at school.

We were too big to be slapped and even sending us to bed early was a problem since we already went there so early. Isolating us from the family seemed to be an option, like not talking to us and ignoring our presence, but we were never that involved in the first place so it didn't make much difference. However, the worst thing, the punishment we dreaded most, was the continuous scolding, never being allowed to forget or be forgiven for our shortcomings, having our petty sins being dredged up time after time. 'And who was it who left a pin on the sofa?' or 'Who left the light on in the lavatory last Tuesday?'

I think our real sin was to be there at all, and who could blame them for getting sick and tired of children who were supposed to be staying for six months and were already well into their second year, leaving clothes in the wrong places, losing our pencil cases, not liking to eat marrow, being found under the sheets with torches trying to read in the dark and running down the batteries to boot? Well, what do you think? I think that now I feel rather more sorry for them than I do for us. But it wasn't like that then.

But there was worse to come than Epsom salts.

Almost as if the evil could be purged from us through inner cleansing, the family considered it essential to have a more thorough intestinal clean-out once a week. This entirely medieval concept of internal corruption was quite à la mode with the family; they would, for instance, talk of pimples and spots as the sign that the naughtiness was being squeezed out of us, a bit like Pinocchio's nose growing longer with each lie he told; it was evidence of wickedness for all to see; or an ulcer on the tongue found you guilty of telling lies.

Still, I was talking about the other evacuations that we were faced with. Not content that we were refugees from a fate worse than death, and I did sometimes wonder what the fate was that no one would discuss, we had to swallow, under the beady eye of Dor-Dor, a vile reddish brown pill each Friday night, that brought on, the following morning, a total turn-out of our insides. This meant that while our school friends were plunging in and out of the water at the Bulawayo swimming baths, we three girls were plunging in and out of the lavvy, convulsed and trapped by the sheer ferocity of this emetic pill called Alophen. Impossible to forget the name, or the pungent pong of Jeyes fluid and other noxious things that hung about the 'smallest room in the house', as Dor-Dor called it. But I guess that we were more than fortunate not to have been subjected to enemas too.

My aunt was a religious woman and that part of her life not dedicated to the practical service of Mavis and the family was devoted to the pious service of her God. She usually had a prayer book to hand, with home-made markers for the prayer of the day, the collect for the week, for the lesson and for reading. She found inspiration in *The Lives of the Saints* and followed *In the Steps of the Master* by H. V. Morton. She spoke eagerly and admiringly of the 'Arch' (Archdeacon of Bulawayo) and waited breathlessly for him to condescend to notice her. She looked forward to visits from members of the Society for the Propagation of the Gospel (in whose name the collection was taken for that Sunday) and sank to her narrow knees by the side of her bed every night to say her prayers (so Mavis reported). She believed in a divine and celestial hereafter and led her life accordingly, chastising her body for the sake of her everlasting soul.

Be that as it may, at that time, in Africa, she walked, by herself, the long road to the communion services two or three early mornings a week and walked with Gyll and me to Matins every Sunday. Mavis, meanwhile, went by car with her parents, because there was really not enough room for us all.

Gyll and I trailed along, hot and dusty, crossing over the bridge that spanned the river that had no water in it for the most part of the year. The rustle of the wind in the fringing eucalyptus trees almost sounded like a river, rushing on its way to irrigate the parched, sparse, uncultivated veldt, which was exciting to hear and reminded us of the Thames in spate at home.

We dutifully followed as Dor-Dor pecked her way eagerly to see the 'Arch' or the 'Bish', ready and willing to render up a tenth of her meagre allowance to the SPG in answer to yet another plea for the missionaries who were busy saving the souls of little piccaninnies and leading them to the path of Jesus and of Righteousness.

Gyll and I, of course, were also expected to put in a tenth of our stingy savings, which would not have amounted to as much as the cost of a yellow duster from Woolworth's in Watford. We did not feel very obliged to put much towards the saving of pagan souls, and became adept at passing the plate with a fumble so that Dor-Dor could not see exactly what we had put in. A tikki?

8

The almost perfect summer of 1939 was worlds away. Here in Africa we had turkey and sprouts in a heat wave and wore cardigans in July. The weather was all upside down. It was hot in a new way for us. The air was dry and the skies always clear and deep blue like a child's picture book. You knew from one day to the next, even one month to the next, that it would not rain. Great weather for picnics. The wind blew off the sparsely vegetated veldt, swirling the dust into spirals; the light was bright and white casting dark mottled circular shadows on the dry ground. Under the scrawny trees that were dotted about the bush like the hairs on a mangy dog a few malnourished and thirsty goats might try to seek shelter from the relentless sun, but the trees gave only slight, almost leafless, relief to the sad animals.

All around were ant-hills, some even taller than me.

The landscape was fairly flat, apart from the dramatic Matopos Hills some distance away. Sometimes you could see the burrows of the wild animals that eked out their meagre existences in the veldt. It was difficult to believe that wildlife could exist in such hot and dry conditions.

But, joy of joys, despite the risk of a horse stumbling into a hole, we were allowed to go riding on Saturday mornings after the evil effects of the Alophen had passed over and out.

We duly dressed up in amazingly baggy jodhpurs, solar topees and sensible, heavy shoes and off we trundled to the riding school that was run by Elizabeth Scott. She taught us about horses, all the anatomy and the names of the various parts of the body, how to muck out the stables, how to clean the tack, brush the horses and, of course, how to saddle-up. I loved all that and of course Elizabeth, and I loved the bay horse, Harry, who was designated as 'mine'. His coat was as shiny as a piece of highly polished mahogany furniture and his jet-black silky mane and brushed and combed tail were my delight.

However, the love affair with Harry was not to last. One awful day when I was getting ready to go out with the others, he planted his hoof fairly and squarely on my well-shod foot. Even so, it was thumpingly painful. I couldn't get him off. Thank Dor-Dor for the tough shoes! But my feelings were crushed. Harry had done it deliberately to put me in my place, I was convinced.

'Whatever are you doing back there?' Elizabeth called. 'Do get a move on.'

'I can't. Harry's standing on my foot. I can't move him,' I squawked.

'Well push him off, you dumb cluck,' shouted Mavis.

'Oh, for goodness' sake,' and Elizabeth came in. She gave Harry a hearty thwack on the rump and he jerked forward and began prancing energetically round the stall. I feared for the safety of my other foot.

'Don't be so feeble. Come on now. Best thing to do when you've had a bad time with a horse is to get on right away. Here, I'll give you a leg-up,' and then she added, handing me a hankie, 'Blow your nose.'

When Gyll and Mavis had stopped laughing I turned to them.

'Please don't tell. They'll only laugh and tease me and, and I can't bear it. No one likes me, not even Harry.' I sat up there and cried.

'Nonsense. Everybody likes you,' Elizabeth said with firmness.

'I don't,' piped up Mavis.

Gyll glared at her.

'And nor do they,' I went on.

'Don't you say a word. You know what will happen,' Gyll sounded pretty upset.

'I was only joking,' Mavis muttered, because she knew in her heart of hearts that the teasing would indeed be unbearable. It was just 'not done' to cry or make a fuss about anything.

Elizabeth raised an eyebrow. 'Come on now. Let's get going.'

We trotted off in single file, Elizabeth at the front, me trailing behind because I was still scared. To tell the truth, I had well and truly got over my romance with Harry. I already trusted few humans and now Harry had let me down. I was very disillusioned.

Maybe Elizabeth might have pondered why I was more scared of what the family might think of such a silly thing than of the whacking bruise on my foot, but I began to sense that she might imagine what life at 12, Bryant Road was like, as after that she softened her tough act and smiled and encouraged us a lot as we all cantered over the open veldt like free kids, laughing.

The time was passing: weeks, months, another year, during which there was little news from home. Mummy had started off writing once a week as she had done when we were at boarding school in England, but the letters soon dried up. I couldn't remember quite how she looked anymore, or hear her voice in my head.

I looked at her dim photograph in the double-sided leather frame, with her face on one side and Daddy's, looking, as it were, directly at her, smiling confidently, on the opposite side. It was only at the last moment that we had thought of bringing the pictures with us. Mummy and Daddy should really have had some good photographs taken of themselves in a proper studio, so that we would have something good to remember them by. But they didn't, partly I suppose because nobody imagined that the separation would be for so long. I don't believe that Gyll and I had been taken to the studio either, for our own to be taken, but then, maybe Daddy had plans already in hand to forget us for ever!

Well, that was supposed to be a joke, but as things turned out . . .

As it was, their likenesses were faded and scratched from their days on our dressing tables at Gardenhurst (possibly because they were covered in a type of cellophane and not glass, which was not considered safe for children to handle). But we could still just perceive Mummy's dark wavy hair and her crooked smile, though I couldn't remember how she felt or what she smelled of – perfume, or cigarettes, or perhaps both? On the other hand, Mrs Marsh, with Dor-Dor in train, would take us to a photographer in Bulawayo regularly, once a year, to have a proper one taken to send home, just in case they did forget us.

Daddy did write sometimes, for our birthdays or Christmas, and he told us that the house in Watford had been sold and that they had moved to Gloucestershire, near the Round House, in the countryside in which he felt at home.

He said that he had joined the Royal Observer Corps, which meant that he watched the dark night skies from a little semi-collapsed hut on the Lechlade to Burford road, waiting for signs of enemy aircraft. He sent us a photograph of himself in uniform and very swashbuckling he looked too. I put it in the frame with Mummy's photo opposite.

Mummy, he said, was 'with' the FANYs, whatever that meant. Dor-Dor did not appear to know and anyway would not use a word like 'fanny'.

Mummy herself once wrote vaguely about 'joining up', which we thought only men did. Then Mrs Marsh explained to us as best she could that Mummy was doing war-work with a group of voluntary (which meant that they were not paid) ladies who did many things for the war effort. It sounded jolly interesting but not a bit like Mummy.

The letters we did receive had been censored, in case of some inadvertent remark that might, for instance, pinpoint where the regiment she was attached to was stationed. We were used to seeing, in England, the large posters that warned that 'Careless Talk Costs Lives' so we were not all that surprised to see large chunks of our letters scrawled all over in thick black pen. Perhaps, we thought, they had messed things up a bit and they had, by mistake, blacked-out the bits in the places where she said she loved us. After censoring, the letters were photographed, put on to negatives and subsequently printed on photographic paper, in miniature. The result was a pygmy page, grey and shiny, with minute writing that was almost impossible to read and hopeless to cherish. We realised that this was all part of the war effort, that sending letters in this way saved valuable space on transport ships, but it was still very sad. And what we wanted, so very much, were letters and contact with home, with the smell and touch of home. As the letters from Mummy and Daddy dribbled to a stop, East the chauffeur used to write from time to time, but when his stopped too we guessed that he had probably been called up and killed at war or perhaps bombed in an air raid. We never knew. Dor-Dor tried to allay our fears by saying that perhaps Mummy's letters had been sunk on the way over and we wanted to believe her, but really, had *so* many ships been sunk? Wouldn't we have heard?

We liked the convent, St Peter's, where we were sent to school. The nuns wore their heavy habits even in the hottest weather, their faces bound round and under their chins with crisp, starched linen, the black veils trailing over their shoulders and down their backs. They wore their religious uniform as if doing penance for some nameless sin.

The nuns who taught us were severe but fair. The school itself was sunny, built round a quadrangle, all the schoolrooms leading out on to whitewashed cloisters that led to the small, dry garden in the middle. As I remember, it was rather rocky. The chapel was cool and dark and sad. We were sent there to think and to pray when we had done something wrong. To me, it was a reward not a punishment.

Mavis and I were in the same form and she was good at almost everything. I would have liked, so much, to excel at my lessons, but the system was different from our little school at Burnham-on-Sea and I never seemed to catch up, not really for the rest of my school days and, anyway, I was just not clever.

Gyll and I made up for our lack of scholastic achievement by entering the weekly competitions in the local newspaper, Gyll inevitably for poetry and me for painting. Small cash prizes were awarded to the winners but the big thrill was opening the paper on a Saturday morning to see our poems and pictures reproduced for all to view. Even Dor-Dor looked faintly pleased, but we were not allowed to tell anyone. 'If anyone is interested,' she said, 'they can look for themselves.'

'Oh, but there was another even more exciting competition to think about, very different and very challenging, given the circumstances of frugality at 12, Bryant Road. We were invited to a fancy dress parade, with prizes for the winners and a promise of a photograph in the local newspaper. It was not so much that we wanted to win, we just wanted to be allowed to enter. All our school friends talked of little else.

From the very beginning it was decided that Mavis should wear her grandmother's wedding frock. We didn't think that the term 'wedding frock' was quite as romantic as 'wedding dress', but that's the way it went, and Dor-Dor was adamant. No Frenchie fancies here.

Anyway, it was a dream of ivory watered-taffeta and lace as fine as cobwebs. We had never seen anything so magically beautiful, the sort of thing that the Little Princess might have worn to a ball, had she not mislaid her father. I thought it unbelievably romantic, though Mrs Bloom, sternly, stopped short of letting Mavis wear the antique lace veil and train. Instead Dor-Dor made her one of mosquito netting which we thought looked pretty good. The frock was a creation to be proud of even though it had to be adjusted just that bit to fit Mavis's eleven-year-old figure. Actually, it had to be let out, not taken in, though Mavis was hardly what you would call plump. She looked like a fairy queen.

'But what about us?' Gyll asked.

'Well,' said Dor-Dor, sitting back on her laurels after her success with Mavis. 'You could wear your pyjamas and go as Wee Willie Winkie.'

My sister groaned in disbelief and disappointment.

'I'll look silly and anyway, that's not fancy dress.'

Gyll cast about for an idea.

'Couldn't we make something, I mean instead of sewing and always having to take it to pieces to sew it again?' This was one of Dor-Dor's favourite ways of keeping us occupied. The stitching improved but not the output. We never finished anything.

'You know,' I said eagerly, 'something like Robin Hood or Snow White or even one of the fairies from the flower book?'

We both loved the Flower Fairy books by Cicely Mary Barker, but we were not quite as tiny and twinkling as her little fairies. If she had had only us for her models she might have depicted something rather more solid, probably dock leaves or ground elder.

As we proffered one of the books my aunt eyed the little creature in blue jerkin and pants, complete with a blue-petalled cap, who represented the Bluebell Fairy. It was so English.

'I don't know. I really don't think, I mean, where would we find the material?' she contemporised.

'What about the Indian shop?' Gyll suggested very daringly, full of hope.

Dor-Dor looked askance. It was a place that she tried to avoid walking past, let alone entering, as if by some absurd chance she might be thrown into a linen basket and transported to an exotic bazaar in the Far East where she would be sold into the white slave trade.

'Not the Indian shop,' she said firmly. 'You know Mrs Bloom would never allow it.'

'But Mrs Bloom isn't here just now and anyway she needn't know and we could say we got it at Miekle's.'

'Oh yes, yes,' Gyll went on, 'and I could be the Blackberry Fairy. Yes, I really could. We could make it together.'

She smiled uncertainly, because she very much doubted her own ability to cut out a costume even from a pattern, had one existed, let alone know how much material to buy.

It could not have escaped Dor-Dor's attention that if Mavis was to go as the Beauty and win all the prizes, it might not go unnoticed that Gyll and I were cast into the role of her ugly sisters. This must have given her pause for thought.

While she muttered on about the gaudiness of the shop, which we, of course, thought to look, as far as we could see from the outside, just like Aladdin's cave, we used all our skills to dispel her fears.

'And it's much cheaper, Margo Thenner told me,' Gyll lied in part – indeed it was much cheaper, but she had never said a word to Margo about it.

'And they are very polite,' she added hopefully.

'Yes dear, I am thinking' was all Dor-Dor would say, but it seemed to us to be as near a 'yes' as possible.

And so she finally agreed to go shopping, just the three of us. It was with colossal bravery that she finally crossed the threshold of the oriental shop, decked with bolts of cheap, brightly coloured satins and silks and hung about with gauzy scarves and beads and braids and heavenly gold-embroidered materials for saris. A treasure house. We stood astounded at the glamour.

Dor-Dor gamely bargained for the minimum she thought she could get away with and once the slippery material had been measured, cut up, packed in brown paper parcels and tied with coloured string, which she immediately thrust into her shopping bag so that if she met anyone they would not know which emporium she had been patronising, she nervously took out her purse and settled up.

We skipped joyously on to the glaring white pavement.

'Thank you, thank you, thank you,' we cried rushing out of the shop to follow her as she scuttled off to a less dangerous and better part of town.

'I think it best if we keep all this to ourselves. Not to chatter too much in front of the family.'

We received the message that she was trying to give us. Good old Dor-Dor, we thought, for once on our side. How devastating if we had actually won a prize, knocking Mavis from pole position, but there was not much chance of that, not with our lack of skill in designing and our frightful crooked hemming. Still, we were happy.

Back at 12, Bryant Road Dor-Dor opened her sewing box, which contained a hoard of carefully rolled pieces of old lace, tape, trimmings of all sorts, pieces of elastic secured in little rolls with a pin, buttons, hooks and eyes, just about anything that could be rescued from a cast-off garment that she might eventually need for some other useful purpose – the covering of hangers, wastepaper baskets, pin-cushions, sewing-wallets, lavender bags, and even more sewing boxes. The collection was phenomenal and in its way beautiful. She assiduously kept a compartment for each item. She used the finest of fine needles and possessed a collection of scissors equal to none. They were never to be used for cutting paper (family please note). Her shears were old and heavy but they sliced through cloth like a hot knife through butter. She also had a little place for her silver thimble, worn shiny on the top with age and use, so that if we tried to use it ourselves, our needles would slip off the smooth surface. She herself had no difficulty, her nimble fingers making tiny invisible stitches as she patched and mended the household linen, made elegant handkerchiefs and embroidered initials on pillow cases. After she died I inherited her silver thimbles, her reels of real cotton thread and a hoard of very small pearl and ivory buttons.

It is a shame that I have no photographs of Gyll and me dressed as fairies. Cicely Mary Barker would have been a bit surprised at our interpretation of the delicate drawings in her book. Gyll seemed appropriately rounded to be a berry, but she had to wear her hateful brown socks and sandals which rather spoiled the effect she had striven for, i.e., a fairy about to fly away on gossamer wings.

For me, my best moment was slipping into the costume and feeling the soft electric-blue satin sheer against my skin. Luckily for me I had a pair of blue bedroom slippers which did not exactly match the rest of the costume, but at least looked less obvious than clumpy sandals. The little satin-covered cardboard pointy hat I made kept slipping off, but Gyll fixed it for me with two large hair-grips.

Mrs Marsh was finally let into the secret, after much elbow-digging and coy giggling, as if she had not already guessed what was going on with the house littered with little bits of material and the rapid concealment of what we were up to each time she came on to the veranda.

She pointed out that it might be nice if I actually carried some bluebells, but as far as the garden stretched I could see only zinnias and flashy shrubs. Still, miracles do happen.

Mrs Marsh had a friend who had an 'English' garden. Us kids were so used by now to the uniform khaki-coloured grass and neat sparse planting of the local gardens that our breath was stolen when we entered the dream of Mrs John's enchanted oasis. It was damp and shady and smelt of an English summer's day. Water tumbled every-where, and there were pools and waterfalls leading down to a dell where one would be sure to find the real Bluebell Fairy, lurking amongst the primroses, lilies of the valley and narcissi. It was like a soft day at home.

It was with some difficulty that I was restrained from going berserk amongst the flowers; I just wanted to touch and smell everything and to pick great clumps of flowers that had no connection whatsoever to bluebells. Still, I filled my little wicker basket and watched them shrivel the moment we went into the sun. But I didn't mind. I had seen paradise that day.

Of course Mavis won first prize but we didn't begrudge her that one little bit, and anyway I pressed the flowers between sheets of blotting paper, keeping them long after the colours had faded, and they had become as transparent as tissue-paper. I seem to remember that the kind judges gave us an honourable mention – but I also seem to remember that all the other children got honourable mentions too.

Mavis and I had our twelfth birthdays and felt a lot older. One of the best things was being allowed to have a bicycle, a first and great step towards independence.

But there were hazards, one of which was the completely terrifying experience of being caught in a locust storm. I nearly fell off my bike. I nearly fainted, I very nearly died, but no excuses were permitted for not getting back to 12, Bryant Road on the dot, so there was no choice but to carry on.

The massive dark swarm engulfed me, clattering round my head as I ducked my chin and pedalled furiously for cover. All round the air vibrated with the roar of their giant wings (spanning up to five inches), which almost drowned out the sound of the desperate clanging and banging of tin drums and corrugated iron as the garden boys tried to protect their crops from the voracious insects, which could strip a garden bare in a matter of minutes. It was thought that locusts did not like noise but it did not seem to deter them much and the place still looked like a blasted heath as I rode on to seek cover. Oh to get back and empty my clothes of the beastly things. I even found them in my satchel and tangled in my hair. Ugh!

The other hazards of cycling were quite good fun, though they could have been deadly. For instance, we learnt to ride extremely rapidly round any snakes loitering across the road and on one famous occasion I was swept away by a flash rain storm and found myself thrashing about in a drain filled with filthy muddy water. I went under a couple of times but I was far more worried for my bike, because I knew that if I lost it it would not be replaced and I would have to trudge on foot to school and back. Luckily as I bobbed to the surface, strong brown arms stretched down for me and hauled me from the water and the bike got lodged in a tree stump further down the drain. When I thanked the men it was not for saving me but for saving my machine.

After the rain had stopped, when the land had slaked its thirst and the dormant weeds and grasses had had a chance to drink, all at once the veldt became green and sweet smelling, miraculous and beautiful, just overnight, it seemed.

It was a wonderful day when we were judged to be careful enough to cycle off on our own into the veldt, of course with strict injunctions to be back on time. We wore our cotton sun-hats or scarves knotted round our heads (like our present dear Queen), in order to protect the back of our heads from the sun. We were warned about sun-stroke – that it could cause grown men, mature women and children to be struck down in their prime, driven first to madness and then to death, all as a result of being careless about head gear.

We set off three in a row, as there was no traffic to bother us, and shouted and sang as we swerved across the empty riverbeds and around the kopjes, over huge burrows (rabbits? Dogs? WOLVES? I never knew but I don't think there were ever any wolves in them there hills) and round the prickly thorn bushes.

On yet another bright day Gyll pulled Mavis and me behind the tool shed in the garden. Tangly things grew there and I didn't care for it and neither did she, so it obviously had to be an important and secret meeting.

'I predict,' she started off, 'that if we pray enough and believe enough in miracles, the war will end.' She sounded like Elijah himself.

'Oh, for goodness' sake, you've been reading about St Theresa again, and Bernadette Soubirous. You remember, those miracles.'

'But you haven't seen any visions or heard any voices, have you?' Mavis asked in a practical sort of way.

Gyll shook her head, flushed with impatience. 'Oh ye of little faith,' she said solemnly, 'I know, I know.' She sighed at our evident stupidity. 'But what I am telling you is that it is true, really. If we believe it hard enough the war will end, I promise you. There will be a miracle.'

Mavis and I looked at each other and smiled uneasily.

'Come on,' ordered our leader. So we went.

It was to the veldt that we pilgrimaged on the occasion of Gyll's Great Prophecy. Without giving any hint to the grown-ups of the purpose of our picnic, we managed to obtain permission, lemonade and sandwiches, and arming ourselves with a prayer book and cross, set forth. We also took our penknives, as Gyll suggested we might while away the time by becoming blood-brothers with Mavis, which would involve cutting our fingers and mingling our blood. But I wasn't too keen about this as my penknife was very blunt, and, in the end, since no one was prepared to make the first incision, we abandoned the idea.

Anyway I was, as always, Gyll's humble servant and her religious fervour was so intense and righteous that I thought it quite likely that she might manage to pull off her miracle, in which case I wanted to be part of it. Mavis had probably come along out of curiosity, because apart from the fact that she had never seen a miracle (at which fact Gyll feigned surprise but refused to go into any details of any that she herself might have witnessed, not even small ones), she had not so far become well acquainted with my sister's more dramatic performances. We found a goodish spot from where we could neither see anyone nor be spotted by anyone. We sat down together, closely, holding hands.

The prayers took quite a long time, but we were fairly convinced that we had a good chance of succeeding.

At about eleven o'clock, as the sun hung high in the summer sky, the same sun that stretched over Europe and to England (but not at quite the same time), Gyll thought that it was probably a good moment to have lunch. Then we wouldn't have to waste time later on, when the miracle was happening. So we did that fairly hurriedly, in order to get back to the praying.

Mavis asked Gyll, 'How will we know when the war has ended?'

Gyll eyed her a little crossly. 'We'll know,' she said firmly, looking round hopefully for a sign of victory.

'But how? Will there be a big bang or bells or bonfires, like the olden days?' I asked.

'I expect so,' she replied in a fairly confident tone.

Mavis winked at me, which I thought was pretty risky and very irreverent. She evidently didn't understand my sister's power of thought, but I felt sure she would soon be very impressed indeed.

At one point, a small group of skimpily dressed, shoeless African children began to gather around us, appearing as if from nowhere. They came singly and silently, uncertainly and slightly bewildered, then holding hands, with baskets and pieces of wood balanced on their cropped, curly heads. There were perhaps ten or twelve of them. They regarded us with curiosity. How could they even begin to guess what was going on? They leaned lazily, relaxed, against the skinny flat-topped trees, silent, staring.

Gyll was so intent on her powerful prayers that she didn't really see them, but then one boy, who was a bit taller than the others, probably aged about ten, moved forward quietly, with even steps, until he was only a few yards from us. He wanted, I am sure, to see what was going on. Magic perhaps? All at once this enraged Mavis who jumped up and waved her arms about fiercely.

'*Voetsec*,' she shouted, '*voetsec*, get out of here, you skellums.'

She looked so wild and big compared to the skinny Africans that they turned tail and disappeared back into the veldt without a sound. They just went.

Mavis looked pleased. 'That's the way to treat those kaffir skellums,' she said with satisfaction, then threw herself back on the ground and laughed.

About two o'clock we got up and went for a bit of a poke around, looking for Matabele ants and spiders and other nasty things; then, feeling a bit peckish, we ate our tea.

'The war will end, *must* end, please God,' chanted Gyll and added, 'Jesus said "Pray unto me" and that is what we are doing.'

'But nothing is happening.'

'Just wait. It's still quite early, silly.'

'Look, man,' said Mavis, 'I'm getting tired. I want to go home. They will be cross with us for being out for so long. I didn't know that miracles took all day.'

I was becoming tired too, but dared not admit it.

Gyll sat on the ground with her eyes shut.

'I know it's going to work,' she said.

At five o'clock it began to grow dark.

Silently we packed our things and cycled back into Bulawayo.

'I mean, perhaps no one knows yet,' I whispered consolingly. 'I mean, England's an awful long way away. It would take time for the news to reach us and anyway it's nighttime there.'

Gyll's eyes brimmed with tears. I could see she felt so let down by the God she believed in.

'I shan't,' she said finally, 'ever ask Him a favour again. I shan't ever believe in God again.' She could not understand why God did not hear us and respond.

Beyond the immediate disappointment in God's apparent unwillingness or ability to perform miracles for us lay the savage realisation that without His divine intervention, it was becoming increasingly unlikely that we would ever get home. Nobody spoke anymore of a return journey, of victory or even of seeing Mummy and Daddy again. It was as if all that part of our life was now over and done with.

Mavis was very decent. She never mentioned this tragic episode, which was a mercy, because Gyll and I both knew that if the family heard about it, they would mock us to death.

This teasing thing may all seem very trivial to you, but believe me it wasn't. It was an art, perfected over the years, which had become a sort of gladiatorial torment.

It had gone too far; probably initially it was quite a light-hearted sort of game that had evolved in order to point out the foolish way some members of the family might have behaved, but now it had become too much, and no one was excluded, not even Mrs Bloom (though she rather cleverly claimed that she couldn't hear what was going on), from the sometimes unkind or even quite malicious attacks.

Of course, it was nearly always the most vulnerable, those who could least defend themselves, who took the brunt of the teasing. In our case being young and inexperienced at the 'game', we had no shields with which to stave off the attacks and we dared not use our feeble spears for fear of even further retribution.

I had once tried to make what I had stupidly imagined to be a funny remark about Dor-Dor's face spoiling my photo album (well, it was a thoroughly thoughtless and foolish thing to say, but truly meant as a joke and most certainly not unkindly, I would never have dared), but despite tearful apologies she purposefully chose to take it the wrong way. There was hell to pay. Quite apart from not speaking to me for days on end, she did not even look at me.

However, it was all thought to be great fun and I think that they really believed that every child should undergo being put in their place, being pulled down a peg or two, for their own good, of course. But in our case, being pulled down to where, when you are already at the bottom? I do think, though, that we were altogether too naive and laid ourselves open, so thoughtlessly and far too often, to their strange sense of humour.

Certainly no one in the family ever got away with showing pride in anything, even though the achievement might only be most modestly mentioned and perhaps well worthy of a little praise.

Naturally we two were labelled 'conceited' as, initially, we chattered openly about our little successes, as we had been encouraged to do at home, but soon we no longer even dreamed of talking about our achievements in the newspaper competitions. It was simply no longer a subject.

'Oh my,' one of them would say. 'Look what a big mouth Susie has.'

In the bathroom I peered into the looking-glass to see if my face had changed, my lips suddenly become gross and ugly as they described. Puzzled, I couldn't see any difference.

I was that naive.

In a way I became a bit of a cold fish, learning quickly to avoid the pitfalls; to shut up. But Gyll was so volatile, pitching in at the deep end before she had tested the water. Her emotions smouldered under the thinnest of skins, erupting into agonies of embarrassment, hurt and confusion before she could stop herself.

'Someone will need her frock letting out again,' Dor-Dor noted as Gyll accepted a second helping of dreary old silverside (again).

'Perhaps she didn't have any breakfast!' Mrs Bloom would add, maliciously.

'B-b-b-but I did!'

'Ha-ha, ha-ha, Dumbkopf,' said Mavis, and added, 'Dumb-cluck.'

Too late Gyll would realise her mistake.

Alone, I said, 'I promise, Honest Injun, that you're thin,' but she didn't believe me.

'I'm f-f-fat.'

'No, promise.'

'P-Promise?'

'Promise.'

Nobody seemed to worry about her stutter, which was getting much worse. They teased her merrily over that too, imitating her until she was on the point of tears. They laughed.

I'm not sure what sort of a sense of humour a 12-year-old is supposed to possess to counter constant teasing. We certainly lacked the necessary verve to answer back. We were so feeble. We did our best to avoid the traps, to dodge any of the 'not done' things that would give them ammunition to poke fun at us, but we were such gullible, simple targets. For them it was a way of life that we didn't understand – and the more we didn't understand the worse it got.

How awful, though, it must have been for the family. The two sullen English cuckoos, growing larger every day and taking up too much space, increasingly unlikely to fly the nest. Unlike wild fledglings, who eventually take wing, we were truly trapped; there was to be no relief for our proxy parents. We were dutifully fed and watered, with efficiency and firmness, but as with the birds, love did not enter into the relationship. We longed to fly away; they probably (and who could possibly blame them?) longed to be rid of us; but as it was, our little visit became an interminable sentence for us all.

Now, it has been pointed out to me that this account is all about 'poor me', or 'poor us'. But, well, just think about yourselves being in this same place at this same time. How would it have been for you, or can't you accept the miserable things that happened? Perhaps thinking about it makes you feel uncomfortable or maybe you don't think things were that bad anyway? Well, that's up to you, but since this is my story I will describe things as I want, and truthfully, too. Of course there were some good happenings as well; we were not always cast down and we had some very happy times but we were not at home. We needed to be at home. We needed our hugs and cuddles.

'Do you know,' Gyll said one day, 'I don't think they like us.'

* * *

The notion that we were unpopular within the family, even disliked, took a bit of getting used to.

Up until now our lives had been so small and unimportant, so that little of what we had done back in England had ever elicited or warranted any positive response. I suppose we had even been rather negative, like Mummy, and had largely gone unnoticed, except by Alice, our most beloved nanny.

Now, far from reaping any sympathy for our orphaned state (Gyll loved the word orphan), if we displayed any sign of homesickness (and I mean the real kind this time), we only incurred their irritation. We were being ungrateful. As we continued to think that we were charity children, we sped into a downward spiral, quite unable to 'pull our socks up' and wanting only a comforting arm around us to stop the spin. But the sadder we got the angrier they got and then we felt even worse. Mind you, we had each other.

Gyll summed it all up, as we lay in our beds, staring fixedly at the knotted mosquito nets that probably harboured whole families of deadly spiders, waiting to drop on us as night fell and the nets were unfurled.

'You know what it is,' she whispered, 'we're just refugees. We haven't even got passports; no belongings; nothing.'

'It would have been better if the Na-a-a-azis had torpedoed us on the way over.'

'And we'd got drowned.'

Death seemed a fairly acceptable alternative.

'We can't run away anywhere. There's nowhere to run to; we can't go to the veldt at night and I can't think of anywhere else.'

'And we haven't any money.'

Doom.

Running away figured quite highly on Gyll's list of intended adventures, but it is always as well to have some cash and as we shall see later, somewhere to run to. I thought of the pocket money we used to have at home and realised sadly that here we would never have enough. Running away is quite an expensive business.

'Do you remember,' I asked Gyll, 'when we went with Alice on Saturday mornings to spend our pocket money?'

'Sixpence each,' she smiled a touch ruefully. 'That wouldn't get us far.'

'Do you remember that little shop on the corner on the way to Daddy's, where they had those shelves of things for a halfpenny, a penny or even tuppence? I wonder what happened to the toys we bought? Broken, I suppose.' I sniffed. No, I wasn't crying, really.

'I wonder what Mummy did with all those dusters?' Gyll asked, in a little voice. 'We must have bought an awful lot.' She wasn't crying either.

Woolworth's was further down the High Street, and by the time we arrived there with Alice holding our hands, we had never managed to come up with a better idea than a yellow duster to take home to Mummy, to make her happy.

We wanted to cheer her up and when we first saw the bright yellow fluffy dusters with the red stitching all round the edges, we knew at once what we should buy. Repeated visits, well, almost every Saturday, yielded rather a lot of dusters.

Alice would say hopefully, 'Look, Gylly, Susie, I see something very pretty over there for your Mummy.' But we ignored the flowery jam pot covers, the tortoiseshell hair slides, the Apostle coffee spoons, and the spotted egg cup, which was quite pretty but unfortunately Mummy didn't like eggs. Alice laughed at our determination to buy the dusters. Poor Mummy, heaven only knows where she hid them all, but we only wanted to make her smile, to make her happy. Perhaps they did make her laugh, just because they were what they were, but I don't think I ever saw her using one.

'Those dusters, the yellow ones, I wonder what happened to them?' I asked Gyll. Toys broke, but dusters?

'I wonder how long the war will go on for?'

'For ever. I heard it said on the wireless. Unless the Germans invade; gosh, perhaps they already have. What will happen to Daddy? Will they shoot all the men?'

'Maybe they'll shoot Dick.'

Gyll pondered about that for a moment.

'I shouldn't think so,' she said, 'he's still at school.'

'Well? And anyway, he could be killed by a bomb.'

'I expect so. But I'd rather be there than here.'

The monstrous truth overwhelmed us, but having come to this frightful conclusion, we realised that there was absolutely nothing that we could do to improve the situation.

'Well, since we can't escape,' Gyll remarked gloomily, 'what shall we do?'

'There isn't anything we can do, though we could try writing to Mummy or even Daddy.'

'Fat lot of good that would do. You know Dor-Dor always reads our letters. And what could they do anyway? There is a war on. That's why we are here.'

In my mind's eye I could see Mummy and Daddy, Margaret and Dick, all crouching in the Anderson shelter, the sky bang-crashing with explosions.

'Oh well, maybe we could try to be naughty. Then we would be punished for something we really have done,' I suggested.

'Hm. Let me think about it' and she looked quite interested. 'But look, I've written another poem.' And she passed me the latest effort.

THE EXILE

We are exiled many miles away
From England, Home, and Beauty,
I would not care if Germans came
To raid and steal their booty.

I'd suffer terror, fear and fire
Unrest and burning pain,
I'd suffer agony,
To be in England once again.

I'm exiled many miles away,
In a town to me unknown,
My sister and I stand by ourselves,
Together – yet alone.

I'd give near everything I have
To return home, once more,
Alas! I stand here quite alone
And face a locked door.

Gyll A. G. H. Edmonds

'Well, it's all right,' I said, 'a bit sad, and I'm not sure about the part about you standing alone in front of the door. I'm here.'

'Oh, of course I know, but I had to make it rhyme,' she said, exasperated. 'And anyway, I meant that we were both alone together.'

I didn't altogether understand, but I liked the poem really, so I didn't say anything else.

However, a couple of days later Gyll suggested that we do something really, really naughty, to cheer ourselves up.

'What sort of thing?'

'Well, you know we are supposed to go to the rehearsal for the dancing display on Thursday afternoon, well nobody would notice if we didn't turn up.'

The dance display consisted of each class in the school putting on a little show for the parents at the end of term. My form skipped around in bare feet, wearing skimpy little short frocks, while we bent and wove through imaginary fields of flowers, gathering them in our arms and tossing them into the air. We also did a wonderful dance, still wearing the same airy-fairy clothes, pretending to be warriors of ancient Greece, taking two steps forward, two back, our right hand to our foreheads, our left arms supporting imaginary shields as we gazed at the supposed enemy, all to the music of the rondo of Beethoven's piano sonata in C minor (The Pathetique). Excellent stuff, but as a dance, we had already practised it enough.

'You daren't miss practice.'

'Oh yes I do. I thought we might go to the cinema,' Gyll said casually.

I was aghast. How could we possibly go unnoticed, quite apart from the fact that we didn't have any money for the tickets?

'How are we going to pay, and anyway, how are we going to get there?'

'Well, I've just enough in my piggy bank and we'll go on our bikes, silly.'

Oh, the sheer audacity of the plan. I could see that it would be naughty, and that was what we had planned to be, but could we get away with it? These qualms did not bother Gyll.

'Tell you what. When we passed the cinema on the way to church last week I saw the advertisement for a film with someone called Tyrone — Tyrone — oh somebody. It's terrifically good. Margo said so.'

'But we can't!' I squealed in fear.

But as you already know, my sister could be very persuasive.

So we went to the bioscope (cinema) and it was one of the best things that we ever did, sitting there in the dark and lost forever in the gloss and magic of the screen and both of us hopelessly in love with Mr Power and his long-lashed glowing dark eyes.

We were drunk with excitement and mad with desire to see another film by the time we finally left the gloom of the foyer and emerged into the startlingly bright street. But we were altogether too careless as we staggered towards our bikes. Because then . . .

'Oh crumbs,' Gyll gasped. She blinked.

We had arrived face to face with Philip Moore, the curate at Dor-Dor's church. He was a young man and quite good-looking, though not in the same mould as Tyrone. But he wore a sheer white dog collar, which added to his appeal and which gave him an aura of something special and authoritative.

He looked straight at us, head on, recognising us at once. He glanced at his watch, rolled his eyes as if to indicate that we should pass as quickly as possible, and seemed to indicate, ever so carefully and lightly, that he had not seen us at all.

Gyll turned very bright red and slid past.

'Do you think he'll say—?' I was trembling as I asked.

'Of course not. He's in love with me,' she avowed, and smiled her very secret smile.

What, Mr Moore the curate in love with Gyll? But what could I say?

Anyway, he didn't split on us but we never plucked up the courage to go again.

9

Although Mrs Marsh, Mrs Bloom and Dor-Dor did not want us to grow up, it's the sort of thing you can't stop, especially in hot countries where girls mature physically rather earlier than those, for instance, in wartime England, as we were to discover on our return. But for the moment, despite the boys' clothes that we were made to wear or the occasional party frock out of which popped our busts (as Dor-Dor would call our budding breasts) like semi-ripe melons, we still were expected to look like children, and no wonder this suited the family.

Maybe they knew, maybe they only surmised, briefly, what might be going through the mind of poor old Augustus. I feel sure that if they had permitted themselves to think the unthinkable, then they would have dismissed such a disloyal thought just as quickly as possible. They probably asked God's forgiveness for having had wicked thoughts about him.

But the fact was that, at thirteen, Gyll was very pretty and nicely curved in the right places, and Augustus was an unstylish precursor to Humbert the Hum, with no glamour and little cunning. Gyll was no Lolita, being innocent about sex in the way that no child today would begin to understand, but she was perfectly aware of the lecherous longings of Mr Bloom and was shocked and embarrassed when he put his hand up her skirt and tried to get into her knickers, no mean feat as they were the sort of pants that had elastic round the thigh. He also aimed passing sweeps of his hands over her breasts, when he leant over her to look at what she was reading or working at. The most difficult moments came when we took it in turns to pass the sweets round the table after Sunday lunch, our one big treat. When it was Gyll's turn she turned puce as she stood by Mr Bloom, his hand groping at her under the capacious white tablecloth while he took plenty of time to make his choice.

Nowadays a child would be knowledgeable enough to complain. The randy old man might even have ended up on a sex-offenders' list, but in later years we always thought about him with sympathy and affection. He was a kind and gentle man, just very, *very* lacking in self-control.

As a reason for liking him, it must be declared in his favour that he did play the piano beautifully and I simply loved that – Schubert, Schumann, Chopin – though, it should be mentioned, never, ever any Mendelssohn, because Prince Albert liked his music and the family did not like Prince Albert. Foreign upstart, they called him, which was a bit surprising to say the least, all things considered.

Unfortunately the inflamed feelings that Augustus felt for Gyll allowed themselves to go too far for comfort. He followed her into our bedroom, I assume having made sure that the rest of the family were well occupied elsewhere and pushed her backwards onto the bed. He then, clumsily and heavily, because he was not a slightly built old man, fell upon her. She yelped with surprise and he at once drew himself up and rushed out of the room. She didn't know what was happening but she knew it wasn't right.

'What shall I do?' she asked me.

'Tell Dor-Dor,' I advised quite wrongly, but as we didn't realise the implications as to what had happened we could not foresee the consequences.

'But they will blame me somehow.'

'Of course not. How could they?'

'You'll see,' she said knowingly and of course she was right.

Unfortunately Dor-Dor doubled the mistake by telling Mrs Marsh and Mrs Marsh quadrupled the mistake by telling Mrs Bloom.

Mrs Bloom summoned Gyll. You can guess the rest.

Suffice to say that Gyll was debarred from family meals until the Blooms set off for their annual holiday at the Cape, this time (no surprise) a month earlier than normal, just two weeks after the awful row. Mr Bloom looked very depressed but the blame was still laid at Gyll's door. She was gated for a month, except for going to school, and was not allowed to stay for the readings after supper. Poor Gyll. It was so unfair, but then you need to learn to be silent at times.

Still, it is possible that Mrs Marsh might have wondered how Gyll could have let all this happen and I suppose she realised that we had had no sex education whatsoever, even though Gyll had started her monthly periods. That was no fun as we had to make our own pads from gauze and cotton wool, which involved cutting up yards of material and the result was about as effective as the absorption found in a single Kleenex tissue today. During this part of the month, Gyll did not move around much! It was not until we went to boarding school that we realised that it was possible to buy something that really worked.

So Mrs Marsh summoned up her courage and took Gyll into the grandparents' sitting room, closed the door firmly behind her, drew in a deep breath and started the discussion on matters sexual, though as Gyll told me, she never actually used that taboo word.

Unhappily, the normal familiarity of a mother and

daughter was sadly lacking, but Dor-Dor would not have been the most informed person to perform this task. Anyway she had practically no relationship with us either.

It was probably the first time Mrs Marsh had had a private conversation with Gyll and now she floundered helplessly in a welter of descriptively unpleasant words that left Gyll totally puzzled, a little in the way that the mother of a friend of mine, when climbing into the carriage to start her honeymoon, was whispered to by her mother, who said, 'Don't worry about anything Gerald might do to you. It's all right.'

Mrs Marsh painted such an extraordinary picture of bodily functions, describing a variety of holes and horrors, that Gyll eventually asked why, if it was so dreadful, any woman ever had a second baby, thinking of the pregnant Mrs Cox who had been befriended by the family because she came from Sevenoaks. Gyll reckoned that she must be a fool to undergo, for a second time, such terrifying ordeals as conception and birth.

When we were alone we discussed the whole sordid business, as we discussed all things together, growing closer, more dependent on each other, as the months dragged by and the months expanded into years.

'I'll tell you what,' she announced one day, 'I'm going to try to borrow Margo's mother's book. It's called, *Sane Sex Life and Sane Sex Living*. She found it on top of her mother's wardrobe.'

'What's it about? A whole book on sex?'

'Well, yes, I suppose so. She was showing it to some of her pals. I'm sure she'd lend it to me if I asked her. She's awfully nice.'

In due course Gyll arrived at 12, Bryant Road with the book concealed, with great care, in her satchel.

'Here, let me see.'

I flipped through the pages, not quite sure what I was looking for.

'What are these drawings?' I gasped. 'They are of naked people!'

'Well, Mrs Marsh said that they take off their clothes, especially their knickers.'

'But like this?'

I pointed to the rather badly drawn depictions of positions that the book said could be 'adopted' during sexual intercourse.

'I don't believe it, I just don't believe it.' I thrust the book back at her.

'Mrs Marsh says that even dogs do it,' Gyll replied giggling.

Was it true? I couldn't think that Margo Heller's mother would take the trouble to hide the book if it wasn't true.

Gyll shrugged and looked a little superior.

'Well, you'll grow up. You'll see.'

She was all of thirteen.

The whole subject seemed to me to be utterly remote; I couldn't get personally involved and yet I felt that there was something missing. In all the pages of the book and in everything that Mrs Marsh had said, I realised that the word 'love' had never figured very prominently. I had been, back at home, given the impression that making babies was to do with love, despite the fact that both Dick and Gyll said that some tramp had just left me in the garden and that Mummy and Daddy had taken me in because Gyll and Dick had begged them to.

But with all this new and very suspect knowledge just acquired, I had to ask myself if Mr and Mrs Marsh did 'it', or how else could I account for the arrival of Alfred and Mavis on the scene? Would there be a new brother or sister for Mavis, heaven forbid?

I thought that they were probably too old and the whole business would be too disgusting for a genteel person such as Mrs Marsh, but Gyll thought not, because of the 'you-know-what' that sometimes got left in the bathroom. It was with frightened eyes then that I first regarded the awesome and nameless equipment, which until then had escaped my naive attention. I can remember quite clearly the day that two and two began to make four.

Mrs Bloom was actually by far the most physically attractive woman in the house, possessed of china-blue eyes, a charming round face and wavy silvery hair; a picture-book grandmother, but with the bearing and hauteur of old Queen Mary. Maybe this was how she saw herself, but actually her family had been in trade, just like ours, so there was little reason for her to look down her nose at Mummy and Geraldine, even though the latter was employed by her family. Mummy had been an exceptionally pretty child, with round solemn green eyes and soft brown ringlets, probably rather a challenge to her own child, Iris. Iris and Mummy had played together as children, under the watchful eye of Geraldine, and now she saw Iris's daughter and Mummy's daughter repeating history. I imagine that it irked her. I am sure that she could not help it, but she disliked me. I was never ready for her anger, which showed a side of her character few of the neighbours in Bulawayo would have expected.

She could be very sharp-tongued, as Augustus knew to his peril; she was also very badly educated and sometimes, like Mrs Malaprop, she got so muddled in her speech that it was comical: 'Augustus, oh Augustus, Amy Johnson has just flown round the world in a fish moth.' Just the sort of thing that we loved and which was told and retold amongst the family. Her mistakes made Mrs Malaprop look super-fluous. That was one side of her.

Now I saw the other side, as she burst in upon me while I was having my meagre bath – five inches of water, and Gyll would have to use the water after me. But it was wartime, you know, and while the British were suffering at home, we had to suffer with them. No sugar in our tea and, for instance, no second biscuit at teatime. I often wondered who ate the things that we were expected to leave on the serving plates, which were whisked away into the kitchen; probably the boys in the kraal at the back, but we ourselves had to learn the lessons of frugality.

Although I was used to my aunt popping in and out whilst I was bathing, seizing the clothes that I had just taken off, picking the pockets of my shorts for anything I had been silly enough to leave in there and at the same time, no doubt, probably looking for evidence of some wrongdoing. But what I was not used to was being accused of trying to murder my aunt.

I was standing up in the bath, prior to climbing out, when Mrs Bloom marched in, with Dor-Dor close on her heels. I was twelve and upset to be found in such a vulner-able state, without even a towel to wrap around me, but the angry old lady ignored my evident distress. I was shy, especially of her.

I think that in interrogating a prisoner, with their clothes stripped off, the plight of nakedness renders up all sorts of confessions that perhaps more complicated torture would not; though in my case, standing there quite bare and being stared at by Mrs Bloom was torture enough.

'Your aunt has told me,' she said in a voice that I recog-nised instantly as being very bad news for me, 'that you left your penknife open in your pocket!'

'My penknife?'

'Your penknife,' she said again, with a hint of menace.

I was beginning to get quite worried, but I managed to stutter, 'But it's blunt', which was very true, and since it was almost impossible to open once it had snapped shut, I had taken to not closing it at all. The problem was my bitten fingernails. Without my penknife I could not cut, slice, splice, peel or even make arrows for my bow. Or my bow itself, come to that. It was no use asking Gyll or Mavis if I could borrow theirs because they were mean and anyway most likely using them themselves.

Meanwhile, Dor-Dor was clucking and darting about like a deranged chicken in the background. It is always possible that she had not intended to involve Mrs Bloom in this farce, but unfortunately bumped into her in the corridor while she was examining the knife. Pity really, that Dor-Dor had not stabbed her to death (by mistake, of course) then and there, and then there would have been an end to all this continual harassment.

'Blunt? Ha?' And she seized it from the by now trembling hands of my aunt. She held up my little knife with the shagreen handle that Daddy had given me one day at home.

'Of course you know,' she said, 'that if your aunt was to cut the sinew between her thumb and forefinger she would get lock-jaw.' And then she added, 'And would die in agony.'

I think by this time Dor-Dor was beginning to believe this nonsense herself.

'But it is really, really blunt,' I said again. 'I'm sorry. Really sorry. I didn't mean to hurt her. It's not sharp enough to make arrows for my bow and I can't even cut my skin so that I can become blood-brothers with Mavis.' Then, from the looks on their horrified faces I realised too late what a terrible mistake I had made.

'Blood-brothers? Blood-brothers?' Mrs Bloom's voice began to rise.

I thought that Dor-Dor would faint and she took a step back, her hand to her mouth. But if I had hoped that Mrs Bloom might be equally enfeebled I was wrong.

'How dare you do such a thing?' she cried, 'God will never forgive you. I have never heard anything like it, and plotting a deliberate attack on your poor aunt's life!'

I shook my head in disbelief. Evidently – and not surprisingly – she did not read the same sorts of books that we did, in which becoming a blood-brother was a seriously good thing, especially if you were a Red Indian.

'Now I can see just what a truly bad child you are, trying to murder your aunt and to harm poor little Mavis. Did you tie her down to do this dreadful thing or did Gyll restrain her? Poor, poor little Mavis,' she repeated, never giving me the chance to explain that it took the agreement of two people to become blood-brothers.

Mrs Bloom continued, 'There, I can see just how evil you are. What you wanted to add to your sins was to see your aunt unable to swallow, back arching and snapping until death took her.'

I now realise that the symptoms she described are akin to those of tetanus, but just where she had dragged up the idea that I might have even thought that a cut on the hand could lead to such a fate I cannot imagine. But at this moment all I could do was to protest again and again that I never wanted to hurt Dor-Dor. How could I? And anyway I would be far too scared to contemplate murdering even Mrs Bloom, who possibly deserved such a fate.

It was at this point in the endless tirade in the bathroom that my eye fell upon the strange red rubber bladder, complete with flexible tube and long thin nozzle, that was perched, only partially concealed, behind the bath taps. Unnoticed by all of us up to this dramatic point, I now gazed at it with new and curious eyes. I leant forward in rising panic, my attention diverted from the main action, in order to peer at it more closely.

'Listen to me when I am talking to you,' snapped Mrs Bloom angrily.

Then, suddenly noticing what it was that had distracted me, she bent forward and gave me a really sharp slap on my bare bottom. Swiping the intriguing article from under my surprised nose, she stamped out of the room, leaving Dor-Dor wittering in consternation.

'What was that?' I asked, too amazed to consider what I was saying.

'Nothing that concerns you.' She pursed her lips and then added, 'Curiosity killed the cat.'

She employed a collection of sayings and proverbs when all else failed, which was frequently, which did not help to add much to my inadequate store of knowledge.

I was finally dragged up in front of Mrs Marsh, who when confronted with the story, looking up from her book, merely said, 'Oh dear, Geraldine, are you all right? Quite sure? You look a little pale, come, come and sit down.' She pushed a chair forward for her to sit on and then turned to me and said, 'And Susie, do try not to frighten Dor-Dor, there's a good girl.'

Mrs Marsh just smiled. Mrs Bloom on the other hand was so angry she had to go to her room.

On a previous occasion I had been accused of wishing to kill Dor-Dor by carelessly leaving a needle somewhere that she might sit. The needle would pierce her skin, would enter her bloodstream and end up in her heart, stabbing her to death. (It was only recently that I plucked up the courage to consult an acupuncturist.)

What a responsibility for a twelve-year-old, to have death on her hands.

Later, when we were in bed, I asked Gyll what she thought the curious rubber bubble in the bath actually was.

'Oh, for goodness' sake, Susie, it was a douche.'

'A douche?'

'A douche to wash out the babies.'

'What babies?'

Gyll sighed in an exaggerated way, so I nodded.

'Ah.' I didn't understand but I was not going to admit it. I was just beginning to feel very grown up.

The 'Lads in Airforce Blue', as the family called them, were the most exciting people in our lives, apart obviously from Mr Moore and Tyrone Power. Mrs Marsh, being English, unlike Mr Marsh who was born in South Africa, hankered for all things English. So she really felt that she was 'doing her bit' for the war effort by kindly offering hospitality to the young airmen from Britain who were training to fly, stationed at RAF camps in Rhodesia. They were polite, friendly and very kind to us. About four or five at a time would be invited for the Christmas turkey and to hear the King's speech. We all stood together and to attention for the National Anthem while the old boxed and veneered radio wheezed away. The 'lads' saluted. It was a wonderful, loyal moment.

They also came on other special days. I do wonder now what they thought about us children, if they did think at all beyond the formal cup of tea and home-made biscuits.

But Gyll, Mavis and I were in love again.

Trevor Jones.

Even now I can recall his blue eyes, blond hair and pretty tip-tilted nose. We noticed his lovely little knees covered in golden hairs, easily observed since 'the lads' (except for the instructors) wore khaki shorts and knee socks. Trevor had a Welsh accent too.

'Trevor is mine. I bags,' claimed Mavis, as daughter of the house.

'Oh don't be daft. He wouldn't look at you,' Gyll said scornfully.

'But I love him too,' I said, not holding out much hope that he would even glance my way.

But Trevor was a terrifically diplomatic sport. He came with us on picnics to the Matopos Hills; he played cards with us and listened to our favourite records.

> 'Hold me tight I'm falling,
> Woo, Woo, Woo, Woo,
> Hold me tight I'm falling,
> Falling in love with you.'

Oh Trevor, we did love you. How we pined for you. You were only twenty.

'Do you know?' asked Gyll knowingly, 'I think Mrs Marsh is a tiny bit in love with him too.'

'What?'

'What, Mummy?' Mavis was very indignant, not only for the possible slur upon her mother's character, but because Mavis was possessively passionate about Trevor herself.

'The thing is,' said Gyll. 'I am the oldest. It stands to reason that he would choose me. I'm fourteen now.'

'Isn't that just a tiny bit young for him?' Mavis asked sarcastically.

Gyll glowered. 'Well he certainly wouldn't pick you,' she shouted.

'And what about Mr Moore and Tyrone Power?' I asked.

It was all hypothetical anyway and I expect he would have preferred a chap in any case. But we didn't know that then and we loved him. I still have his photograph. After the war was over Gyll wrote to him at his home in Wales. They met for a cup of tea at the Lyons Corner House in Leicester Square, but somehow the magic was gone. And anyway, she had lots of other boyfriends to entrance by then.

10

Two years had gone by and letters arrived for us less and even less often. What was happening at home while we were trapped in Africa? We had no inkling, but I doubt that we would have understood even if we had known.

We were so tired of being away, of not belonging; of not being able to crack the shell of the family who had taken us in; but after all, why should we have expected them to love us? I certainly do not automatically love every child I meet, though Dor-Dor could, should, have been different because she was Mummy's sister, a real relation. After a time we came to understand that we would never be accepted as part of the family; we were simply the tiresome guests who had overstayed their welcome. But we could not oblige our hosts and just leave. We were in the way of their family life and though we longed to disappear, we were stuck.

It was like being outside a cage and yet still wanting to go in.

We lost a lot of ourselves; we learnt to comply, to obey, to be negative. But even Dor-Dor sometimes relaxed her coldness and allowed us to come a little closer. I see now that she was probably afraid of us, perhaps even afraid of losing us if we were to return home. Maybe. Maybe it was just her nature, too used to rejection and unable any longer to risk the chance of rebuff.

The only time we had her on her own was walking to church. On these occasions, when we had her to ourselves, she began to be quite nice to us. She sometimes favoured us with stories about Mummy when she was a little girl and about her brothers and sisters – our aunts and uncles. We were quite happy to hear the same stories again and again and I suspect she quite enjoyed the repetition too. She would also tell us about her own life when she had first arrived in Africa and about the little school she ran, first for Alfred and then for Mavis, but quite honestly these latter stories did not hold the same fascination for us. We wanted to hear about Mummy. But after the business with the penknife, as a form of subtle punishment no doubt, she withdrew these small favours.

Gyll and I, in lowered voices, speculated endlessly about what had happened that evening and why she was treating us the way she was. We felt perhaps that she felt stupid about allowing herself to tag along with Mrs Bloom. We did not think that Dor-Dor liked Mrs Bloom very much – she made such a point of belittling Dor-Dor, implying rather openly that she thought Dor-Dor to be an inferior person, a servant. Poor Dor-Dor, we thought for once, with her pride in her own family; we really wanted her to hold her head up high and look down on Mr and Mrs Bloom's family. Gyll asked, 'Do you think she's all muddled, sort of being made to go along with her?'

'I don't know, but she is certainly taking it out on us now'.

'I bet she never says sorry.'

'I don't think she knows how to say sorry,' I said. 'Not to us, anyway.'

'Do you think that she really believed that I wanted to kill her, with the knife? I mean, that's daft.'

'Of course not,' Gyll replied firmly.

But nevertheless, whatever Dor-Dor really thought, she looked hurt and angry and was withdrawn and silent. Her little peaky face was stony as she marched forward, with Gyll and me dawdling a few steps behind, miserably clutching our horrid hats in the hot, dry wind.

We hated having to wear hats. Daddy never made us wear them, but then we never went to church at home; we did have pretty straws for the summer sun, with brims laced with artificial cornflowers and poppies. Dream hats, English hats, chosen by Mummy in Harrods and worn under an English summer sun. Now we wore our felt hats with the crowns crammed well down over our damp foreheads. Gyll longed to wear hers halo-style on the back of her head, like the other girls, but this was utterly forbidden by Dor-Dor, ruled out as exceedingly odious and common.

It didn't help that this Sunday in July 1942, as well as everything else that had happend, my aunt was in a bad temper, partly because she said she had lumbago, though for some perverse reason she would not consult a doctor. I found this a little confusing as I thought lumbago was a shrub with a pretty little sky-blue flower. When I asked her about this she shrugged her thin shoulders irritably, but did not choose to enlighten me. She had no intention, I could see, of relenting. I had thought that as it happened to be my twelfth birthday, 18 July 1942, she might have forgiven both herself and me, but no.

However, as we pursued her down the road, like Alices after the Red Queen, over the bridge of the dry, bush-ridden river bed, she finally and reluctantly confessed that she had news for us.

'You are going to boarding school,' she remarked shortly. Gyll and I looked at each other, completely taken off our guard.

'Where? Will Mavis come too?'

She nodded, pursing her lips.

'When?'

'Soon. The school is called Kingsmead. It is in the Union of South Africa. In Johannesburg.'

'Is that far?'

'Two days in the train I believe.'

'Will we have to —' I corrected myself. 'Will we come back for the holidays?'

'What will you do? Will you miss us?' asked Gyll.

'Of course not,' she replied with asperity, 'Why ever should I?'

'Well, I just thought —'

'Well, don't,' she countered tartly, the response I had more or less expected.

She had a way of saying things so that I never knew if she was joking or being serious; but she never, under any circumstances, admitted to any affectionate feelings. That did not surprise me either, but even so, I was really upset that she had said she would not miss us. I always hoped she might drop her guard one day and say at least one kind word, but she obviously liked to keep us guessing and if we made the wrong assumptions, made a mistake in interpreting her mood, she never bothered to correct the impression. Petty, really, and silly, if it had not been so sad, since we craved the chance to be able to love her.

But I wonder. In retrospect, I wonder.

Gyll asked when we were alone, 'What do you think that Dor-Dor will do when we all go away to school?'

'I don't know, I suppose she'll have to stay here.'

'But she's supposed to be Mavis's governess. There won't be anything for her to do.'

'Will they pay her?'

'Do they pay her now?'

We didn't know. She certainly never seemed to have

any money of her own, but then she needed so little, just a small amount for the collection in Church, for a tube of denture paste, for writing paper and stamps. Pocket money? Most certainly she could never have saved enough to be a lady of independent means.

'I don't think she could go anywhere else. I mean, who would give her another home? And she can't very well go back to England. Not in the middle of the war.'

'Maybe she'll die.'

'She's not that old.'

'She looks a hundred.'

'Maybe she'll die of grief at losing us,' and we squealed with laughter at the very thought.

'No, but really, whatever happens, we'll be bound to get the blame.'

Which was not so far off the mark. If the decision had not been made to send Gyll and me off to boarding school, for whatever reason, maybe to get us out of their hair, maybe to save Augustus from Gyll's wicked seductions, then darling Mavis would never have been sent away at all. As it was, she couldn't very well be left behind and anyway, she was looking forward to escaping as much as we were. Naturally the fault was ours and the guilt inevitably ours, or so it appeared to be from the sighs and from the frowns with which Dor-Dor now regarded us.

Mr and Mrs Marsh never displayed the least sign of dismay or resentment at the continuing prospect of housing an unemployable old lady ad infinitum. They continued with grace to share their home, a home that in truth had never ever been their exclusive castle anyway, what with the grandparents, Dor-Dor and now us.

For Dor-Dor, it would mean feeling useless and unwanted for which she over compensated by mending even more worn-out clothes and effacing herself even more – perhaps even further self-denial (if that were possible) right down to the refusal of the accustomed and very modest glass of sweet sherry before Sunday luncheon. That would therefore mean that the only alcohol to pass her lips would be the communion wine received at Church. Gyll and I joked unkindly, amongst ourselves, about the number of times she attended the services.

Dor-Dor did eventually come home to England to die in a hostel for retired governesses (towards which she had apparently made pension contributions during her salaried working life) some fifteen years later. She had initially, on her return, lived with Mummy for a short time. But Mummy had shingles in her eye and hair after falling and breaking her wrist badly, and she could not cope with looking after her elderly sister properly.

By the time she left Mummy she was so thin that she almost disappeared completely between the crisp white sheets. Forlorn and tragic, having abandoned her God and eschewed all his works, she slipped from life blaspheming, swearing and cursing at the one passionate thing that had held her life together, her motive for living, and her *raison d'être*; in other words, her faith. The good people who looked after her thought she had gone mad, as did everyone else.

Mr and Mrs Bloom, on the other hand, soldiered on to an even riper old age, surviving their son-in-law by some years. Poor Mr Marsh, he never did get to be the true master of his household.

Dor-Dor could never have envisaged a life without her religion, but she must, at that time, have asked herself what life would be like without family or friends, without anyone to look after, not even us.

Still, with stoicism she prepared our trunks, while we

sewed on name-tapes and marked our pens and pencils. It was a nice change for us anyway, an improvement on hemming and unpicking and hemming again the trial scraps of material on which we usually practised our sewing. Not that this boring task did me much good, because although I made both my wedding dress and all my small trousseau, austerity and rationing still then being a major factor in what we could buy, my daughter recently described my stitching on a nightshirt as naive. What a blow after all that effort!

So now we were hardly grieving at the thought of leaving it all behind us – except for Trevor. How would he manage without us?

But the prospect of escape to school was extremely alluring. We would not miss the goodnight kiss, the touch of the comforting arm around us, the warm smile; we would not be homesick since you cannot lament the loss of what you never had.

As it was, the naughty but harmless Augustus was the only one who now touched us (both) these days, so school was bound to be better than anything at 12, Bryant Road. We were not to be disappointed.

On the day, when we were at last all packed up and ready for departure, Mr and Mrs Marsh took the three of us to the station. The platform was filled with excited children, school trunks, suitcases and wistful-looking parents. We were all to travel south together, to a set of different schools in the Union, some only travelling as far as Plumtree and others going right on down to the Cape. We were to stop off at Johannesburg, or Jo'burg as we came to call it.

We found our compartment, the top bunks folded up against the wall. Gyll and I and Mavis shared with one other girl, Maureen, who was also going to Kingsmead, but who had already been there for a year. As we had no idea what the school was like, since we had not been shown the prospectus nor any photographs, she was able to tell us all about the journey and much about the school. It sounded just wonderful and since we had never had to sit any entrance exams, I think the good nuns of St Peter's must have given us delightfully acceptable references.

While the girls were grouped together in the first-class carriages, four to a compartment, the boys were relegated to second-class, six at a time, with three bunks tiered one above the other. On one extraordinary journey, the boy in the middle bunk had slid out of the window of the moving train in the middle of the night. They found him curled up, wrapped in his bedclothes, fast asleep beside the track. After that the boys had to keep their blinds closed at night.

The concept that if the sexes were in different parts of the train they would somehow not get to meet each other was rather fanciful. It was not long before the boys were crowding the corridors, peering in to each compartment to search for pretty girls, not that anything untoward ever took place. It was the first time we had met any boys that had not been handpicked by the family. It was such freedom and such fun.

Two days on the train, meeting other children, especially the ones going to Kingsmead, was heaven indeed. Unaccompanied by any grown-ups, we revelled in the enjoyment and excitement of the journey.

When the train stopped to re-water, we ran down the tracks and spent our limited pocket money on unsuitable purchases. We punched holes in tins of condensed milk and shared them around, sucking out the gluey sweetness. I don't know why we did not all die of ptomaine poisoning. Some of us were a little sick, though.

Arriving at the school, our first impression, after the dryness of Rhodesia, was the leafy greenness of the grounds that surrounded the simple buildings. Scarce financial resources (the school was still quite new) had not been spent on unnecessary trimmings; indeed the dormitory windows initially lacked glass, though during storms canvas sheets were hung across the openings to keep the borders dry. We were never cold. Open air was considered good for us and a lot of lessons were held in the garden in the summer. Whatever the reason, no one minded.

'D.V.' aka Miss Doris Vera Thompson, the headmistress, was a very remarkable woman. She had founded the school, having first been educated at Cheltenham Ladies' College, which is rather ironic, as you will see later. She fought to form and maintain Kingsmead according to her high ideals for girls' education. So far as Gyll and I were concerned she was a teacher, visionary, sage, scholar, idealist, philosopher and mother all wrapped into one. She had a tall, stooping figure and her thin grey hair was gently pulled into a low bun at the nape of her neck to frame her oval face and serious, concerned blue eyes. She tried to teach us to love God, to be self-reliant, generous and tolerant. Such gifts. I regret to say that in the matter of God she had arrived on the scene a little too late to make much difference to Gyll (following the failed prophecy), but even if you did not believe in Jesus, at the very least you would find something to learn from his good example and the wise things he said. There was comfort and peace in the way that D.V. taught us to listen, to learn and at the very least to recognise Jesus as a good man and a prophet. Oh, such gifts.

The school was run on the Dalton System, whereby we spent a good part of the school day working independently, using the library for reference. Every two weeks our work was assessed by D.V. herself, from form report cards listing our marks and the time spent on each subject. She discussed with us our achievements, or our lack of achievements, and suggested remedies, which usually worked. More time spent on this subject and less on that. She knew and she was always right. We finally began to make a little scholastic progress.

She also took us to a township outside Johannesburg, called Sophiatown, populated uniquely by black people, where we helped a little with their community projects and raised funds for the children with sales of our handcraft work and with concerts held in the white world. We became acquainted with the terrible poverty and hopelessness of these people, who were eventually forcibly removed from the pathetic hovels they called home and dumped in Soweto. Sophiatown was knocked down and rebuilt as a whites-only town, renamed Triomph. 'Triumph' of the well-armed and rich against the non-armed and poor. It happens all the time, everywhere in the world.

The small chapel, run by the girls who wished to be involved, was an important part of school life. Under the benign influence of Canon Tonkin, who conducted the services, we came to love the quietness and tranquillity of the little thatched building. Canon Tonkin had the sort of looks that you would expect to find in a Hollywood movie concerning a much loved, gentle and ageing priest. We all adored him; helping to prepare for, and serving at, the services. It was a true privilege. No wonder we all (except Gyll) wanted to become nuns! If I could have invented a school that was better than any other, then I would have modelled it on Kingsmead. If I could have chosen a headmistress I would have picked D.V.

Apart from the lessons, we had a wonderful choir. I was

a fourth, which clearly did not require much skill other than to keep your own tune in your head against three other concurrent tunes, but Gyll was often picked as solo. She played Hiawatha, 'Come away, awake beloved', and had a leading part in Schubert's 'Lilac Time'.

'Oh gather ye rosebuds while ye may, Old Time is still a-flying / And this same flower that smiles today, Tomorrow will be dying.' The music was from heaven; the words were by Robert Herrick and had been arranged to Schubert's music by our music mistress. The productions were worked and reworked until they were perfect. How we loved it and you can image that Gyll was in her element.

Our school uniform included long-sleeved pale-green smocked blouses. In the tight-wristed, voluminous sleeves I was able to keep my beige mouse, Tyrone, the darling of my life, well, nearly the darling. I had not been so entirely disloyal as to forget Trevor, but, well, Tyrone was different. It was possible that Tyrone was a girl, but I couldn't tell. He had been given to me be a day-girl, Georgina, who had many mice, but none as special as Tyrone. I knew he was unique the instant I touched him in the mice's big box and he ran up my arm. Not only attractive, with his fine beige coat, but clever too.

There was also a mulberry tree in the garden at Kingsmead. Mulberry leaves are the only food that silk-worms really like, so I kept some of them too, watching as they changed from caterpillars into cocoons, made from the finest, brightest sunshine-yellow silk thread imagina-ble. The only trouble was that there was a limited number of things that could be made of yellow silk, book markers being the chief use, but after making about six for the Sophiatown project I rather went off the whole produc-tion business.

The only clouds on the horizon were going back to Bulawayo for our school holidays, and the fact that the war seemed to be no nearer to ending.

Naturally, South Africans were not one hundred per cent interested in the news of the progress of the war, leastwise not at school. We were kept informed of any victories, real or fabricated, and any major defeats, but we did not really know what was going on in Europe. Being at Kingsmead had considerably improved our happiness but we still longed to get home. We began to think that a declaration of peace was not necessarily a prerequisite for our return and we were only too ready to face the hazards of an enemy action, bombing, invasion, whatever, if only we could sail back to England.

Daddy wrote once and said, with no explanation whatever, that since Mummy had now joined the Polish Army we had better stay where we were as there would be no one to look after us at home. The Polish Army? Why on earth? And anyway, were the Poles of more importance to her than us? It didn't make any sense, but we would have been prepared to face the enemy entirely alone, without Mummy, rather than spend yet another year away from England.

We also puzzled as to what on earth Mummy could be doing in the Polish Army, and surely, if we did get home, she would leave them and come and look after us instead?

Our fourth Christmas was gloomy. We sat around the dining table at 12, Bryant Road, each member of the family with their presents placed in front of them. Naturally Mavis's pile was biggest, because she had lots of relations out there, aunts and uncles and cousins and godparents. But I was overjoyed with the exquisite marquisite pendant that Daddy had given me and was content with just that. Until, that is to say, I saw that Gyll had an identical pendant. But it was not until Mavis opened a little white, similarly packaged parcel, that I saw that Daddy had also given her one, the same as ours. Gyll and I looked at her in an agony of jealousy. I behaved very childishly. I threw my pendant out of the window and ran out. Nobody followed me, but after a time Gyll came and found me sulking in our room.

'It's not fair,' I cried. 'Mavis has so much already.'

'Oh I know, but probably Daddy sent them some money for presents for all of us. To be fair.'

Mavis wore her pendant but we never wore ours.

But it did set us thinking. If Daddy could send money for presents, why couldn't he send money for other things? Like clothes? Like fares home?

It was in that same Christmas holidays, in 1943, provoked by the tensions arising from the pendant episode shared by all at 12, Bryant Road, that Gyll and I dreamed once more of going home. It seemed just possible that Mr and Mrs Marsh's thoughts were beginning to come closer to our own. We decided that we would press our case further, knowing now that it was not necessarily up to the family to pay for us to get home. If we didn't try harder, it was clear that we would be there for ever.

We tackled Mr and Mrs Marsh when they were alone. Perhaps we had all, unknowingly, been sharing the same thoughts. What surprised us was their willingness to listen. For the first time they took our pleas seriously. Maybe they felt, like us, that if something didn't happen now, it never would. If Britain lost the war before they got shot of us, they would have us for life, but I hope it was because they minded that we were so unhappy and that regardless of the circumstances in England, we would be better off there. It was the right moment.

Ships were beginning to take civilian passengers back

to England, despite the danger at sea being considerably more serious than on our outward-bound journey and the girls at school encouraged us to think that it might just be possible.

'Go on. Try!'

I can't remember how we found Miss Balmforth. Was it D.V.? Or Mrs Marsh? Or us? Or, most likely, the mother of one of the girls at school? Anyway, she appeared on the scene, a retiring missionary on the way back to England to care for her sick mother. Her mission in life had been to work with fallen women, with unmarried mothers (white, of course, for naturally it was thought that African women gave birth (married or unmarried) like the sub-humans they were considered to be – more like animals really, and certainly not worth wasting time on trying to bring back to God's good ways). And she called herself a Christian? Oh well.

Now that Miss Balmforth was planning to return to her own fold, tentative discussions were held and she agreed to be our chaperone, for a price. Somehow tickets were acquired, with Gyll and me urging and pushing and fighting every inch of the way. Being older (thirteen and fifteen) gave us more influence and of course we were considered more able to look after ourselves. Somehow we were going home but was it because Daddy was also involved, wanted it, or had he been by-passed? There must have been correspondence between him and the Marshes? Had they pressed for our return, or had he pressed them to get us home? It was never discussed.

We were at Kingsmead when the news came that we should proceed to Cape Town and wait there for a ship. Of course we couldn't write to Daddy and tell him, because of the censorship of all letters, particularly in regard to the movement of shipping, No careless talk or letter writing from us, after all it was our lives that were at stake.

Nobody came from Bulawayo to Jo'burg to see us off, to give us a hug or even make a telephone call to say how nice it had been having us for four long years, and for our part, we never had the chance to say, ever so nicely and very politely, 'Thank you for having us.' We threw ourselves into fits of giggles at the joke and said goodbye to our friends at school instead.

We had to leave our few possessions, such as they were, those that is to say that had not been needed at boarding school, behind at 12, Bryant Road. Not that we cared, we were just so excited.

The mother of one of our friends, Mrs Andrews, knowing about clothes rationing in England, took us shopping to buy us some warm clothes, which she paid for herself, on the understanding that our oh-so-grateful parents would reimburse her in due course. The outfit consisted of a woollen suit, a blouse to go with it, a good pair of shoes and a shoulder bag. This last item caused us irrepressible joy. We had never had such a luxury before, though at the time we had nothing to put into them since our passports and papers rested safely in their little linen bags that Dor-Dor had made for us, to strap round our tummies with stout tape, never to be removed under any circumstances until we arrived home.

My only sorrow was to leave Tyrone behind, and also Mavis, who had become almost like a real sister. Being away at school together had helped with the cementing of our friendship, although we had never managed the fearfully surgical business of becoming blood brothers. Still, I gave her the most precious thing I had, Tyrone, and Mavis said she would look after him/her and send me news of his/her progress, not that she ever actually got around to it. Maybe he died of sorrow at our parting and she could not bring herself to tell me, but at the time the gift to her helped to soothe the pangs of parting from her/him.

Our names and addresses were painted on to our tin trunks and we said our goodbyes. It was awful leaving D.V. She looked sorrowful and seemed to want to say more, but held herself back. In retrospect, I think I know what was troubling her. But of course, I can't be sure.

The whole school was at the windows, waving, as we drove off in our taxi one evening, to the station and the train that was to take us to Cape Town and Miss Balmforth, where we were to wait for our ship. We did not know how long that wait would be, but we were on our way home and that was all that mattered. It was July 1944, one month after the Allied landings in France and just in time for Jerry's new toy, the doodlebug.

On the train, a ginger-haired man sat next to Gyll in the dining car and undid his flies. He showed her something under the tablecloth that made her go very pink. Really, she just was the sort of person that these things happened to. Anyway, she was very calm. After all, she was fifteen years old. But on another occasion, an elderly man sitting opposite me shot up his elbow in a very determined fashion and his index finger approached his nose, apparently on very serious business.

Gyll said 'Ugh – you would think he would be too old for that sort of thing', but it was really a bit of a whisper, and we collapsed again, tittering, until he took out his handkerchief and blew his nose properly.

In Cape Town, we stayed at the Colonial Club, a plain and demure hotel for women only, originally designed as a refuge for newly arrived female teachers pending their appointments to schools in other parts of Africa.

Although we met Miss Balmforth, we did not see

much of her. We found her to be a spectacled lady with a sensible Eton crop and very sensible clothes. She did not seem to know much about young girls and even less about adolescents, though they must have figured as clients somewhere in her good works. I think she was probably scared of us, I can't think why; so she left us to our own devices.

We put on our new clothes, warm though they were in this southern climate, and sallied forth to gaze in wonder at the smart models in the windows of the shops.

'Gosh, look at that,' Gyll said with her nose pressed against the glass. 'Look at those shoes and, golly gosh, the handbag.'

It was slung carefully over the glassy model's arm, a particularly violent shade of green, to compliment the crocodile shoes and pale pink suit.

'It's an awful shame that we bought our things in Jo'burg,' Gyll said, 'the clothes here are much more exciting. I just love the colours.'

After all the drab shorts, occasional dismal frock (or our school uniforms), at 12, Bryant Road, we were mad with joy about these exotic emporiums, never giving a thought to what would happen should we take home these very unsuitable clothes. In any case it was too late; our outfits had already been bought.

We had no idea how long we might have to wait for the ship. We could not afford to spend too much money, just in case there was nothing left when we got to England, even though the wait went on for weeks and weeks. But we did go to the cosmetics department (cosmetics was a new word for me) and bought some proper shampoo, instead of the horrid Lifebouy that we were given at 12, Bryant Road. We were told it would bring out the red highlights in our hair. I can warn you that if you are so stupid as to use carbolic soap on your hair, followed by a vinegar rinse to get rid of the scum, you will be left with something unspeakable. Whereas, we noted, if, like Mrs Bloom, you went to the hairdresser and had perfumed shampoo, you were left with a cluster of silvery curls.

We found buses and went to Sea Point, where we knocked about looking at the beach and Windhoek, which was quite adventurous (and expensive). We went to the shops most days, just looking, but sometimes buying lipstick, silk stockings and even cigarettes

If anything, this all frightened Miss Balmforth more than ever, and it was clear that she was totting up how much of our limited cash we were spending so wantonly on unnecessary luxuries. Would there be enough left of our pocket money to pay our expenses once we arrived in England?

We went to the bio almost every afternoon, sometimes even twice in one day. Oh the freedom. We were independent. In the six weeks of waiting, four years of repressed adolescence burst forth with the energy and joy of a released champagne cork. We were free – but not all that free, as we were far too coy to even dare to return a smile to anyone wearing trousers.

We thought that we were being frightfully adventurous and avoided Miss Balmforth at mealtimes if we possibly could. She didn't comment if we did not turn up to lunch or supper. I suspect she dare not think what we might be up to, though in actual fact we were reasonably timorous. Still, we did a lot of growing-up in that brief time and in the absence of any tempering guidance, it all came out rather lop-sided.

My fourteenth birthday: 18 July 1944. How very grown-up to be in Africa, just with my sister with no highly organised tea party with polite school friends (girls), sitting round politely, eating my birthday cake, politely, in almost complete silence.

I hadn't liked my birthday cake, so I left it. What an unkind thing to do. I should, at the very least, have pushed it round my plate with the fork.

As we waited in Cape Town we did the same thing but on our own: had a birthday tea, but at a smart and overly expensive tea-shop near the Club, but this time enjoying every little crumb of cake.

I looked up and saw Miss Balmforth peering anxiously through the shop windows, scanning the tables for a sight of us, her hand held to her head against the light. She looked embarrassingly ill-mannered.

'Hard luck, old bean,' Gyll said, 'she's come to join us. Look, quick, finish the cake.'

Irene C. Balmforth stumbled into the shop and blundered her way across to our table. Her hair was unruly and we could soon hear that she was out of breath.

'Where have you been?' she started off rapidly, 'you should have been at the Club. I told you.'

'But it is my birthday.'

'You should have been at the Club,' she said again, continuing breathlessly, 'You were asked always to let me know where you were. What about the messages?'

'Messages?' News to us.

'Well, there are messages. Urgent messages. Come at once. Here, give me the bill and get your things together. No, don't finish the sandwiches. Hurry, hurry.'

She was in such a rush that she did not even notice the large size of the bill.

Gyll and I sort of guessed what the panic was all about, at least we hoped so.

It had been six weeks of waiting and now at last we were called. Time to pack, time to pay the Club, visits to

the Embassy, visits to the doctor, the emigration department and the ticket office, all the papers for which Miss
Balmforth allowed the clerks to hand directly to Gyll and
me, so we popped them into our shoulder bags which
Miss Balmforth never considered we might lose. Now it
was time to think about the glories that lay ahead.

End

I I

How different was His Majesty's Transport Ship, *The Andes* – HMTZ 76 (also known as *The Vomiting Venus*), from the grandiose *Cape Town Castle*. Four years ago the latter had risen from the dockside with a newly painted gleaming hull and a dazzling funnel topped with bands of red, flaunting all the stateliness of a monstrous swan. The ship that now lay before us was sinister – silent as the 'gentleman in grey', the heron. Dressed in dark battle-ship colours, *The Andes* (a defensively equipped merchant ship) had no shiny paintwork and neither did any of her angles reflect the light, as if she were smothered in mould or lichen. The whole vessel gave an impression of dulled uniformity, the caked salt, the rust and camouflage protecting her secrets as she ploughed stealthily through the ocean, hoping to foil the enemy who lurked beneath the waves in their submarines or above in the heavy skies, armed with bombs and guns.

Once she had been a cruise ship, no doubt as sparkling as the *Cape Town Castle*. Now she was a troop carrier and on this particular journey packed with RAF servicemen and their families, plus one or two independent travellers like Miss Balmforth, Gyll and me and also a handful of other evacuees returning home, mostly about the same age as us.

How different too was the accommodation. Once upon a time, we were told by one of the ship's officers, the *Andes* had boasted a glamorous, but small, honeymoon suite, complete with sitting room, bedroom, bath and lavvy. Now twenty of us inhabited each of these state-rooms, with the bunks tiered up to the very ceiling of the airless quarters. When we were not standing in the queue for the smelly washing facilities, we had to lie on our bunks, for there was little space for forty people to stand around at the same time in two such meagre rooms. There was one porthole in each of the rooms but we were not allowed to open them under the pain of death, possibly real death. No one, of course, was permitted on the deck after dark and absolutely no one allowed to smoke a cigarette once dusk began to fall, for fear the enemy might catch sight of the glow.

Once again the ship zig-zagged across the black, swirling waves and once again our insides swirled too. We were all dreadfully ill. This time it was distinctly worse, partly because of the pitch and roll of this particular ship and obviously because of the terrible stench in our cramped and airless quarters. The air was fetid, to say the least. There was no obliging stewardess to clear up the vomit and change the bed linen and we longed for a breath of fresh air. But did we care? Oh no – it was paradise! We were going home at last and nothing mattered except the pot of gold at the end of the rainbow.

Of course it did not escape our notice that the 'powers that were' had kept us safe from the Hun in Africa for four years only to let us return during possibly – no, probably – the most dangerous time for shipping. The Germans were desperate to score a victory anywhere and anyhow, especially against a defensively armed merchant ship such as ours, carrying troops and their families.

When we clustered round the ship's padre for the Sunday service on deck, surrounded by the crew and the airmen, all smartly dressed for the parade, the families marshalled to one side, we felt a nervous chill. We sang again, as we had on the way out, 'For those in peril on the sea', and prayed that we would be spared as we gazed at the threatening sea and speculated how long we could survive in such deep, cold water. Would anyone look for us, wearing our orange life jackets armed with a whistle but no lights? What would it be like to be a fish? How did they breathe under water? But still, it was all a splendid adventure.

One of the mornings when we got up early enough to see the dawn, we could just make out, through the mist and the sun in our eyes, the pale outline, on the horizon, of what could only be land. As we approached, we saw a port.

'It's Freetown,' one of the passing sailors said. 'West coast of Africa. Didn't you know?'

Well, no we didn't. The ship was always shrouded in secrets and no one had explained to us that the *Andes* was stopping en route, to load or off-load anything. It was quite a surprise. Here was yet another country, Sierra Leone, but we didn't set foot upon it. Our ship was anchored some way out and everything was brought out to us by ferries and tankers. The only lively interest, as we hung over the rails, was the little flotilla of craft manned by small, shiny, smiling black kids, who called to us to drop coins into the waves for them to dive for. They were really very clever, catching everything that fell into the water beside them, often going quite deep and popping up like corks, grinning, with hands held aloft with their booty. Eventually we ran out of coins so they waved and paddled off back to the dock.

We guessed, as we left the coast of Africa behind us, that we would probably be heading out into the Atlantic again, as we had on the way out. Once far, far out to sea, we would turn north, loop over the top of Ireland and steam down the Irish Channel to Liverpool. It was a long and complicated journey, zig-zagging all the way, to avoid the German U-boats. It was fortunate that we did not know then that 3,500 merchant ships, and I mean merchant ships, not warships, but the sort of ship that we were sailing in, had been sunk since September 1939. Some of the ships carried food, supplies from Uncle Sam, or others passengers or wounded servicemen or women and children. Were we still children, or would we have been counted as women in their statistics, I wonder?

I suppose that we were quite lucky to get away with it not just once, but twice. But then of course we were unaware of all these horrors, as we sprinted round the outside decks, flinging quoits into the water at imaginary subs until we were told to stop. Children, I think.

I am not sure what Miss Balmforth felt about the good times that we were having with our new shipmates, but we could guess. She was not too happy. We learnt very little about her life and she seemed disinclined to get involved with ours. Her duties as a chaperone led her to attend lifeboat practice with us, so that in the event of disaster we would at least all die together. But apart from that she avoided us as much as was possible in such enclosed circumstances. She left us more or less to our own devices or under the casual eye of the occasional harassed RAF mother who might agree to watch us for a bit. This arrangement left a lot of leeway for us to roam the decks with the other children, getting Hershey bars from the sailors and generally having an excellent time once we had found our sea legs.

At night Miss Balmforth, with a gentle sigh, would open her Bible and close her mind to all the baffling things that were going on around her. As she lay on her pillow her book would slip from her fingers, her spectacles slide down her nose and her loose jaw drop back to allow a loud and regular snore to fill the cabin. Then we knew that Miss Balmforth had surrendered herself to her God, at last asleep, the moment we had been waiting for. The snore was the signal for Gyll and me to climb down, very stealthily so as not to wake her, from our berths above her. Gyll, of course, had taken the top bunk and I was like a filling in a sandwich between them. We would make haste for our assignations with our loved ones on the deck beside the swaying lifeboats, until a passing ship's officer ordered us inside and we settled down instead, cross-legged on the floor in the corridors. Love will find a way!

For we were both in love again, Trevor almost, but not quite, forgotten. Leastwise, I thought I must be in love. I had never been alone with a boy. Boys had not featured strongly in the Bulawayo programme and, of course, there were none at all at school. The object of my desire was a downy-cheeked youth called Arland. In retrospect I rather think that it was my sister that he really fancied, but she was obviously and enviously busy with several other slightly more mature suitors of fifteen or sixteen. So in an attempt to get close to her, Arland got close to me instead. It wasn't the first time that I found myself to be a go-between or a substitute for my sister and it was certainly not to be the last. But I wasn't proud, I was just curious. Gyll's lips were fairly well sealed when it came to discussing her own affairs, though she did not hesitate to talk about anyone else's.

I had told her about Arland, about the way I kept finding him looking at me and I said as we stood on deck, 'You know, I wouldn't mind being kissed; for the experience,' I added quickly.

'But Arland? He's a bit young isn't he? And he looks, well, just a bit feeble.'

'Oh, I don't know,' and Gyll turned to him and threw him a kiss, waving her fingertips as if she was a fairy. He perked up a bit at that and I could have hit her.

'You've got tons of boyfriends. You leave him alone,' I said despairingly. 'Go on, go and get one of your own.'

Arland had shifted his position and it looked as it he was going to walk over to us, but at that moment Gyll got up too.

'Silly thing,' she said, laughing at me, and then a very small thought crept into my head that she might, just might, have someone else in mind. I imagined that she was searching, all the while, for someone in the crowd, behind the advancing figure of Arland. I dreamt that I could see a tall-ish boy of about sixteen or seventeen, with neat black hair, beckoning Gyll to go and look at the outlines of a blacked-out Liverpool with him.

'I wasn't waving at Arland, it's the one standing just behind him,' she whispered to me.

But I still didn't believe her, until she tripped past Arland, who, once started on his trajectory in our direction, could only smile weakly as Gyll flashed past him on rather more senior business, and by then being unable to stop landed at my side just as I was about to start crying with both anguish and anger.

Arland came up to me as I stood there, tears brimming. I think he felt sorry for me and didn't quite know what to do; for one awful moment I had a terrible feeling that he was going to cry too.

But he didn't. With astonishing confidence he put his arm around me – he was only thirteen – and offered to kiss me. I was completely bowled over. I didn't think that love affairs started this way. In the event, it was a terrible disappointment. His breath smelled awful; he probably hadn't brushed his teeth since getting on board. He spent quite a few boring minutes clinging like a limpet to my firmly closed lips, but when he released me he smiled apologetically and rather nicely, so we took each other's hands and went over to look at the docks outlined against the smoky sky. We hung over the ship's rail so that we too could see England at last and what war really looked like.

I have a clear memory of seeing England again. It was 12 August 1944. It looked as grey and dismal as HMTZ *Andes*, without colour or lights. Liverpool, England. Home. Four years had passed since we were last here. We crowded on to the deck and hung over the rails, everybody cheering and crying, because we were home and safely delivered. Of course the dockside was empty because no word had been sent ahead of our impending arrival; there was no welcoming party and no band.

The RAF families were processed by the force's authorities and soon there were only a handful of independent travellers left, poised on the empty ship, and not knowing quite what to do; some of us were reluctant to disembark. What would we find? Would we be bombed? For the first time I felt afraid.

But the skies were fairly quiet and there were no bombs that night.

Quietly we stepped down the gangplank; subdued, we hovered in the customs sheds, while we were given our ration books, gasmasks and identity cards. We were at home and it was still wartime.

Miss Balmforth evidently had an urgent appointment elsewhere and simply left us there. Poor lady, if anything had gone wrong she would probably have been blamed. As it was, she still needed to travel to Fairford to collect, personally, her (no doubt paltry) payment. Daddy could be unbelievably mean at times. Whenever he responded to a request for any extra cash it was always with the proviso that we should understand that if we asked for £10, he was really giving us the equivalent of £20 or even £30, depending on what the Chancellor of the Exchequer had chosen to demand by way of tax.

It was with mixed feelings that we saw her take off in such a hurry. Obviously she wanted to see her mother as soon as possible, as we did ours, but in her excitement she seemed to have forgotten that there were no further arrangements made for us. We were on dry land and that was that. The bargain was fulfilled. Our thanks to her and our good-byes must have sounded pretty limp, but in a way we felt glad to see the back of her and her prayers and her snoring.

But there were other things to think about. It was dark and for some reason our trunks would not be unloaded until the following morning. The RAF families had other arrangements for their luggage and had quit the quay pretty promptly, so there was no one that we could ask what to do next.

One of the ship's officers came up to us while we were standing there awkwardly, waiting for something, anything, to happen.

'No one to meet you then?'

'Well no, actually,' said Gyll coolly. 'We couldn't tell our parents of course – censorship, you see.'

'Otherwise Mummy and Daddy would have come,' I added.

'Well, it's too late to do much.' He looked at his watch. 'How about an hotel?'

'Hotel?' Gyll echoed, knowing that we had spent nearly all our money already.

'Yes, I could get a taxi for you. Would you like that?'

'Shouldn't have spent so much on the way over!' Gyll gave an embarrassed but brazen look and smiled at him evenly. I guessed exactly what she was up to. The officer smiled back uneasily, but eventually he put his hand in his pocket and came up with a white, papery fiver. He held it out.

'Oh no, we really couldn't,' I said quickly.

'Well, we could,' countered Gyll, 'so long as you give us your name and address so that we can repay you.'

'Fine,' he said, 'fine,' relieved, I suppose, that he wouldn't have the responsibility of looking after us all night.

'A taxi then,' he said, after which he added, 'The Adelphi. Very good watering hole. Top hole, top hole,' and then, to our surprise, 'Do not pass go; do not go to jail, collect five pounds.' Now this was a joke that we could understand.

He summoned a taxi and stood on the pavement, smiling and saluting. He was really very handsome.

Through the cabbie's window, Gyll said airily, 'The Adephi please.'

'Adephi?' queried the taxi man, surprised.

'Gosh,' I whispered to Gyll, 'I jolly well hope we will have enough left for the train tomorrow.'

Gyll waggled the fiver and jingled the very small amount of change in her pocket. 'I think it will be OK,' she smiled. 'Yes, the Adelphi,' she repeated in what we both agreed later was a very commanding tone.

'Cost you,' he said then.

Gyll ignored the warning with an aloof smile. 'Our father will repay us,' she announced grandly. 'He's very rich,' and with that she stepped majestically into the cab.

God only knows what the receptionist must have thought as we staggered into the plush, marbled foyer, two teenage girls with smudged make-up and no luggage whatsoever.

'Double room, is it then?' he asked, scanning the ledger.

'We have come,' Gyll said, 'from Africa.'

'Oh yes,' he replied, in a matter of fact voice that did

not encourage us to pursue the point. 'That will be ten and sixpence.'

We opened our new shoulder bags and carefully examined the contents of our purses. Gyll handed over the five-pound note and waited calmly for the change. It would be all right if we did not have any supper. A very young porter (too young to be called up, we guessed) showed us to our room but we dared not risk spending anything on a tip. He shrugged, looking tired, and disappeared without telling us where to find the bathroom. Luckily we had passed the sign for the lavatory on the way down the dimly lit corridor.

The room was huge and gloomy, the feeble lights only faintly illuminating the reddish hangings and vast double bed. The curtains were hung with thick air-raid protection curtaining, so we turned out the lights before daring to pull them back – just a little, to see what lay outside. Gyll opened the window. Liverpool smelt different to Africa. There was acid in the air, the whiff of dead, burnt buildings. Decay. Large chunks of Liverpool were entirely missing. Of course it was what we expected, and yet the reality quelled us. We were scared and felt a bit guilty for having run away to somewhere safe when all these dreadful things were happening, but given the option, even after looking at all the blackness around us, we both knew damn well that we would rather have been here all the time. After the war quite a few people would remark, from time to time and even today, that we were lucky to have been able to be away during the worst of the war. Lucky? I really minded this. I used to want to say, 'Maybe you would have preferred to be where we were,' or else, 'How does a child of nine get to have a choice?' But I generally kept quiet because it was all too awful to explain.

For a brief moment we contemplated ringing Daddy right then, late as it was, to tell him the wonderful news, but we did not have the telephone number of our new house in Gloucestershire. The only number we knew was that of the shop in Watford. Obviously it was long past closing time and no one would be there.

In the absence of any pyjamas or washing things, and anyway we were too tired even to wander down the corridor to find the bathroom to wash our faces, we just slipped off our top clothes and crawled into bed. I had not been in a bed with Gyll since we were at Shalford Cottage, because we were not allowed to get in together at 12, Bryant Road. Now we snuggled up, feeling for the first time the chill of England's summer, and hugged each other with triumph, relief and happiness to be home.

We chatted briefly, anticipating the excitement of tomorrow, the joy of seeing Mummy and Daddy once again.

'Won't they be pleased?' Gyll said. It was not really a question, it was a fact.

In the morning Gyll bravely picked up the telephone and asked the operator for the Watford number. She liked a challenge. I felt quite giddy with apprehension. Would Daddy be there? The lady at the switchboard said no, but she would get a message to him.

Gyll said, 'Ask him to meet us at Oxford this afternoon.'

The operator then said she would tell him if she could find him in time.

Rather troubled at the looseness of this arrangement, we went to the dock and collected our luggage. We had already calculated that if Daddy was not there to meet the train we would have no money to travel anywhere else.

When we eventually arrived at the station, we saw there was no roof on it. Of course not. The glass-and-steel stanchions had long been bombed away and now it was beginning to rain. Drip – drip. We did not like to leave our trunks unguarded, so we simply sat on them and got soaked. The wool of our jackets gave off a homely smell, a bit like a laundry. We were in for a long wait.

Finally, with much shunting and letting off of steam, the train arrived, though by the time we had hauled our luggage into the goods van all the seats were taken. We were quite happy to stand in the corridor but it was very squashed, and we had to wait again because of an air raid near by. The already packed train opened its doors at Crewe and even more people sardined in, until it was impossible to shift up or down the corridor or get to the unsavoury lavatory. Mind you, neither of us felt the urge to go. Apprehension dries you up, I think.

It had become quite sunny when we reached Oxford around teatime. The platform teemed with activity; students, soldiers, civilians, all milling around and moving in every direction. The number one thing was to get our luggage off before the train moved on, so we pushed our way to the van and as there were no porters here either, we set about shifting our trunks on to the platform.

I hardly dared look up to see if Daddy was there, because if he wasn't I didn't quite know what we would do. My heart thumped. Four years of longing were caught in one anxious moment.

'Is he here?' Gyll asked, boldly surveying the crowd.

'I don't know,' I hissed, suddenly overwhelmed by embarrassment. 'Come on, help me with this trunk.'

We made a pile of all our kit. It wouldn't be too difficult, I thought, for anyone to recognise us as our names were plastered in white paint all over the luggage, in humiliating boldness, but the platform was still full. I cast a furtive eye around.

'There's a man by the entrance,' Gyll said, 'I'm sure it's him.'

I glanced up. 'He's not Daddy.'

An indifferent gaze fell on me for a moment and then swept on. The man had a curious, tight expression on his face.

The platform began to clear. The man stood still, now openly watching us, as we continued, self-consciously, to straighten our crumpled jackets and skirts and to smooth our hair.

'It's him, I know it's him,' said Gyll, in her best actress voice.

'It's not,' I said again, 'he's too old.' I was afraid of him. He looked remote and stiff.

But nothing would deter my sister. With a dramatic little cry, she tripped across the platform in her newly acquired high heels, wobbling a bit, calling 'Daddy, Daddy', in an unusually high-pitched voice.

The man stepped forward. He looked so old and so stern and so tall. He was not in the least what I had expected, but then I suppose we were not quite what he had expected either. I was nine when we left home. Now I had just had my fourteenth birthday on the ship. I was pretty grown-up too, I thought, and also wore high heels and carefully applied bright-red lipstick. And I had a wonderful Americanised/South African accent, chewed gum (both habits acquired on the ship) and smoked the odd cigarette.

If Daddy was appalled at the sight of his erstwhile baby daughters, clothes rumpled after the journey and hung about with cheap accessories, he did not do much to disguise it. A look somewhere between surprise and despair flitted across his face before he pulled himself together and said, rather brusquely, looking at his watch, 'Come on now, girls. I have black market petrol. Shouldn't really be here at all. Better get going.'

I looked up at him. I was expecting an acknowledgement of some sort, hello or maybe even a kiss or a hug, or at the very least a smile, but he seemed too shattered to contemplate any such thing. I think he was ashamed of us, the way we looked, how big we were, how we had changed. He couldn't cope. Gyll for her part looked quite dumbfounded, waiting for a hand, a touch, anything to let us know that he was happy that we were home safely. War had changed him, I could see.

Gyll and I looked at each other uncertainly. We had imagined this moment so often, dreamed of meeting with laughter and love and tears, and here we were with this perfect stranger. We were not what he wanted. We hardly allowed the thought to enter into our minds that he was perhaps not what we wanted either.

Docilely, almost guiltily for keeping him waiting, we loaded the car, heaving the heavy trunks into the boot, and climbed in. We both sat in the back. Whatever had happened? The joy had gone. Maybe, I thought hopefully, he was shy like us. Yes, that had to be it. Given time he would come back to us to be the father we had known before the war.

In the car, once out of Oxford, he inclined his head a little towards us and explained that as Mummy was away, he had a housekeeper.

'Away? Mummy's away?' I asked, shocked.

'Well of course, she didn't know that you were coming.'

But surely, whether we were expected or not at that particular moment, she should have been at home anyway?

'What about Margaret?'

'Oh, she does the cooking and cleaning. Mrs Dalton does the housekeeping and drives the car and does my secretarial work.'

'Oh.'

'I'm sure you'll like her.'

'Yes.'

The house was far grander than anything I had imagined and beautifully decorated with fitted carpets everywhere and chintzy curtains in the bedrooms and velvet ones downstairs. The bathroom, with cream porcelain fittings chosen from the 1939 Ideal Homes Exhibition, was a knock out, complete with a punch ball from floor to ceiling (as if either he, or Dick, were a first-class boxer), a bidet, and a silent flush lavatory, the handle fixed to a small cistern at the back, instead of the swinging chain from above that we were used to in Africa. We were impressed. It was all so luxurious.

Mrs Dalton, flitting about in an ecstasy of organizing, shook her hennaed red head at us and said, 'We thought you might have your mother's room. It's so pretty. We've had twin beds put in there this afternoon.'

'But where will Mummy sleep?'

'Well, dear,' said Mrs Dalton, patting the back of her abundant red curls, 'your mother is not here, is she?'

Not ever?

Confused, we inspected our room and admired the beautiful furnishings, the green china basin on a smart modern pedestal, the three-sided bevelled looking-glass on the elegant, draped, kidney-shaped dressing table and the cream telephone on the table between the beds. The beds had new coverlets and a lush pale-green carpet stretched to every corner. It was like a dream and about as familiar as a palace. I wondered what had happened to our beds that we had had at Watford, indeed to all the furniture that we had had there, for I recognised only one or two things, like the old television set (not working) and the sofas, now covered in dark-brown velvet.

We went as soon as possible to find Margaret in the kitchen, with her baby. She had written to us in Africa asking us to choose a name and I had asked for David, because it is my favourite name and reminds me of blue. He was a beautiful boy with a soft engaging smile and we could see at once where Margaret's priorities now lay. But all the same she kissed and hugged us and pushed the hair back off my forehead and said, 'Of course your Mummy loves you. Of course she will come home now.'

We plucked up courage and asked Daddy if we could telephone Mummy now.

'Not before six,' he said, 'she'll be busy until then. Best to phone at six,' he repeated, as if it was something he knew only too well. We looked at each other, crippled by disappointment. The joyful bubble of our anticipation had been well and truly punctured.

In the sitting room, Daddy seemed at a loss as to what to do with us. Had we been younger he could have told us to go out and play, or had we been older he might have told us to take the car and go and explore. Clearly he now felt that the situation called for something more than the cursory, actually cruel, reception that we had so far been awarded. All Gyll and I wanted to do was to recount the adventures experienced on our long journey home. Home? At that moment it didn't seem to be much like one.

After we had examined the bedroom for any signs of Mummy (there were none, which was rather odd), we unpacked and put our small collection of clothes, mostly Kingsmead uniform, into the empty drawers. We came downstairs to sit, side by side, on one of the big sofas.

Waiting for Daddy to say something, while we looked around ourselves at no particular thing, I started nibbling my nails. Gyll nudged me.

'Don't do that, you know that Mummy doesn't like it.'

'Oh you, always telling me what to do, or not to do.'

I didn't often get cross with her.

So we were a little surprised when, without much difficulty, he persuaded Mrs Dalton to take a seat at the piano. He regarded her with a measure of pride while she launched into an instant and melodramatic rendering of a song that she said was 'something' from *Pelléas et Mélisande*. It might have been all right (because she could reach the high notes and sang, relatively, in tune) had she not had a cleft palate. I am ashamed to say that Gyll and I were at the age when we thought that sort of thing either embarrassing or funny. We couldn't understand the innocent flaunting of her voice in this way, especially as it had a distinct nasal twang. She could never have got away with it at 12, Bryant Road. It was such an odd scene, so random. I wanted to laugh or cry. I certainly wanted Mummy and not Mrs Dalton.

After that, Gyll just stood there, swinging her arms around her like a much smaller child, while I tried to suppress my giggles. I nudged her and we edged towards the door.

'I say, Christine,' Daddy said at last, as if he had just thought of something that would amuse us as we waited for the call to Mummy. He pulled himself out of his big deep chair, and said, 'What about Jasper?'

'Jasper? Well I suppose so.'

Mrs Dalton looked a little uncertain. Daddy came up behind her while she hesitated, her hand on the doorknob. Gyll and I exchanged nervous glances. Who, or what, was Jasper? No one had said anything about anybody called Jasper either living or even working in the house. Daddy prodded her, a little as a farmer might prod a beloved cow.

'Perhaps he is the gardener?' I whispered to Gyll, because by this time Daddy and Mrs Dalton were heading for what turned out to be the dining-room door. We had neither inspected nor even discovered this room yet.

Daddy flung open the door and, with a flourish, popped on the lights. We looked for something, anything, that might remotely be named Jasper. Jasper, the sort of name you would expect to find in a romantic novel, or even, perhaps, it could be the name of an old dog, to be found snoring noisily by the cold cinders of yesterday's fire. But we couldn't see anything that might be called 'Jasper'. The walls of the room were lined with shelves, which held a grand and impressive collection of old books. Gyll and I were surprised to see such a large number of them, since we certainly did not recall them being in Shalford Cottage and guessed, rightly, that they were a newish acquisition. Well, a library, even if it shared itself with a dining room, needed books. It occurred to me later that perhaps he had bought some of them to impress. Then Daddy strode to the window and gestured towards a very large glass tank. We were astonished to see that it was a filthy green aquarium. The water was disgusting, nearly opaque and strangely motionless, with only a few bedraggled plants to be seen, trying to make their way towards the light.

Then, oh just then, the smallest flash of light, as from a tiny diamond, pierced the murky gloom.

'I think Jasper Pike might be hungry,' Daddy said. 'Go on Christine, give him a finger.'

Christine, appalled, backed away and tucked her hands firmly behind her back.

'Go on girls, then.'

But we hung back, horrified, at the very idea of going anywhere near the hidden secrets of that water, let alone to dip in the tips of our fingers . . .

'Oh well,' our father said with a sigh, and allowed his own finger to slip into the end of the tank where we surmised Jasper's tail to be. But with a whip-lash turn, looking like a piece of mobile steel, the enormous fish turned within the boundaries of the moss-covered greeny glass and made a dash for Daddy's finger.

'He likes worms,' Daddy said, all innocence in his wolf-ish smile, 'doesn't he, Christine?'

She looked repelled, but turned to us, as we cowered in the corner away from the threatening tank, and said by way of explanation, 'Your father caught him in the river and meant to take him down to one of the new lakes, but he forgot. He threw him into the horse trough in the yard, and poor Margaret, when she went to fetch a bucket of water, found him one day and couldn't stop shrieking.

'After that, Jasper, when he was still quite little, was popped into this handy tank. Poor thing,' she added, eyeing Daddy warily, for signs, we thought, of disapproval at her concern for the condition of Jasper's prison, 'this tank is not really big enough.'

She went on, 'He has grown so much, but I don't know why he is so big as he doesn't get a lot to eat, what with rationing and forgetting and one thing and another – there are hardly any scraps anyway; we eat everything there is. He should really be allowed to go back to the river.'

She had certainly won our approval, both for the thought, and for defying Daddy, since we could never even imagine having the courage to stand up to someone like him. Quite a good sport in some ways, we chatted when we went to bed, but not all that clever; but then, had she been anything else she would not have been Daddy's handservant.

'Well, we all have to tighten our belts in wartime,' Daddy reproved her, with a wink that we could just see, 'but Jasper belongs to Dick. And that's that. Now girls, we had better go and try to telephone your mother.'

We trailed after him, too shocked then to say anything. Gyll pulled a face at me, and we left the dining room without a backward glance, leaving Jasper the pike to his hungry darkness and confined sleep. Mrs Dalton stayed behind us to shut the door firmly, in case, just in case, he might escape. You could never be too sure.

Then, at exactly six o'clock, Daddy said, 'Perhaps you'd like to try the telephone now.'

The operator, who since calls went through the local exchange appeared to know all about us, took a long time to get through to Scarborough, which was where Mummy was working. Even when we got through to the number that we had been given it took several minutes to get her to the telephone.

Daddy said, 'Look Joan, surprises! The girls are back. They arrived here today. What about coming home now, old girl? – What? – No, I know – but look – have a word with Gyll.'

He held out the telephone to her and, putting his hand over the mouthpiece, said, 'Get her to come home, there's a good little thing.'

'Little thing,' I asked myself. Ha! She was nearly sixteen.

'Hello Mummy, it's Gyll.'

At last it was my turn. Mummy's voice was so faint. She sounded a tiny bit upset and tired but she said that she was 'pleased' we were home. We must go and see her soon. It sounded rather vague.

'Can't you come here – tomorrow?'

'No, darling, I have a job. I'm in the army, you see. You ask Daddy to let you come and see me here.'

'Oh – I thought you'd come home, now we're back. Daddy said.'

'Daddy knows perfectly well that I can't do just whatever I like. But dear, you must come and see me, just ask

Daddy—' but then the telephone clicked, pipped three times and went silent. I stood looking at Daddy who looked away.

'She said to ask you something,' I said. 'I think to take us up there.'

'Well, maybe soon,' he answered briefly.

Mrs Dalton got up and straightened her skirt. She gave a sympathetic sigh and went to find Daddy a drink.

Gyll seemed determined not to allow anything to spoil such a very special day. 'It's the most wonderful thing in the world to be home with you and soon we'll see Mummy.'

Daddy glanced at her out of his dark eye. He did not answer.

'Really, Daddy, it's so – so—' she was lost for words.

'For goodness' sake, old girl,' he said at last. 'Let's not get all sentimental.'

That stopped her in her tracks. For a second she looked at him, unbelieving, then seeing he was serious, half cross and half embarrassed, the tears brimmed in her eyes and rolled down her flushed cheeks. It was as if she had been hit. There must be some sort of mistake, I thought.

She pounded from the room.

Daddy said, 'She's all het up, with the excitement, I expect.' He did not seem too worried.

Later, at supper, he mentioned schools.

'School? But we've only just got home.'

'Well, you can't hang around here all the time,' he answered. 'Everyone has to go to school. Remind me, Christine,' he turned to Mrs Dalton, 'to find the prospectuses.'

Gyll and I looked at each other in despair. It didn't seem quite believable.

Gyll said, 'But Daddy, I'm nearly sixteen. I didn't think I'd have to go back to school.'

'School-leaving age may be fourteen in Africa,' he said evenly, 'but not where you two are concerned. Whatever did you think?'

The truth was, we had not thought at all. It had never occurred to us that further education awaited us, and oh so soon.

'Margaret, where are all our things?'

'Things, Susie?'

'Well, you know, the things we left at Watford. Our toys and books.'

'There aren't any here,' she said, 'or I would have seen them. Better ask your Daddy.'

'Daddy, what happened to all our things?'

'What things?'

'The things we left behind.'

'Good Lord, those things . . .'

'Yes.'

'Well, I don't really know. Maybe they got lost in the move. Anyway, what would you want with them now? Just baby things I'm sure.'

I wanted to say that he had got rid of everything because he didn't think we were ever coming home again, but I didn't dare.

'Maybe he thought Britain was going to lose the war so we'd have to stay in Africa for ever and ever,' I said to Gyll, by way of explanation, but she had a funny expression on her face.

'It's not fair,' I continued crossly. 'We've brought nothing with us from Bulawayo and now we have nothing here. No dolls, no books.'

'You're too old for dolls,' she replied flatly.

'I know, but it would have been nice—'

Gyll cut across me. 'Do you know,' she said, 'I think they just forgot.'

'Forgot?'

'About us,' she said at last.

We looked at each other. At last the truth dawned on us. They had not expected us back. In fact, in their minds we had been, conveniently, cancelled.

The next day, Miss Balmforth arrived to collect her cash. She must have travelled by train to Oxford and then caught the local line which meandered through the countryside stopping at all the ten or more villages on the way until she arrived at the end of the line, Fairford.

Once the financial transactions had been completed, in a fair amount of secrecy, Gyll and I were most relieved. We were never too certain that Daddy would honour his debts. But she seemed content and he even brought out the visitors' book for her to sign.

August 15th. Irene C. Balmforth, of Alexandra Park, London.

Daddy said, 'Come on girls. Put your own names in too.'

Reluctantly Gyll picked up the pen. What a charade. She made a face at me, then wrote,

> 'Aug 14th Gyll Edmonds from Bulawayo
> To Home
> Aug 14th Susie Edmonds from Bulawayo'

I glanced up the page. My cousins Diana and Victoria de Rin had been to stay earlier in August, with their mother Blanche, my mother's youngest sister. And before that, but still on the same page but with no date, Mummy's writing. I would have known it anywhere, it was round and pretty and a touch continental. There was no name, simply 'Nameless and aimless, address only temporary. Polish Rest House, Scarborough, Yorks.'

I showed Gyll when we were alone, and then we pored over the previous pages.

Lots of shooting parties and lots of lists of birds shot and bagged, lots of fun had, and really rather frequently too. When they were not shooting they were fishing; no wonder Daddy didn't have time to write to us. As we understood it, the wartime shortage of food meant that they were all on the edge of starvation, and I could see the point of birds and fish for the pot, though I hadn't noticed that Daddy or anyone else was particularly thin. What upset me was the realisation that Daddy was living the life of old Riley, killing things on a very regular basis, while we waited in the hope of just getting a letter. Just one letter would have done. No wonder he didn't want to have us back, to interfere with his plans to entertain his boozie fellow sportsmen. Which is not to say that he should not have had a good time while we were away but to say that there could have been some sort of balance in his activities. That is how we saw it.

I read, for instance, on one day, 31½ brace partridge, 3 hares, 3 rabbits and un-numbered pigeons; in the evening of the same day, 12 trout and 3 grayling. We examined the names of the participants, men who we would get to know well in the forthcoming years. These were men who not only came for the sport of shooting but to play cards in the evening, to smoke, drink and generally ignore Gyll and me as if we didn't exist. The funny thing was that I didn't even remember Daddy owning a gun before the war.

We noted too the procession of lady visitors who had come to enjoy the dubious hospitality of the Manor Farm House, or the Manor, as Daddy preferred to call it. Even our mother's father, our grandfather, had been to stay there. I learnt, only a couple of months before writing this, that he died shortly after our return from Africa, but no one bothered to tell us. I didn't mind because I didn't really know him except from what Dor-Dor had let slip, and from that we didn't think he sounded all that nice. In fact, perfectly horrible, but I had thought him long gone to his hell.

But most surprising were the many Polish names, Jan Grochowski, Stefan Radłuski, Roman Pilch, Janina Kochan, Jan Sobkowiak, Stanisław Pietkiewicz, some giving addresses in Poland, others writing just briefly, Polish Forces P/53A. So they had existed and visited, but were they still alive then, at the time we read their names? Did they survive the Allied Landings in Normandy? How little we knew.

After five or six days of agonising delay, it was at last decided that we should go to Scarborough to meet Mummy. We had waited anxiously every day for word of a visit.

We were to travel by ourselves, but first we went to Watford to see Alice. It was all just the same as when we left; the road, the little flat in Mildred Avenue, Alice and Eddie. She kissed and cuddled us and cried and laughed and nothing had changed. She said we were her babies (she had none of her own) and that she loved us. She arranged for us to stay with Eddie's sister in York on our way up to Scarborough to see Mummy. She was rather silent about our proposed visit and our plan to bring Mummy home with us.

We could barely stay still and the train was very packed. We had one seat between us and took it in turns to sit or stand in the corridor, which was rather good fun. Lots of soldiers squashed past, which was about the closest I had ever been to a man, because I didn't really think of Arland as a man. Really more of a boy.

We were fairly timid with Eddie's family, which was

odd since we had managed, more or less alone (we didn't really count Miss Balmforth) from Johannesburg to York, but perhaps it was the thought of what lay ahead that made us afraid. We simply did not know what to expect. We couldn't help but notice the reluctance of anyone to talk to us about Mummy. Was there a problem? What could the problem be? We couldn't think of anything.

We were just pleased to be on the train again from York to Scarborough the following morning. Of course there was no one there to meet us, but we had been told to take a taxi to the Fairfield Hotel, where Daddy had explained to us that Mummy was working in the Polish Rest House. Had I been a sophisticated child of today I might have thought that a 'Rest House' was a brothel, but it wasn't. Since the Polish soldiers had no homes to go to when they were given leave, the Rest House had been organised to give them a bit of a holiday by the sea, not that there was much for them to do because the beach itself was out of bounds, set aside for military purposes, but they could walk through the rather war-jaded resort, stroll down the shabby Esplanade or go to the Pier or the Dance hall. Actually, now that I think of it, I suppose that wasn't too bad, but it wasn't home for them – and we could understand their feelings only too well.

We had secretly rather hoped that Mummy might have been there at the station to meet us, but after carefully scanning the platform for yet another parent whom we might not recognise, we gave up and hailed a taxi as we had been told.

The Fairfield Hotel, which had clearly seen more genteel days in the years before the war, was now dressed in rather shabby white paint, but there were beautiful full-length windows on the lower floors, looking out towards the sea and the windy cliffs.

The shallow, wide steps stretched up in front of us as we nervously made our way to the big front door. Once upon a time, perhaps, there would have been smart porters, wearing white gloves, to welcome us and take our luggage. Now, as we clumsily slumped down our cases in the big hallway, we were surrounded by very fat old Poles and very young, slim and beautiful Poles. They stared at us with curiosity as Mummy stepped down the broad, elegant staircase in her khaki uniform. It was like something out of a film (without any music), only the balustrade was dirty and chipped and she looked older than we had imagined. The uniform, though, was *very* smart.

She was tentative about holding us closely, then and there, in front of the soldiers. Unbelievably cruel? Maybe she was scared of us? Perhaps she thought we were too big now for overt signs of affection. Quietly, almost shyly, she led us upstairs to her little bedroom, which had a view of the backs of other hotels and of the town. There was no sign of the sea at all. It was all very simple, with the minimum of furniture. I could see no luxuries, no civilian clothes, no pictures of her two daughters.

Then, when the door was closed, she turned and kissed us lightly on our foreheads and looked into our faces and held us for a moment while she smiled her pretty, crooked smile. She looked so different; she had changed so much; it was almost as if she had laid aside, physically, purposefully, the pain-filled years before the war and her terrible, sad, burnt self and had emerged as the woman she was now, confident in her uniform, in her new-found organizational abilities and her mastery of languages. She was assured and happy in her role of army officer and she found herself to be needed in ways other than the docile wife and mother she had been, because she had found her own place in the world. Was it for this brief happiness, these war years, that she had suffered through the flames and agony and had not died? She had come a very long way to be here, independent, free and in (of all places) Scarborough. We saw it, we understood that she did not mean to let her freedom go, fleeting as it might be. It was, as it turned out, to be a very short parole indeed, just the duration of the war and a couple of years more, but for Gyll and me the timing was not good, as it was obviously not good for so many children of our generation. Countless women of her age had had to make some difficult decisions, to commit themselves elsewhere than with their families and their homes, unexpected and temporary winners in a loser's war, financially and emotionally independent from their husbands and families for the first time in their lives.

Make the most of it, little birds; fly away, fly away while you can.

★ ★ ★

'But what did you do, How did it happen? I didn't know you were in the *real* army. Daddy said you were in something called the "Fannies".' Gyll giggled at the word which was prohibited at 12, Bryant Road.

'Oh, well, yes, in the beginning I *was* with the FANYs. Up in Scotland. I don't know, it was supposed to be a lady-like thing to do I suppose, because to begin with one didn't get paid. I'm sure my father would have approved of that.' She laughed shortly.

'But how did you get into the *Polish* army?'

'Oh that,' she said, as if it was a sort of everyday thing that one did, dismissing the subject, though she rested a finger on the medal that hung below her breast pocket – the same medal that was eventually placed on her coffin before her cremation.

But then she decided to change tack.

'If you really want to know – do you? – it's a long story.'

She took a deep breath. 'FANY stands for The First Aid Nursing Yeomanry. Oh, years ago in the Crimean War, perhaps before,' she looked vague, 'there were these ladies who used to drive the dead and wounded soldiers from the trenches to the field hospitals in horse-drawn trucks! Some of them even rode the horses to bring help, medicines and bandages to the front line, all dressed in long skirts and wearing hats. And in all that mud. But not now, my dears, not now. Why, we have cars and trucks and I drive them! Imagine! But war is pretty stupid anyway. Enemies just aim to blow each other up, young men they don't even know.'

She gazed out of the window at the dusty, dirty walls and shrugged, sadly.

I don't think either Gyll nor I had ever thought anything much about war, not the whys and wherefores. The good people believed in God and the enemy did not, we had been told. The fact that the enemy might also believe in God had rather escaped us. Everyone, good and bad, bombed and killed each other and families were parted. War was terrible, we knew.

Mummy seemed to be finished with the explanation, but Gyll was not finished. After all, if she intended to join up, which was already a possibility in her mind's eye, then there was a lot to learn.

'Then what happened?' she asked Mummy eagerly.

'Well, I suppose what happened next was Dunkirk (English spelling à la Mr Churchill), when the Germans pushed all the Allied Forces towards the British Channel, where they were all stacked up waiting to be rescued, awful, because the Germans were going to kill them other-wise. There were a lot of Polish soldiers there too. Do you know anything about this?'

'A bit. We were told a bit.' (Not enough by half.)

'Do you want me to go on? You must have heard of Dunkirk?'

'Mm,' Gyll murmured, 'but not much.'

'Well, a lot of small boats and big ships came from England and took them off the beach and sailed them home across the Channel. A lot of soldiers were killed, but the ones that did get back, and especially the Poles, had nowhere to go. They couldn't go home because the Germans had taken their country. It was bad, you know.'

'Oh?'

'Well, camps were set up for them in Scotland and we were sent to look after them. We did rather well, in fact.' She smiled. 'When the old ladies who ran the FANYs realised just how well we were getting on with the Poles, they decided to send all their women back south.'

'Oh,' we said, innocently.

'We had done so well, learning to speak Polish especially, that the Polish Army didn't want us to go either. So they offered me and five of my friends commissions as Liaison Officers in their army. So we said yes.'

'What's a Liaison Officer?' Gyll asked.

'Well, it's someone like a go-between. The Poles couldn't speak English but we could speak French, which most of the Polish officers and cadets already could, and then also, luckily, some of us were good at languages and learnt to speak Polish quite quickly – so we helped to interpret and generally do things for them, to look after them, because when they first arrived after Dunkirk – now, you've heard of that – they were complete strangers in Britain. They didn't have any homes, or families, or houses, or barracks or anything. Nowhere to sleep except in hurriedly-put-up army tents. Not that much of a welcome home, was it?'

Home? Gyll and I looked at each other. There was almost nothing to say.

Mummy continued, 'But that is what war is all about – about fighting.' Well, at least we did not have the fighting, yet.

'But these men, these here, they seem all right.' I wanted to know why she was in Scarborough and not at home.

'Well no, not really. They're on leave. They have been fighting in France, after D-Day, with the Allies against the Germans, and they need a rest. They need to get the energy to go on fighting. Of course they've fought in lots of other places before now, like Norway and Italy and North Africa, Tobruk. You know, everyone says how unbelievably brave they are, how hard they fight, but they die, they die.' And then she looked at our faces and realised that we didn't understand much of what she was saying.

Well, we didn't know much about war and especially not about the fighting. To us, war meant being sent away and coming back to a different world.

'So you look after them?' Gyll said. 'What else do you do?'

'I drive trucks, three-ton ones, and I drive army cars for important people,' and this was Mummy talking, who never drove anywhere before the war. I didn't even know that she could drive.

'And oh yes, at the beginning, when I first joined the FANYs, we were sent to Perth one day. There was quite a gathering of the top nobs, army and civilians, oh, I don't really know who, we were never allowed to talk about our work But all these men needed driving to Gask, which was a really lovely old house out in the country. The Polish officer that I was driving from Crieff told me, and I suppose that he really should not have said anything about it, that it was an important headquarters for the Army. Well, it was difficult to find a space to park the car, after I had dropped him off at the steps, so I had a bit of a cold walk back to the house. I was asked in to recover.'

Mummy warmed to her subject. It was the first time that we had seen her so animated. She positively glowed, and we listened quietly and in anticipation of something really exciting about to happen. We waited a little impatiently for her to get on with the story.

'The house was huge and very grand. There was a big sort of lobby, circular if I remember rightly, and that was why we could see everyone, coming and going. We were standing round the edge of the hall, just chatting, when there was a bit of a flurry and then silence and then a Polish driver standing next to me said that the officer who had just come in was the President of Poland. Imagine! Anyway, he walked past us, having a word here and there, and it was explained to him that I was English. He stopped and smiled, but sadly he did not take my hand to kiss it. Oh I wish he had. What a hero. His name was General Sikorski and he had come for this big meeting. He was head of the Polish Forces as well a President. How about that!'*

Gyll and I were quite impressed, but, well, not all that much, until Mummy said, 'He's dead now. Some people think that he was murdered. He was drowned when his aeroplane fell into the sea just after taking off from Gibraltar.'

'Murdered? Why? Why murder someone like that?' I asked, horrified.

'Politics,' she said shortly. 'Stalin or Churchill – who knows? He was very powerful and commanded a great army but did not always agree with the other big chiefs. Oh, war. And, my dears, he was so good looking. Hard, but handsome.'

'So what happened? Did they ever find out?'

'Sometimes it is as well not to know,' she replied softly. 'He was not the only Pole to die. Just think of the troops that I trained with before D-Day. A lot of them were killed. They were so brave because they were fighting for us but also so that they could get Poland back from the Germans and go home.'

'Were soldiers that you knew killed?'

'Yes,' she said, and left it like that.

'Oh.'

She shrugged and we could see that she wanted to forget that sadness.

---

* The conference was held in May 1941, shortly after Rudolph Hess had crash-landed his aeroplane in Scotland, ostensibly to broker peace between Germany and Britain.

'So what is happening now?' Gyll asked. She always got to ask the questions that I wanted to ask.

'Well, just now an underground uprising has started in Warsaw. We don't know what is going to happen next. It started while you two were on the way home, actually at sea, so that's why I couldn't come to Fairford. You see, it wasn't a very good moment. These men here got so excited when they heard that America and Britain had told them that it was a good time to start an uprising . . .' but she drifted off when she saw that we didn't really want to talk about the Poles but about her.

'Mummy, when are you going to come home?' I asked.

She sighed. 'Look dears, the war isn't over yet, the battle in Poland is not going quite as well as everyone had hoped . . . you do understand, don't you? Say you do? But if help comes . . .'

Oh we understood well enough. We understood exactly what she was saying, that she wasn't going to come home under any circumstances, that she was going to stay here or wherever, looking after these men, these Poles.

From our hurt and confused faces Mummy could not help but see what she was doing to us. She blundered on in an attempt to make us understand.

'The Americans and the British *said* they would help. They *said* that they would parachute in supplies, food and medicines and, above all, ammunitions to General Bór Komorowski, the head of the Secret Army there, the soldier who had organised this well-planned uprising, so that they could fight those brutal Germans who are in their Warsaw, and who are murdering hundreds of Poles everyday. They *said* that the Russians would come and help – after all, they are very close with their tanks, just the other side of the river – but no food has arrived and no ammunition either and now the Russians won't move to help. I sometimes think that they don't want to help. You know, I don't trust those Russians.' (And how right she was.)

She stopped and it seemed that she brushed away a tear. I had never seen her cry. I had never heard her swear, but she did now.

'My God, blast the lot of the filthy brutes, the Russians. Damn them to hell and, for that matter, Churchill, and that Roosevelt too, he's always thinking about his popularity back at home in the US, while thousands die. It sickens me.'

Gyll and I exchanged stricken glances. It was the very last thing that we had expected and hoped for in our first meeting with Mummy. She seemed for a moment to be quite mad. But then she stopped and looked at us quietly and sadly.

'It's so difficult that you two have arrived just when everything is going wrong.'

'It's all right, Mummy, we do understand,' Gyll said at last, but she didn't, not really.

'Oh dear,' Mummy said, 'I'm sorry, really sorry. Now let's have a hug,' and all at once she was a different person.

We sat on her bed, one on each side, and were quiet for a moment. Actually she didn't put her arms round us or anything, but we just sat there and it was all right.

By this time, Gyll, in her eagerness – oblivious to the true nature of the disaster unfolding before us – had worked out that if she could join the Polish army then she could stay with Mummy. She could see only one thing, herself in uniform.

Like a small child, she stood rather shyly, her arms held straight in front of her, fingers turned inside-out, while her shoulders rose in a 'please don't be angry with me' sort of way.

'What is it, Gylly?' asked Mummy, only too eager to change the subject, and knowing there was a question to be asked.

She grinned sheepishly. Mummy looked questioningly at her. 'Well, could I join the army? I know I'm old enough.'

'But darling, you don't speak Polish.'

'I could learn.'

'And anyway, I am afraid Daddy would never let you. You have to go back to school you know.'

'You could never learn to speak Polish,' I interjected. 'You can't even speak French and you've been having lessons for years.'

'Oh shut up. You don't know anything.'

I looked at Mummy. She was lovely. She wore her soft brown hair just short of her pale-khaki collar and her small waist was nipped in by her buckled cross-belt.

'Every time I say I'm leaving they give me a new uniform or a medal or something. I'm not really worth it but there isn't anybody else just now, you do see.' She touched her medal again, as if it were a talisman.

Well, I did see and I didn't see. We needed her too.

There was a light tap on the door and a young soldier popped his head round. His hair was nicely ruffled, I thought. A bit untidy.

'*Dzień dobry* Pani Edmonds!'

'Romek. Come and meet my daughters, Gyll and Susie.'

Romek smiled brightly and clicked his heels together neatly. He stopped short of bending over our hands in a more formal greeting. Gyll and I were speechless with delight.

'Hello Gyll *i* Susie.'

We grinned back weakly.

'*Pani proszę*, Lieutenant Szumski is waiting for you.'

'Good gracious,' Mummy exclaimed, looking at her watch. 'Is that really the time?' She picked up her shoulder bag. 'Listen, you two; I have to go now. I'll be back soon. Perhaps you'd like to go for a walk? Look around? There's a nice sea-front –' she tailed off.

Then she added, turning to Romek, 'You will show them, won't you? *Proszę?*'

'*Tak, proszę, Pani, tak,*' he said and clicked his heels again. Mummy vanished down the stairs.

Romek informally saluted her parting back, grinned at us and leapt down the stairs in front of us. From the hotel steps he pointed to where we should go.

'*A bientôt,*' he said and vanished inside.

'That's French,' said Gyll, 'I'm sure.'

'Well, you should know,' I remarked tartly.

'Maybe he speaks French as well,' Gyll mused. 'I shall have to learn to speak both fluently. Not too difficult.' She had an air of absolute certainty.

'He's rather super,' she said a little time later.

'Hmm.'

It occurred to me that we hadn't even been shown our room and that our cases were still in the hall at the hotel. Oh well.

That evening, after supper with the officers and Mummy at the big table in the frowsty dining room, where we ate some sort of dumpling, sour cabbage and apple compote with currants, we crossed the wide corridor to the canteen.

Here the soldiers were served inexpensive snacks and hot drinks that we made for them from behind the counter, which spanned the back end of what probably would have been the spacious lounge of the Fairfield

Hotel. There were small tables dotted round the large room and lots of lovely soldiers who regarded us with some interest. We pretended not to see them, the way young girls do, as we busied ourselves preparing trays of *kanapki*. These were a sort of open sandwich made from thick sliced bread smeared lightly with pale margarine and then cut diagonally across and decorated with thin slices of cold, spicy sausage and bits of salad. Sometimes, when we were in a Scottish camp, Mummy would find big fleshy kippers, but these were eaten uncooked. We thought it savage and quite disgusting, but I get ahead of myself.

However, urged on by the desire to communicate with these lonely young men, we soon learnt to say '*Dzień dobry*' (good day) and '*czy Pan chciałby szklankę piwa?*' or '*czy chciałby Pan kawałek tortu?*'*

What a frightful hash of communication was made at the Tower of Babel!

Luckily it was no time before we understood '*Ja kocham Cię, moja ukochana,*' to which we replied, giggling, in English, 'Yes I love you too!'

It was, we discovered, a great deal easier not to try to spell anything but to listen carefully. Fortunately Mummy was fluent in several languages and especially in French and Polish.

On our second night there local girls, recruited from goodness knows where, were brought in to a dance held in the canteen, always under strict supervision. Not that they needed much watching over. They seemed content to chat amongst themselves, sitting together on the chairs lined up along the sides of the canteen, looking a little askance and surprised at the temerity of any Pole who

---

* 'Would you like a beer, sir?' or, 'Would you like a piece of cake?'

dared to ask them for a dance. For most of the time they blithely ignored the young men, who were so desperate to touch just an inch of chaste, female flesh.

'*Ja nie tańczę!*' I murmured on being asked to dance, because I didn't know how to. Ballroom dancing had not been on the curriculum in Africa, though I could do a good imitation of a wood spirit.

'*Ja nie tańczę!*' I repeated shyly, though I was just longing to try.

During the day Gyll and I mooched around the town while Mummy was working. If the weather was fine we would walk along the cliffs, looking down into the turbulent, cold sea; if it was warm we would find a sheltered spot along the grassy hollows, where we could read our books, or, more often, discuss our progress with the glamorous Polish cadet officers, quite a habit. One of them, Zbigniew, had promised to send me his sweet ration when I got to school, if I was unlucky enough to go to one. We had put off thinking about that.

For the moment we strolled down the promenade humming:

'Oh I do like to be beside the seaside
Oh I do like to be beside the sea,
Oh I do like to walk along the prom prom prom,
With a passionate Pole tiddley om pom pom.'

We giggled and flopped about, hell-bent on picking up anyone who would talk to us in English, or, even at a pinch, in elementary schoolroom French, a last ditch effort to communicate with someone. Anyone.

We went to the dodgems by the pier and even ventured into the dance hall where servicemen and women on leave were doing some very serious jitterbugging. Still in their uniforms, they jived the afternoon away, throwing, or being thrown about by their partners, legs akimbo around male hips or knees pressed neatly together as they slid swiftly between strong thighs. We were overcome with admiration and jealousy. The Poles seemed pale in comparison and Gyll and I like a couple of lumps of lead.

At lunchtime and for supper we returned to the hotel/ Rest House, where we continued to eat strange mittel-European food concocted for us by the chef, who had collected our ration books on arrival. Actually, I rather liked these meals. But it couldn't go on.

The news from Warsaw was becoming very alarming and the first intense happiness now changed from hope to fear and frustration. Whatever had happened to the Allies who had first encouraged them to rise up against the Germans and then failed to honour their promises of help? What was wrong? The Russians had not budged from their positions only fifteen kilometres away to come to the aid of the desperately beleaguered Poles, the food and ammunition had not arrived and the Secret Army was beginning to run out of supplies. The Germans, in their turn, were beginning to fight back and to reoccupy much of Warsaw, killing every living thing in their paths.

Mummy was totally distracted, red-eyed and taut and it was all too clear to us that we were in the way. The cheer-ful optimism of the Rest House evaporated and so did we. After what seemed like a dreadfully short visit, during which we had so little time to be with Mummy, she tele-phoned Daddy and said that it was time we returned to Gloucestershire. A school had to be found. Decisions had to be made for our future. Never in our wildest nightmares did we dream what that was to be.

A Note on Bad Timing:

1 August 1944	Start of the Warsaw uprising, the first week victorious.
7 August 1944	Himmler orders the Germans to kill all the inhabitants of Warsaw. Fifty thousand Poles are killed.
12 August 1944	Gyll and Susie arrive in England
20 August 1944	Uprising turning. Gyll and Susie arrive in Scarborough.
26 August 1944	Really bad news in Warsaw, Gyll and Susie depart for Gloucestershire.

12

Back at Fairford, Mrs Dalton produced a clutch of prospectuses for us to look through, but Daddy had already made his choice.

'Please not Cheltenham, Daddy, please not Cheltenham Ladies' College.'

'It's a good school, only twenty-four miles away, and who knows, it might even make you two into ladies, though the chances seem quite remote at the moment.'

He was disinclined to discuss the matter; he was not very interested, it seemed. End of subject.

But we had scrutinised the prospectus, examined the photographs, read the text. We personally fancied the friendly convent in the next village, St Clothilde at Lechlade, or St Mary's Wantage or St Mary's Calne.

Cheltenham looked vast and forbidding compared to the parochial atmosphere of Kingsmead. Its mock Gothic architecture was looming and chilling and the pictures of the neat girls in neat clothes doing neat things scared and depressed us. We couldn't, in any case, see why we had to be sent away so soon. We had only been at home a couple of weeks but the school term, which was also the beginning of the school year, was due to start in September. It seemed to us that if we were to be packed off to school at all, it would only be reasonable to wait, at the very least, until after Christmas. In addition, we simply could not understand why Daddy had chosen the only school to which we had taken an instant dislike, but he was adamant.

'Over eight hundred girls,' Gyll remarked in despair, 'it'll be so big.'

In a tearing rush (my goodness, he really did want to get rid of us!) we were hauled off to Cheltenham to be interviewed.

When we came down the staircase at home, dressed in what we felt to be our best clothes, Daddy looked at us incredulously.

'You can't wear those,' he said, eyeing our colourful suits with disdain, as if we had had any choice. 'Ladies don't wear red, and just look at your shoes.'

Gyll looked down at her feet and gazed guiltily at her high heels.

He looked disgusted with us.

'Go up and change into something suitable for an interview at the Ladies' College.'

'But they're new,' I exclaimed, aghast. 'Mrs Andrews bought them for us in Johannesburg, because of the clothes rationing – we said you'd pay her.'

Daddy raised his eyebrows, but we couldn't think why. We were very attached to those garments, the first that we had ever chosen for ourselves; especially I liked my cerulean-blue suit and pink blouse, and Gyll adored her red jacket and skirt. Yes, perhaps the outfits had got rather out of shape during their damp journey from Liverpool, but they were just so much more grown-up and more bold and beautiful in colour than anything else either of us had ever worn.

While in Africa we did not fully understand about rationing or coupons or utility books and furniture, but we knew perfectly well that almost everything was in short supply and that sailors were drowned bringing food and other essentials to Britain. Nothing should be wasted, even less, if it were possible, than at 12, Bryant Road. We thought that it would please everyone if we arrived kitted out with some warm clothes, for what we anticipated would be a cold winter ahead.

'My dear girls,' he said in that tone that men sometimes use, somewhere in between impatience, ridicule, boredom and condescension, 'clothes coupons are *not* a problem.'

'Oh,' remembering the shop.

'And naturally any member of the family has a 22 per cent discount.'

'Oh.'

We felt subdued and also worried because we could sense that he was about to make a problem over repaying Mrs Andrews: he implied that she had interfered unneces-sarily. We were both dumbfounded and ashamed.

I just wondered if Mrs Marsh had suggested to Mrs Andrews that she might take us to buy some clothes before sailing back to England, because otherwise we only had our Kingsmead school uniforms with us, designed for sunny days in a warm climate.

'But Daddy . . .' we fretted.

He laughed. We did not know either what he meant, or what he intended to do about it. In fact to this day I do not know if he ever repaid Mrs Andrews, but I hope to God that he did.

So all right, we did still have our school cardigans with us and our pale-green smock-topped blouses with the wide sleeves in which I brought up Tyrone, but the Kingsmead uniform just did not look right in England. Mrs Dalton, asked by Daddy to go and find something even remotely more suitable for the interview, rootled around in our not very tidy cupboard, and produced, like a rabbit out of a hat, our green skirts and school shoes too.

Gyll groaned. 'I'm not putting on those,' she declared.

But she did, in the end, even the socks and shoes. It was

both ridiculous and sad that no one had thought of taking us shopping since arriving back, and we were left with nothing else to wear, giving us no choice and leaving us no self-esteem. It was not as if we did not have access to clothing coupons, unlike everyone else who could manage just one new outfit a year, and if they were lucky, just one sheet. Otherwise it was a case of make-do-and-mend. Sheets with holes in the middle were mended sides to middle. Everyone did it, after four years.

Our confidence in ourselves, in our family, in England, was beginning to get very crumbly round the edges.

The interview at Cheltenham was a terrifying ordeal. The school was empty because the term had not yet begun. The vast corridors, chequered white-and-black marble, the gaunt and forbidding halls and classrooms overwhelmed us. Miss Popham was elegant and blue-rinsed and not our idea of a headmistress at all. She had a trim figure and wore classy little black dresses and high heels. She had very good legs and twinkly little feet as she moved briskly from one place to another.

Settling herself down, she launched into the subject of the 'Umpire', which baffled me completely until I realised that she was speaking about what we called the Colonies, towards which, she said, she and the College Governors seemed to feel some sort of attachment, an affinity. Gels from the 'Umpire' would be found places in college, but these things took time. She smiled brightly at Daddy, as if expecting him to understand.

He leant forward, frowning. Even he was taking a little time to adjust to the broad long vowels – umpire/empire. Oh Daddy, do try. Please.

'Well, the gels will need to be tested in any event,' she remarked. She rang a bell and her secretary came to the door.

'Take these gels down to Miss Blandford in the Lower Hall,' she commanded and we were whisked away down the slippery staircase and hard, unforgiving marble corridor, which looked out over a perfect lawn stretching uniformly from one huge school building to the next, criss-crossed by obligatory paths; obligatory for the grand design of the quad and obligatory in the sense that we had to walk on them and NOT on the grass.

Nervously we took our places at the desks indicated by a large woman, definitely more of a bull than a cow. She eyed us with annoyance, as if we had interrupted some important piece of work.

'You may look at your questions now.'

It was a nightmare. I could do no part of it. I was overawed by the heavily carved wood everywhere and ecclesiastical glass windows that cast pale-coloured stains on my desk. The syllabus from which the questions had been drawn was entirely alien. The maths paper looked like double Dutch. I wanted to go to the lavvy but dared not excuse myself. I would never have known where to find it anyway; and my mouth was so dry I thought that I would probably not be able to get the words out. I had become dumb.

When the hateful ordeal was over, the mistress collected the papers and told us to go back to Miss Popham's study. But where was it? We floundered round the corridors and eventually found a recognisable landmark. We climbed the beautiful, curved, highly polished staircase, the kind that you might have expected to see the young Victoria descend, in glory, to meet her ministers assembled and waiting humbly below.

Now we mounted it, tapped on Miss Popham's door and waited to be told to enter.

'Come,' she called, in a stately sort of way. Gyll and I were far beyond seeing the funny side of it.

While Daddy was sitting hunched in a deep armchair (there to embarrass parents who were not too limber at climbing out of it), trying to look in command of the situation, we were more than astonished to find Miss Popham sitting daintily on a soft rug in front of the unlit fireplace, one hand resting gently on a panting white dog, whom she introduced, with great affection, as Peter. She popped her smile at him and he smirked slothfully in return, well, it was probably more a look of 'Hey, here I am, your faithful admirer, and where's my sweetie?'

Miss Popham and Daddy had obviously been talking about Gyll and me; they stopped the moment we walked in. Well, I can't think what else they would have been talking about during that frightful three quarters of an hour we spent at our desks in the Lower Hall.

She explained to us that she had been telling Daddy that all the Boarding Houses were full and that we would have to join a waiting-list, always supposing that we had passed the exam. There were many other parents, who were no doubt equally desperate to get their daughters off their hands and into very secure keeping. We felt enormously relieved at this news. A reprieve! But then Daddy made the most awful tearing sound which came out somewhere between a strangled choke and a sob.

We looked away in embarrassment, because we were beginning to get used to his tricks, but Miss Popham looked concerned. Maybe she was afraid that he would break down altogether. What an embarrassing situation she would have on her delicate little hands then.

'Well—' she started hesitantly, a hint of promise in her voice.

Daddy put on his beleaguered air. 'I should have realised that such a fine school as this would have no vacancies, forgive me for being a silly old fool.' But he couldn't let such an opportunity go. 'But it's so difficult . . . their mother . . . being evacuees . . .' and then he embellished that. 'Refugees returned home to a difficult situation . . .'

What on earth was he trying to say?

He paused, allowing the utter dejection of his attitude to be recognised as fully as possible. 'I am at my wit's end . . .' he almost sobbed.

'Maybe –' Miss Popham began again.

Daddy looked up, seizing on the second of her weakness, suddenly all hope, or was it cunning? He flashed his warm brown eyes and smiled, stroking up the ends of his generous moustache. What with his flowing bow tie and rather eccentric ways he could easily be mistaken for a Continental gentleman, except that he was almost too big to be a foreigner. He was well over six foot tall. His imported mannerisms, designed, I suspect now, to conceal a multitude of complexes (some of them quite inferior), probably were the consequence of not being very well educated, though he claimed to have been to school in London, France and Switzerland (and he used to mutter about his time at the Sorbonne in Paris). Neither was he in the least bit genuine. On the other hand, he was very well read and up to date with politics, past and present, and interesting on all manner of subjects. But Miss Popham? She was a real challenge. Genuine or not, he was beginning to make headway with Miss Popham; it was the performance of a lifetime.

'Maybe,' she pondered, 'maybe they could go to the Sanatorium.'

'The Sanatorium,' he breathed, as if he thought it was the most wonderful idea in the world. 'What do you think of that, girls? Miss Popham is offering you the Sanatorium!'

So far as I could see, she was not 'offering' us the Sanatorium at all. It was just a rather unpleasant idea that she was turning over in her mind, in a half-hearted sort of way. But he chose to misunderstand her. His swagger was quite restored. I was horribly embarrassed by his false exuberance – or his naiveté. I had a vile feeling that he thought he was playing a board game – a game he wanted to win regardless of the prize – just so long as he could get rid of his unwanted pieces. I couldn't bring myself to look pleased or to smile and Gyll was looking pretty downcast. It was so obvious that the school did not really want us, that the notes on our exam results that had been handed to Miss Popham by her discreet secretary just after we had returned to her study, and which she had scanned but briefly, were not up to scratch. How could they be? Our scholastic standards were too low, we did not measure up to their yardstick, and our personalities were entirely unsuitable. It would have been best to give up there and then. We were just evacuees with common clothes, common accents and a different kind of education. Why bother with us? Why try to fit fat bulging pegs into neat square holes?

I hated the thought that Miss Popham was doing Daddy a favour, a colossal favour. It put us in such a subordinate place, having to grovel and then be grateful, but he couldn't appreciate that, and the die was cast. When I grew older I learnt to recognise all Daddy's ploys; I also learnt how easily women gave in to him though they probably saw through his flattery, his tactics. He was a bit of a sham really, but fun in his mischievous way; the trouble was that too often the consequences bounced off on to us, the pigs in the middle. Those people who might have taken pity on us in our loneliness or felt it their duty to be kind to us gave us a wide berth, nervous of becoming unnecessarily involved with the kids of such an apparently embarrassing and unpredictable man.

★ ★ ★

Daddy was very cocky about his little victory. Anyone would have thought, from the way he bragged to his friends and gambling mates, which included the priest of the local Catholic Church and the family doctor, that we had entered college through our own merit, had passed incredibly difficult exams and personality tests. It was as if getting into Cheltenham had proved something about our worth, not only Gyll's and mine but his own too, and that of the whole family, on a par with being accepted in court circles and being presented to the King. All of which was ridiculous because there was nothing snobby about Cheltenham, no special value attached to background or wealth. The most respected virtue, the one most admired, was the ability to conform, so all the good girls tried to be as much as possible like all the other good girls. It was a ridiculous boast too, because Daddy, of all people, underneath all the swagger, longed to be different.

One thing was certain – he was disarmingly naive about social graces, having, apparently, absolutely no good taste whatsoever. But he had his interestingly unique preferences which included an eclectic art collection (mostly by unknown but interesting impressionist artists, which was generally OK and good fun), muddled in with a hideous Boule cabinet, from his time in Paris, and utterly awful furniture, probably pieces picked up for an irresistible song, or less, from a sale of utility furniture in the shop. He was an entertaining raconteur and a great bluffer; honesty was not his strong suit. Things went wrong when he tried to be someone that he was not, which was quite often. Just now, Gyll and I both wished that he would not brag about us being accepted for College and preferred not to think about the melodrama we had witnessed in Miss Popham's study. His version of us conquering untold odds through our amazing scholastic achievements combined with his own version of Mummy's background seemed just so much more fun to him than the truth.

To be fair to my father, he did believe in education for girls, for everyone in fact. And to be fair again, I am grateful that he sent me to school. I just wish that it had not been Cheltenham.

Daddy's enthusiasm took a bit of a dip when he saw the formidable clothes list. He was annoyed to see just how much we needed, suggesting alternatives that could be obtained from his own shop, which, he said, had a perfectly good school outfitting department, albeit, he admitted when pressed, for Watford Girls' Grammar School and not for Cheltenham. Still, the knickers . . .

'No, Daddy. They're blue. Ours must be green.'

'Nobody will see them.'

How wrong he was. Old ladies in Cheltenham seemed to lurk on almost every pavement and complained constantly about a flash of pink thighs between stocking top and knicker elastic, when they watched for those girls senior enough to be permitted to bicycle to school. As a consequence, all girls were liable to be stopped at any time by a prefect and challenged to lift their skirts so that it could be seen whether the lisle stocking tops were well covered by the green woollen underwear.

'But six pairs,' he protested, 'and linings. Whatever are they?'

'They go inside.'

'What, two pairs of knickers at once? That's ridiculous.'

'Yes, Daddy,' we said with glee.

We refrained from pointing out that if he had chosen the convent nearby we could have bought our knickers wherever we wanted to – say, in Watford.

It was out of the question that he would patronise a rival

establishment, so the fact that Daniel Neal was the chosen supplier of the uniform truly maddened him. The very idea of dealing with a competitor! Daniel Neal was to be eschewed as the provider of underwear and anything else on the list.

Instead he took us to a private costumier recommended by the college, a Madame Forma, who occupied a select, terraced house in Montpelier, which was considered to be in one of the more superior parts of the town. Madam Forma had firm, rounded bosoms, hung about with amber beads, and matching sausage curls, neat as anything – which betrayed the perfect symmetry and orderliness of an absolutely awful wig. We were transfixed. It was also rumoured, we found out later, that not only was she bald but also that she had no ears. How heartless are schoolgirls and how tragic the afflictions of poor Madame Forma.

However, Daddy gazed at Madame Forma with admiration (the old rogue) and confided his problem. Two daughters, no mother to look after them. Madame Forma threw herself into the task of providing every single item on the list. There was no arguing; Madame Forma made it completely clear that College regulations required us to purchase the lot and as he was by now so deeply under her influence he was incapable of protest. He accepted the green Harris Tweed skirts, the flannel Sunday suits, the blouses, winter coats, ugly hats, blazers and cardigans—

'With every button done up.'

'With every button done up,' he echoed, and she added, 'No petticoats may be worn.'

Well, that's a relief, he must have felt, at least I don't have to pay for those – regardless of the fact that wearing Harris Tweed close to the skin is equal to the punishment of a hair shirt.

He sighed with a sort of acquiescence and nodded in

agreement, still transfixed by her lists and samples until, that is, she went too far and too fast, so that he could not cope with the mounting number of garments nor the ascending total of the bill.

He let out a suppressed sound as if he was being throttled as she went on and on. She had by no means finished.

'What,' he queried, 'lisle stockings, vests, gym shoes and three dozen white handkerchiefs – each?' He turned to us with a wild look and I could imagine him eyeing these items in the tidy glass-fronted drawers of his own establishment. He exclaimed with pain, 'But I have my own shop, Madame. These things,' he gestured at all the stacks of knickers and stockings, 'can be bought there.'

Madame Forma ignored him as if she had not heard him and went on counting.

We almost felt sorry for him.

With mounting passion, Madame Forma (was that her *real* name?) held up two pairs of hideous, high-laced brown walking shoes, each.

'And two pairs of indoor shoes each,' she emphasised the 'each.' She gestured towards the ugly shoes of the type that we had last seen in 12, Bryant Road, complete with the heels shaped like the pedestal of a lavvy, and with thick cross bars over the instep, the buttons of which were almost impossible to do up, since the leather was thick and rigid. It was possible to buy button hooks but Daddy most certainly was going to economise on those.

'Now then, green silk summer frocks for Sundays and special days,' Madame Forma's face was gleaming with the exertion of selling to a man like Daddy, who by now had his head in his hands. She seemed to be oblivious of the sense of rising panic in her parlour and I thought, and rather hoped, that he would, goaded by the sheer profligacy of the costumier, leap up and cry 'No, no!'

But alas he caved in, staring with quiet obliviousness around him at all the tissue paper and boxes and yards and yards of ugly cloth draped about the furniture. It was called school uniform.

With mutual anguish Gyll and I stood slackly, in the middle of the room, in order to be measured for the unutterably repulsive frocks, which Madame Forma insisted would later be tailored to fit our individual figures. My eye. Alas, the shiny material appeared to defy her professional manipulation. In the event, the parts that were supposed to hang loose certainly did not. The box pleats, which fell from the high yoke at the front of the bodice, with the intention I imagine of concealing our Jane Russell-type breasts, allowed them to burst out like footballs.

Daddy made one last ditch attempt to pretend that everything was all right, but even he knew it wasn't. Madame Forma had of course persuaded him to buy extra large, to allow for growth. Now even he looked doubtful as we shrank inside the horrid green cloth. Of course what was really bothering him was not so much the sheer beastliness of the uniform, nor the bill, but the fact that he suspected that she was trying to get rid of her stock regardless of the correct sizes, the sort of thing he might have been suspected of doing in Watford. Not that he came that close to the shop floor, but he could always issue orders to the staff.

I guess he couldn't see a way to wrangle even a 10 per cent (trade of course) discount from such a redoubtable saleswoman. For once he had been hoisted by his own petard. But wait! Yes, Madame Forma would, as a special concession, sew on the name-tapes in the very short time that remained before term started (two days) and free of charge! I dare say she sewed on every girl's name-tapes, but Daddy pretended, to us anyway, that he had at least scored one point.

It was agreed that we should return in two days to collect our clothes, on our way to the Sanatorium. That meant that in three days time we would be in the huge building called College.

Now here, to amuse you I hope, is a well-known inscription on a tombstone in a Cheltenham Churchyard, but I'm not too sure which.

> Here lie Mrs Brown
> And her three daughters,
> Who died of drinking
> The Cheltenham Waters,
> Had they stayed
> With Epsom Salts
> They would not lie
> In these cold vaults.

Well, I'm not at all sure about drinking the Epsom salts. Did they really come from Epsom and travel all that way to Bulawayo? Or had they been concocted by a Mr Epsom, a pharmacist of course, for Mrs Epsom, who suffered from all manner of ills and therefore needed them to take her mind off her troubles? They didn't do me much good in Africa, so I surmise that drinking the Cheltenham Waters might be an equally foul-tasting and disappointing experience.

13

'Now then, who is that girl who whispered something about frying pans and fire? Step forward that girl.'

It all sounds so simple, doesn't it? Two little girls are sent away to Africa for four years and are unhappy. All they want to do is to come home.

Two rather larger girls come home – home? Happy?

The Sanatorium on Leckhampton Hill reminded me of illustrations found in creepy storybooks; it was a tall and narrow Gothicky building like College itself, shrouded by dark trees and a high wall. My first impression, as Daddy's car swung up the steep drive, was that it looked sinister. But this feeling of uneasiness was immediately dispelled on meeting Miss Davison, the Matron. She seemed old to us because she had silvery-white hair, but she had lovely blue eyes set in a pretty, gentle face. She wore a nursing Sister's uniform and had a Matron's belt round her slim waist, adorned with a silver buckle. A white veil hung to a point at the back of her neck and a watch was attached to the front of her trim bosom, fixed with a silver pin. An older Mary Poppins of the nursing, rather than the nursery, world.

Gyll and I were taken in, in more ways than seemed apparent at the time.

Daddy supervised our luggage and Madame Forma's numerous cardboard boxes. He had a quiet word with Miss Davison and handed over our pocket money and his responsibilities.

Miss Davison took us to meet the other girls, who had evidently been squeezed into College at the last moment too.

Extensions had, in the past, been added on to the Sanatorium to cope with epidemics of one sort or another. It was difficult to imagine any circumstance in which all the beds might be occupied simultaneously, since as I later discovered to my pain, the harsh no-nonsense attitudes of the House Matrons generally did not allow that any girl was ill unless she had a temperature of more than 100°F. Otherwise you were dismissed from Nurse's surgery with a warning not to be a fusspot, but if by any chance you threw-up in said surgery (hopefully over her), you were simply sent to the sickroom and neglected there for a few days. The majority of girls queuing miserably at Nurse's door were regarded by her with hostility and dismissed as malingerers. The nursing staff were far too preoccupied with scraping our scalps with sharp-toothed combs to see if we had nits, or spying on us to make sure that none of us were getting too 'friendly'. None of us could imagine why being friendly with another girl could be wrong. I mean, how could it?

It was stupid of the House Matrons to be so dismissive of anyone feeling sick because not one of us, after a first visit to the San, would ever willingly be sent back there again, so we would never feign illness. When I finally landed up there it was after an emergency operation for appendicitis. It had to be an emergency complete with a wailing ambulance, because Nurse had left it too late to call the doctor since I didn't have a temperature. But my God, I had a red-hot bellyache.

The air in Cheltenham town was described as 'enervating' despite the fact that it was a spa town renowned for its healing waters. In fact, the mists tended to linger in the bowl formed by the encircling Cotswold and Malvern Hills, which probably accounted for the endless chesty colds and bronchitic coughs to which the girls succumbed even in the summer terms. After four years of war, food rationing, and little winter heating, it was not altogether surprising.

Normally at the San the girls who were not considered to be at death's very door, just inconveniently unwell, were lumped together in one of the wards, which had narrow white metal beds and small lockers. There were also rails hung from the ceiling so that curtains could be suspended, and then drawn round the patient, when necessary, just like a real hospital.

This was to be our home until such time as a place was found for us in one of the school Houses. We breathed a sigh of relief when we saw other perfectly healthy girls standing by their beds or perched upon them, in the long, narrow ward.

'*No* sitting on beds,' Miss Davison remarked briskly, as she swept down the dormitory and showed us where we were to sleep.

The girls, I could tell at once from their silence, were new girls too. Like us, they had come either from the Umpire or, also like us, had other urgent, or awful, family problems. There was Mary whose mother had been killed right at the beginning of the Blitz, just at the end of September 1939. Her father, to whom she was very attached, had decided it would be better for her to be at school, now that she was fourteen, with girls of her own age. It was at that time, after the first days of the shock of the Blitz, of course, that the Government decided that as many children as possible should be sent away from London.

Then there was Phoebe, whose parents had just obtained

a divorce, a piece of gossip imparted by Miss Davison to Gyll in one of her rather frequent confidential moods. We all regarded Phoebe with absolute fascination, horror and pity. We did not know anyone whose parents were divorced. We whispered behind her back, contemplating the unimaginable awfulness of her situation.

The first evening Gyll and I opened our Madame Forma cardboard boxes (the other girls had trunks) and arranged, on our bedside lockers, our single permitted photograph (Mummy and Daddy in tandem, the one that we had in Africa), our two permitted ornaments, a miniature dog like Sally in Watford before the war, and a carved Kampala deer from Africa. This did not leave us much room for a hairbrush and comb. We laid our pyjama cases on our pillows and filed in to supper. A day room had been set aside for us, which was mostly filled with a dining table, where we could sit and do our prep, mending, letter writing and so on.

Now Miss Davison took her seat at the head of the table, which was laid for our meal.

'Mary, Mary dear, shoulders back. We don't want to look like a hunchback, do we? Now then, quiet please, for Grace.'

Mary seemed unable to get her shoulders back and Phoebe was sniffing quietly. I think that she was crying. Anyway, we all pretended not to notice, and especially not Miss Davison.

In the morning, the eight of us took the bus from Leckhampton Hill to College. We arrived, a motley little bunch of confused schoolgirls, like dispossessed children, quite out of kilter with the rest of the pupils, who swarmed around us with purpose, always in a hurry, but never running, and never so much as throwing a glance in our direction. There Gyll was instantly taken from me and I felt as if I had been struck in half from head to toe, 'split asunder' as the Good Book would say.

The day spun and whirled around me as I was sucked into the streaming mass of girls revolving from one classroom to another (a different classroom for each specialised subject), skidding along the corridors, sack in hand, up and down the stairs to the next lesson, or striding single file down the wide marble corridor, which was flanked on one side by the library and on the other by long windows giving on to the fresh green turf of the quad. There was a perfectly beautiful weeping willow, a tree that was to become the object of many odes that I wrote to it during Latin, and also some quite accomplished, I thought, artistic impressions in pencil at the back of my Kennedy's *Latin Primer*. Silently we fled, beetling after each other, our arms weighed down with books, forbidden to talk, so it was impossible to find out what was going on or where we were supposed to go next.

I saw Gyll once, fleetingly, as we passed in opposite directions going down a darkened passage, but we were not allowed to stop. The prefects saw to that.

The girls in the established Houses went back for their lunches, but because it was two bus rides away from Coll to the San and back, we ate in the Domestic Science Block. We had cabbage pie and railway pudding (a sort of flat sponge) with custard, cooked by the students, which I suppose saved the College the trouble of employing extra cooks, who, in any event, had probably joined the A.T.S. (Auxiliary Territorial Service) or were doing other war work.

That first day, we continued with lessons in the afternoon, but at last the school day was over. We stood by our desks in our appointed form rooms, with our homework crammed into our sacks, waiting for the signal to be dismissed. The sacks, incidentally, were fabricated from strong canvas, with leather straps to act as handles, not quite long enough to sling over a shoulder. I was wondering how I was going to carry everything back to the San.

'Susie Edmonds?'

A prefect stood at the door.

'Come,' she said, in a regal, no-nonsense way.

I followed her but she explained nothing except that Miss Blandford wished to see me. I trotted obediently after her, to the Lower Hall, where I had sat my test exam and where we had gathered that morning before being sent off to our individual forms, where we would have our own desks and own teacher to supervise us. Down here, in this awe-inspiring cathedral of a room, there were a few empty tables down the middle and at the far end, the Head of the Lower school sat at a desk, waiting for me. She did not immediately look up, although I am certain that she knew I was there.

I recognised her as the mistress who had given us the test papers, the one who made me think of a bull. She set down her pen slowly and deliberately, as if having to see me was a very tedious matter indeed.

Now she rose and advanced upon me, as the prefect departed, having completed her task.

Miss Blandford came up to stand very close to me. She examined me in a critical way as if I was an item for sale that she did not fancy.

'Well,' she said, after a long moment, and she put her hands up and pulled my cardigan away from my shoulders, as if she was squaring me up. 'Well,' she repeated, 'what can I say?'

I simply stood there, unable to reply because I didn't know what she meant or what she expected from me.

'I mean,' she said nastily, 'look at this!' Her fat fingers

pulled at my collar and at the buttons on the front of my shirt.

I tried to look down to see what so offended her, apart from the fact that the tie was not too perfectly knotted. I had never done one up before, but I could perceive nothing else exceptional; just me and my large tropical tits. She grabbed my chin and pushed my face up, so that she could stare into my face.

'Don't you look away from me, child,' she spat.

Miss Blandford was of simian appearance. She had narrow eyes, a round head and a solid mannish neck. She also had a mannish haircut and a florid complexion. She put her face even closer to mine, all the time holding on to my (buttoned-up, as per Madame Forma's injunction!) cardigan, touching my breasts quite deliberately. She was an ugly woman, which was obviously not her fault; just bad luck. But now she was wearing, in addition, a venomous expression, somewhere between gloating and contempt.

'Child,' she said angrily, 'have you never heard of an iron?'

'Iron?' I quavered. What could she mean and why?

'These clothes,' she said, eyeing my uniform. 'They are all crushed.'

An iron? Whatever for? An iron, as for pressing clothes? Or something inexplicably to do with horses? Panic. Branding? Hooves? How stupid could I be? I floundered about hopelessly, trying to organise my thoughts.

'A clothes iron?' I asked nervously, completely confused.

'To what else could I possibly be referring?' she asked with exasperation, and then she continued, 'These clothes, your shirt,' and here again she picked at my buttons, 'your College uniform, all crushed. An absolute disgrace.'

Her breath smelt of tea and I drew back my head but

she pulled me towards her once again, until our bodies were touching.

A hundred thoughts swirled round my muddled head, but chiefly I wanted her to let me go. I was so desperate that I even wanted to swap all this and be back in Africa again, hated place that it was. Yes, I actually wanted to be back at 12, Bryant Road.

'What would your parents think, your clothes in this mess? You are not fit to wear the College uniform. You let the College down, you let your parents down.'

I knew that my parents wouldn't think anything. Mummy was still looking after the Poles and Daddy was looking after his Business Empire.

'Take that insolent look off your face, my girl. If this is the way you intend to take advantage of your privilege in being admitted to College, then I can see trouble ahead. Well,' she added impatiently, 'what are you going to say?'

I could think of nothing correct that I could say to her and yet I could think of too much that I wanted, needed, both to ask and to say.

Firstly, why pick on me? Secondly, how did she imagine that clothes delivered in a box to the San could be ironed? We had never learnt to iron in Bulawayo, it was considered far too dangerous as the iron was heated on burning coals, and in any case the houseboys did it. Blame Madame Forma? And thirdly, I wanted to ask her if it was really my clothes that bothered her. It was *me*, wasn't it? Out of all that teeming mass of girls, why was I the one who needed to be reprimanded for personal untidiness? Should I burst into tears or fall to my knees and beg forgiveness?

'Well, what do you say?'

After a moment I said, 'I'm sorry.'

'I'm sorry, Miss Blandford.'

'I'm sorry, Miss Blandford,' I parroted. It was a name I was unlikely to forget.

'You'd better go now,' she said, releasing her hold, but with warning in her voice. 'But don't ever, ever let me see you looking so untidy again.'

I was dumbfounded by the unfairness of it all, and above all else, frightened of the power she had over me; and of her angry, red eyes that chased me as I backed away from her. I was in a stark panic as I fled, without running, which was forbidden in the College or its grounds, to the rendez-vous in the cloakroom where the others were supposed to be waiting for me. Perhaps they had given up on me and gone ahead? We were not allowed to travel alone, so what would happen? Would I be stuck in the school all night? Would the porter telephone for me? Unlikely.

There was an ominous silence in the college corridors. I took the wrong turning, but I eventually found the others who had been hanging on patiently at Gyll's behest. I held back my tears, unable to explain what had happened and the fact that I had died a thousand deaths since the day began, the worst day of my life until then.

Not so long ago I heard Jonathan Miller talking on the radio. He said that some masters at school got a kick out of bullying. If only I had known, understood the least bit, fathomed the sexual innuendos of her behaviour.

In the ensuing weeks, months, even years, I continued to be overwhelmed at the thought of what had happened, and walked in agony thinking that she might catch me again for some spurious reason. What had happened that first day cast a long shadow over my life at school, but so did a lot of other things.

Once I got over the initial hurt and surprise, and that took me quite a time, I simply learnt to hate Miss Blandford, with murderous intent. Yes, I would have killed her, had

I had the opportunity. In fact I would kill her now, if I ever met her again, but I think, I hope, that she is dead and gone to her own hell, hopefully in the company of my grandfather.

But I also learnt something; that if you are not very careful you can become part of someone else's hang-ups and if you let it it can ruin your life. Since all too often we seem to be victims of circumstances beyond our own control, the only way to deal with other people's twisted heads is to shut yourself away from them, surgically and dispassionately. Duck from it, ignore it, because if you don't they will break you. The protective shell that had been growing round my soft centre ever since we had embarked for Africa was beginning to close almost entirely. I was in my carapace and did not intend to venture out to meet the world. All I wanted was to get through each day with the minimum of mistakes and stupidity. There seemed little point in trying to be cheerful or to look forward to anything, except Mummy coming home.

All in all, not a very auspicious beginning to my college career.

'Miss Davison,' I asked timorously, 'could I use the iron please?'

'Good gracious child, whatever for?'

I explained that my uniform was creased.

'That sounds very vain,' she chided, 'and it is quite out of the question for a gel to use an iron. Far too dangerous.'

'But Miss Blandford said—'

'It is simply not possible. Now run along dear and don't be silly.'

Gyll and I wet my blouses and smoothed out the creases the best we could but, really, there were hardly any puckers there and those that were, were all in the correct places. Oh, I was so damned innocent. Blast Miss Blandford. Blast the College for employing her. Blast the war for creating a shortage of suitable women to teach. Blast Hitler and the Hun.

We soon learned that Popeye (obvious nickname), amongst other things, shared the dog Peter with Miss Davison.

He had a problem with either his bladder or his psyche – maybe both – for the wretched creature had to stop every two minutes for a piddle. This was very boring for us as we were expected to take him for walks when he paid his frequent visits to the San (not as a patient, you understand). He generally only went to College if Miss Popham needed him to impress any new parents with her gentle, understanding ways, and surely having a dog must be one of them? Otherwise he passed his free time at the San where there was a garden as well as a hill to climb and pee on. Whenever Miss Davison or 'Davy' couldn't think what to do with us we were expected to take Peter for walks on Leckhampton Hill. Our progress was positively funereal. Still, we would eventually reach the open fields above Leckhampton and there we could feel the pleasure of being alone and free. There was a view that led the eye across Gloucestershire and all the way to the vague shad-owy blue-grey hills of Wales, quite breathtaking in its sweep of the countryside and in its pale English beauty. We would sit on a tuft of wet grass, in the chilly wind, and revel in the luxury of doing nothing other than look about us. For we were almost always kept well occupied both at school and at the San. The general idea seemed to be to keep our minds and hands busy so that there was no time for naughtiness. We know that the Devil finds work for idle hands, don't we?

Prep took us to about eight or eight-thirty each evening, when we had a cup of delicious Horlicks or Ovaltine before going to bed. On Saturday mornings we still had to go down to College. Each Sunday we had to learn, and be able to repeat to Miss Davison or the Junior Matron, the Prayer book Collect for the forthcoming week. Later, when we were placed in a school House, our ability to memorise the Collect was judged by a House prefect. Woe betide if you were not a popular girl and the prefects had it in for you.

At assembly in the Princess Hall each morning, we gathered, a pea-green soup of whey-faced girls, to await the grand entry of our headmistress, flanked by her chosen prefects and led by the divinely pretty red-headed head-girl on whom most of the juniors had a crush.

'Popeye' clipped her way smartly across the platform, high-heeled and elegant, usually dressed in black. She would throw back her silvery head and call upon our Lord in a soulless sort of way, 'Oh Gard.'

It did not sound the same as prayers at Kingsmead. In fact it did not sound very religious at all, just shallow and brittle. I soon came to suspect the hypocrisy of it all and felt unhappy at the mass devotion that we gave to God in words that had been practised by rote rather than with spiritual thoughts.

However, I made up for the lack of what I considered to be true religious fidelity (Gyll, at that time, had given up believing, with great determination), by going to church twice each Sunday, once for Communion and later for Matins, since at that time I still believed that Jesus was not only the son of God but also in the Virgin Birth. However, this concept began to bother me and I needed help in order to continue my faith in the Church. I went to Davy in order to discuss my doubts, but here I suppose she felt herself to be in rather deep waters. She telephoned Miss Popham's secretary and made an appointment for me to go to consult with Miss Popham.

Once again, Popeye was sitting on the floor, but this time the fire was lit, which made the scene appear to be less artificial. However, when I described my doubts about believing in the Virgin Birth, she launched into what I now see as an utterly incredible explanation, which even then I found difficult to swallow. There was a goat, Miss Popham said, in the London Zoo, that had been in a cage by itself for seven years (poor goat, you may think, but I believe she said that it was a rare one and possibly no matching mate could be found). More to the point, Popeye said seriously, rising to her feet with an agility not usually expected of a blue-rinsed lady, that this goat, much to the utter astonishment of the zoo keepers and other animal experts, had given birth to a baby goat, a kid, she called it.

'There,' she declared, 'miracles can happen!' She looked at me in the certain belief that I had believed both her and her reasoning.

But I was taken aback. Was this why I should believe in the Virgin Birth? Because of a freakish goat? And anyway, did she really believe in Jesus herself? I wasn't too sure about that but I did know that D.V. believed and consequently there must be some truth in it. However, Popeye's conjuring trick did nothing to help to confirm my faith. On the contrary, it did a lot to make me very suspicious that we were all being conned, and I began very seriously to consider all the other inconsistencies that I had found in the Bible. But for the moment I continued my visits to church because it was a chance to get out of school and to look at the choirboys in their frilled collars, and it was calm and peaceful and a fine place to contemplate and to believe in the good things that Jesus had done.

Then there was letter writing under supervision. Not for nothing did we head our letters from 'Stalag IV', which we kept carefully concealed from any staff and their prying eyes. Also we had to mend our clothes; everything was mended and mended again, just as at 12, Bryant Road. There was a war on and simply because a hole the size of an orange had appeared in your lisle stocking did not mean that it could be thrown away. At least I could use my needle and darning mushroom with the sort of dexterity that would have pleased even Dor-Dor.

There was no time to sit about and gossip, nor to write diaries or poems; no time for novels or magazines (they were prohibited anyway). But there were less understandable strictures in our lives.

We were not allowed out or away from College during term time except for three Sundays a term – and then not until after Matins finished at 12 noon. We had to be back by 6 p.m.

We were not permitted to telephone under any circumstances, even supposing there had been such a means of communication on the premises other than that used by the staff.

We were not allowed into a shop or a café, or indeed anywhere near the shopping centre of the town.

The short time we had off never gave us a decent chance to drive home, even though home was – as Daddy had said, in order to convince us that it was the best school for us – only twenty-four miles from Cheltenham. The petrol required for the journey was not justified by the few, short hours we could spend at our house, he said. Oh, Daddy, you blackguard.

However, the parents were issued with a list of suitable and permitted hotels; any others were out of bounds because the Boys' College frequented them. Hard luck if you had a child at each school. 'Mother' had to go to the gentility of the Lilybrook Hotel, while 'Father' could enjoy the raciness of the Horse and Jockey. Otherwise it had to be a picnic on the damp grass of Leckhampton Hill, but at least *en famille*.

In addition, there were whole areas of Cheltenham town that we were not allowed to enter and roads that we were not permitted to walk upon. The town was quartered up like a battlefield and displayed on a map in College, indicating where we could go and where we could not, the enemy territory belonging to the Boys' College, the whole being carefully monitored by spying old ladies in Cheltenham (the same ones who split on us to the College about the inadequacy of our knicker elastics) who kept an eagle eye on our behaviour, which was not too difficult, since we were never allowed out except in uniform and thus could be easily identified.

We were not even allowed to attend the same churches as the boys, but Cheltenham being a town of retired and devout folk, there were plenty of churches to go round. In addition girls were not normally allowed to walk down the Promenade, as if some sex-mad shopper from Cavendish House might actually cast a glance our way. What, in our uniforms?

The only time we could wear something other than uniform was in the evenings in the Houses; then we changed into mufti (which other people might call civvies or just ordinary clothes), but even they had to be pretty sober in design and colour.

I think possibly the worst imposition was having to wear our hateful green felt hats whenever we went outside, except for games. We wore them over our ears and we knew we looked horrible. Gyll and I had abandoned all attempts to preserve our newly found femininity, and in a perverse way we revelled in our ugliness.

So a walk up the hill with the peeing Peter was quite an escape. We were supposed to keep going in order to exercise ourselves as well as the spoilt dog, but much to his relief, whenever we could we would collapse on the ground and catch up with each other's lives. There was much to talk about.

Miss Davison was beginning to take somewhat of a shine to Gyll; she would call her into her sitting room in the evenings and promote discussions about the other girls. Although Miss Davison seemed quite old enough to us to be a great-grandmother, I would suppose now that she was probably only around the age when she might be enduring the problems associated with the menopause, in common with most of the other housemistresses in sole charge of the fifty to seventy girls in their care. Oh, so suitable, all these variable women. It was not quite the best arrangement because not only were we totally uninformed about the 'change' (as it was termed) but totally bog-ignorant about the cause of the rapid mood changes and random switches in their behaviour towards us. I suppose too that the cloistered lives our housemistresses were expected to live did not help. Probably both the teachers and the house staff had troubles in common – but did they receive any advice, any help? Did they ever share a gin and tonic and a laugh or a cry over some exceptionally vexatious problem or pupil – or even, more likely, a cup of tea? I am no longer sure for whom I should feel the most sympathy. It was wartime and I imagine that the College governers felt themselves lucky to have any staff at all.

But all the same, the blazing unpredictability of Miss

Davison was pretty frightening. One moment she was all charm and blue sparkling eyes, the next a virago with the ferocity of old Mrs Bloom. All was not entirely well. We could see that Mary irritated her. The girl was hunched and miserable, her nose and eyes red from crying, hugging her bereavement and her despair to her narrow chest.

'Ah!' cried Miss Davison, with what almost amounted to glee, 'here comes our little hunch-back.'

Maybe Mary had a problem with her spine and was in need of remedial exercises. Maybe she only needed a loving arm around her. Uneasily but openly we teased her about her inability to stick up for herself, for being unable to give just a tiny smile. We called her 'pathetic' and 'cry-baby', all the while aware that Miss Davison was pleased that she had carried us forward with her, the leader of Mary's tormentors. We thought about it and tittered again but inside felt a sinking shame for laughing at Mary and for toadying to Miss Davison. Still, we were learning to survive and surely that is what school is all about, even if the lessons learnt were at someone else's expense?

Gyll said to me, when we were alone, 'Sometimes I think we have climbed out of the frying pan and fallen into the fire.'

'Maybe we should have stuck with those awful Epsom salts,' I said. We laughed as we remembered the morning visits of Mr Marsh with his tray of steaming cups. We were doubtful about Miss Dorothea Beale, who founded the school for daughters of Gentlemen in 1873 with generous scholarships for the daughters of clergymen and who also founded St Hilda's College for women at Oxford. Of course we understood enough to know that these good works were both noble and brave, but for us, in another century and different times, we felt ourselves yet again to be caught in a time warp, in the nineteenth century this time, but at least in England.

At about the same time Miss Buss founded Camden School, in London, for the children of the less affluent, and North London Collegiate for the children of the better off. They were both passionate believers in education for women and quite right too, in retrospect.

> Miss Buss and Miss Beale
> Cupid's darts do not feel,
> Miss Beale and Miss Buss.
> Are not human like us.

The twelve-week term crept to a close. Gyll and I wondered if Mummy would be able to leave the Army now and be home in time for Christmas. It did not seem to be such an unreasonable thought.

As we packed our things we heard, unbelievably, that the following term we would have a House of our own. Oh joy! The American Army had handed back to College one of the Houses they had requisitioned as a hospital. With the D-Day landings over, the requirements for the treatment of the wounded soldiers and airmen had diminished. The House we were to be in was called Glenlea, and Gyll and I, together with our companions from the San, were all to go there. We breathed more easily at the prospect of escape from the Sanatorium, with its strange brooding, uneasy atmosphere. Daddy came to fetch us. We asked when Mummy would be coming home but he looked depressed and said he did not know. Maybe, he said, we would telephone her when we got home and see if we could persuade her.

Persuade? Surely she wouldn't need any persuading so long as she had the permission? We had heard of leave on compassionate grounds. Did our need not qualify?

Daddy was morose and as soon as we got back to the Manor Farm House he went to the drinks cabinet and poured himself a large gin.

There was not much for us to do. We didn't know any of the local children and Daddy seemed in no mood to make the effort to introduce us to any of his contacts who might have known other children of our age.

War had most certainly changed him. He was simply not the father we had known up until the day we sailed for Africa, who was nowhere to be found. He didn't even look the same, especially as now he was growing a beard, a very neat one it has to be said, like a Spanish grandee, but he was not the father we wanted back. We speculated about whether he really was the same person.

It was obvious to us that he no longer had the friends we had known in Watford, in fact he had few friends at all, except for the 'cronies' who joined his shooting parties or played cards and gambled with him a couple of evenings a week or more. Otherwise he went up to the Bull to drink with the regulars who were not really his friends. He also went to Watford a couple of days a week, and Mrs Dalton went with him to the little flat over the shop in Watford, the one that had belonged to Daddy's father. We were left in the care of Margaret, and we would settle down happily with her in the kitchen and play with her baby, or, if the weather was warm enough, we might cycle into Cirencester to go to the cinema.

We also walked around the village a good deal, hoping to be whistled at by passing Yanks, who had taken over the local airbase, which was called 'RAF Fairford', though, to be more accurate, it should have been USAF Kempsford, since it was neither an RAF base nor in Fairford. It was ringed by the villages of Daddy's youth, Kempsford and Whelford, very near to where we had spent that precious summer in 1939.

A few locals may have felt the American presence at the base to be oppressive, especially as the US had, in the event of an incident, total military control over all the land and the people within a five-mile radius of the airfield, as at all the American airbases. It made some people feel uneasy, including us.

But Daddy rejoiced, as he had found large quantities of gravel under the surface of his farmland, near Kempsford, the sort that was useful in the making and mending of runways. He palled-up in no time with the top brass in the officers' mess. Was he trying to do business, Gyll and I speculated, as we sat on the rather uncomfortable Cotswold dry-stone wall near the river, the same river that flowed down to the Round House, where we had spent that last, incomparable summer.

'Do you remember . . .' Gyll began, but just then three young airmen appeared, cycling towards us.

'Don't look at them, *don't*,' she whispered, and we pretended to be in animated conversation about the king-fishers by the bridge.

Contact with an airman, any airman, was just what we longed for, but if we were lucky enough to be at the receiving end of a wolf-whistle, we feigned indifference, our little noses in the air, our eyes cast away.

But all at once Gyll cried, 'Oh just observe how that delightful bird flies!' and she looked, not at the airmen, but towards the birds, in such a ridiculous voice that it would fool no one.

From under my eyelashes I could see the young men smiling amongst themselves, and I blushed as they cycled right past us. They couldn't see my red face but I felt awfully stupid. The moment that they were out of sight, we fell about, swooning with happiness and excitement. Had we known then that there were soon to be nuclear warheads at the base, we might not have felt quite the same.

'The one nearest me, he looked at me!' my sister claimed. Oh yes?

But oh yes, truly it was heaven for the girls of middle England, being surrounded by so many bases and so many gorgeous young men, in their divine oyster-and-olive uniforms, their pockets full of dollars.

It was the 'special relationship', you see, which was exactly what Gyll and I were so keen to promote, that lonely autumn of 1944.

As Christmas approached, we did our shopping. I bought Daddy a picture of a hunting scene, but he never hung it up. It was pretty awful, the sort of thing that you couldn't give away at a car-boot sale nowadays.

We didn't know if we should get anything for Mummy; we still did not know if we would be seeing her. We wondered where she would sleep, as we were in her room. Maybe in Dick's room, or Mrs Dalton's, who we hoped might vanish if Mummy was in the house.

Then all at once she arrived, but she was not alone. She had taken the chance of bringing a Polish officer with her, not the glamorous Romek, but a rather sad, aesthetic-looking man, who was about Mummy's age. Daddy was enraged, Mummy defensive and the Pole, Wacek, very embarrassed. I don't know what she had promised him, but it was clear that this family scene was not what he expected.

Daddy took out his twelve-bore shotgun after he had been sloshing back the gin and tonics for an hour or four and aimed at the Pole who promptly quit, leaving his little collection of toiletries behind in the bathroom. Mummy had hysterics and disappeared into the night, not to follow him but to drown herself in the river. Gyll rushed after her, out into the Christmas cold shouting 'Mummy, Mummy', but the wet wind blew away her cries, and it is doubtful whether Mummy would have heard her, even supposing they had gone to the same part of the Coln, behind the railway towards Fairford. But Gyll's rescue attempt was thwarted by three drunken Yanks who had been downing the booze at the Railway Inn, who molested her outside the pub, just by the entrance to our drive.

Mummy decided against death that night, though she was to try again, quite seriously, at a later date, and on more than one occasion. What she did decide, though, was to hot-foot it back to Scarborough, leaving behind her a bewildered collection of frightened and unhappy people.

14

Dick came home on a brief leave from his regiment, the Ox and Bucks. He looked very young to be a soldier and to jump out of aeroplanes (with a parachute!), but mostly he showed us photographs of hunting expeditions in the deserts of North Africa.

He inspected us as a brother might, as if we were a couple of kit-bags. We in turn looked at him in awe, admiring his uniform, his red beret worn straight across the brow and then pulled neatly down to one side, and even more glamorous, the pip on his shoulder. We skirted round him gingerly because although he was our real brother (not in the sense that Mavis wanted to be in Africa, but because we had the same parents), he really was a complete stranger. He had a face that was cherubic and which belied his age, which was five years older than me. Let's see, that made him nineteen. He was separate and a stranger but he had spent his adolescent years as an unexpected casualty of war.

If Gyll and I had been unhappy in Africa, aggravated at the thought that our brother was enjoying the affections of our parents while we were not, then perhaps we should have questioned his lot a little more carefully, left in England, more or less alone, to follow his own path. But I don't suppose that we could have been expected to imagine that difficult scene, him moving from Watford to a fairly hostile situation in the country, with his mother, who would have been accepted in almost any snobby household in the district, nowhere to be seen.

When Daddy uprooted his household from Watford, he had arrived in Fairford minus a wife. He was exempt from active service because of his age combined with the necessity that he should look after his business affairs, but he had the nerve to turn up with a housekeeper-cum-secretary, who did not appear to know about either housekeeping or being a secretary. And soon there was a member of the household who had a fatherless baby. While the child was most certainly not one of his own progeny, he was damned if anyone expected him to go round explaining or excusing himself.

Dick did not find it easy to get to know anyone of his age locally since his father was regarded with a deal of suspicion. Daddy made little effort to ease the situation for him, in fact he actively impeded him from making friends, since he cared so little for his own reputation that he easily, without intending to, infuriated most of the hoity-toity locals – who might have helped with introductions for

Dick. Carelessly Daddy distributed silk stockings from his plentiful supply in the shop; avidly the ladies of the district accepted them, and then being the shallow stuck-up people that they were, whispered and gossiped behind his back, half in fear, half in jealousy. But then country life is like that, isn't it? Poor old Daddy, he too, like us, was too innocent by half.

And as the nobs of the district quite naturally steered clear of this unpredictable man, it made life quite difficult for Dick, who lacked, as a consequence, many friends of his own age or background, save for those that he had made in the army and later at Oxford. No wonder he felt aggrieved.

Poor Dick, too. He looked at Gyll and me, in our bobby socks and odd bits of school uniform, and I am afraid that he was a trifle disappointed, but by now we were getting used to disappointing people. If he had hoped that we might make a contribution to his social life he could see at once that we would be a positive hindrance. Only Alice and Margaret could accept us with unreserved love, disregarding our foreign ways (after all they were foreigners themselves) and demonstrating that they were happy that we were home.

But 'home' was populated with unfamiliar faces and beyond the garden wall we felt the mistrust of the villagers. Daddy did daft but exciting things like taking us, underage, to the local pub or even to dances in the local Palmer Hall, where we were obviously considered to be far too young to be out, far too forward to learn how to jitterbug with American Airmen or to chat to boys in the RAF. Daddy liked going to the Palmer Hall because they occasionally auctioned a gallon can of Tate and Lyle's Golden syrup, which he would always end up taking away with him, having paid above the odds (much to the chagrin of the locals) so that Margaret could make syrup puddings for his shoot lunches.

We also had two pigs, Roger and Francis Bacon. They were friendly, nice clean pigs and liked it when we scratched their backs. Half of each pig belonged to the Ministry of Food, but we did not really make the connection until they were bundled away, one by one, squealing in terror as if they had already recognised that their executions were about to take place. When the halves were returned to us (longways) Margaret would salt the pieces that could not be eaten fresh and at once (no deep freezes in those days), which she did in the long salting-trough at the back of the house, turning the carcasses each day to re-salt and make bacon that could be kept for the future.

It was impossible for us to eat the fresh pork chop on our plates, and Daddy got very angry and said that we had been utterly spoilt in Africa and that we should realise what rationing was all about. Of course, what he did not acknowledge was that while most people were rationed to one egg every week, he had the pick of our farmyard chickens. Still, Daddy and Dick quickly scooped the chops from our plates and looked satisfied.

If Daddy was in a bad mood, then he would shut himself away in the sitting room, emptying packets of unfiltered cigarettes and bottles of gin as if they were going out of fashion, his feet propped up on the chimney breast as he lay thinking and sulking in his big armchair. That was when Gyll and I would don our red sweaters and sit on the low stone wall by the mill and hope that someone would stop and talk to us.

Sometimes Daddy went off on his own up to London for business reasons or to see his brother, our wildly eccentric uncle Stuart. On these occasions you might have thought that Mrs Dalton would entertain us, do something special like a visit to the cinema or shopping, but she had other fish to fry. Mrs Dalton had a caller. He was an American called Sergeant Miller. He was a big, rangy, gentle sort of man, who wore his beige trousers low on the hips, like a film star in a Western.

One day soon after our arrival, poking about on the top floor of the house, near to where Margaret lived with her baby and alongside a couple of empty bedrooms and linen storage cupboards, I was riveted to find, on the floor of one of the larger store rooms, a camp-bed laid out neatly, with clear evidence of someone having slept in it not long before my discovery. Toilet articles were scattered about and there was a mirror suspended by a piece of string from one of the shelves.

I stared around for a bit and then closed the door and went downstairs to find Gyll. It seemed so odd that no one had mentioned that anyone was sleeping in the linen cupboard, especially as there were unoccupied bedrooms close to hand. Eventually we just had to ask Margaret.

'Oh,' she said, without thinking, 'that's where Sergeant Miller sleeps when your daddy's at home.'

'Where does he sleep when Daddy's away?'

Margaret peered at us a little crossly. She wore very thick-lensed spectacles that got clouded with steam when she did the washing up, and she was rather deaf. Just now she pretended to be more deaf than usual. She pushed her glasses up her nose and blinked.

'Tell us Margaret, go on.'

'I don't knows anythings about that,' she said at last, quite adamantly. She spoke a curious mixture of Anglo/ Swiss and deep Gloucestershire; when she was perturbed the accent was more noticeable, a great giveaway. Gyll and I tittered and looked at each other because we suddenly knew where Sergeant Miller slept when Daddy had gone off on his own.

But where, we wondered, did Mrs Dalton sleep when Daddy was at home?

As a matter of fact, we were fairly convinced that it could not be with Daddy because he was far too old and anyway he was married to Mummy. But we liked to tease ourselves with idle speculation. Not a lot else to do, really.

Although Gyll and I lived in dread at the thought of returning to Cheltenham, we could see that it was not an equally sad concept for Daddy.

The trunks were packed and loaded into the boot of the car and tied down with rope. This time there were no cardboard boxes; the clothes were packed with immaculate neatness that would most certainly have found favour with Dor-Dor. Nevertheless I was filled with apprehension that I would never measure up to the strict standards set by the College; that I would meet again the blazing, ugly anger of Miss Blandford. But at least, look on the happy side, we were not to be returned to the San and the arbitrary behaviour of Miss Davison.

Glenlea was a broad-fronted red-brick building, designed and built originally as a College House. Initially a housemistress from another well-established House came to help our own new housemistress, Mrs Garner, to get the House started.

Before we went to bed, each one of us in turn had to say goodnight to her. She was the one who took ultimate control of the House, and whose word was law. If anything had gone wrong, then she would have had to take the blame. Parents put their girls into her care, trusting that they would be taught to behave like ladies (most of them did already), but then there were us wild colonials who

had not been taught how to enter or leave a room grace-
fully, how to pick up a chair – no, don't laugh, you can
look very silly if you get it wrong when in high society –
'proper' table manners, which included how to hold your
knife and most importantly of all, in my opinion, how to
get something you wanted from where you could not
reach it without stretching your arm across the table.

'Would you like some salt?'

'No thank you, but would you like some salt?'

'Oh yes please, I would very much like some salt.'

Now you know.

The Housemistress had also to watch that no man got
near us, except the school doctor, the organist, the art
teacher and the porter. Otherwise, no males, not even from
the Boys' College, which, on the face of it, seemed a safe
enough place to visit, for drama or science or even the
occasional school dance which could have been, under
strict, of course, very strict supervision. After all, we were
not even allowed to walk the same sreets. The virtue of
Cheltenham girls had to be protected at all costs.

I suppose that was why I was gated for two 'out' Sundays
because Mrs Garner, or maybe it was Nurse or a prefect
who split on me, intercepted a smile between a choirboy
and me, and for goodness' sake we had never even met!

However, there was one occasion, quite a bit later
during another term, when if I had been caught I would
have been expelled, and brought my friends some of the
way with me. Actually, it was something for which,
Honest Injun, I could not really be blamed.

One Sunday afternoon, my clutch of friends and I had
gone to the church for an afternoon of ecclesiastical singing. Mm, were we thinking of the choirboys, organs and
oratorios not being near the top of our list of not-to-be-
missed entertainment? Well, my choirboy just happened to

be there, with his pure and divine white ruff and red cassock, but I kept my eyes down, very primly.

However, when we came out into the bright, late afternoon sunlight, I saw the young chorister waiting on the pavement ahead. I asked Foxy, I think it was, to bend down and do up her shoelace, because I wanted to wait and see what might happen next. Whereupon he approached the small group of us girls, lingering while Foxy fooled around with her laces, and came up to us. I expect that we all looked most anxious, to see if there was anyone who might be watching us and report us for looking at a boy, let alone talking to him.

He turned to me (I don't know what his name was) and he asked, quite simply, 'My mother and I wondered if you would like to come out to tea with us?' I looked at the other girls and each one of us was equally stunned. The expressions on our faces must have said enough. The sheer impossibility of the invitation took my own breath away. How could I possibly explain that it was the craziest question I had ever been asked?

'Look,' I said, trying not to sound snooty, 'look, I'm terribly sorry but – look, I can't explain, but we are not allowed out, I mean, to go out, not with anybody.'

The boy looked at me, not really understanding.

I looked at the girls for help, but they just shrugged their shoulders in a let's-give-up sort of way.

There was a woman, about the same age as Mummy, watching us from some little way down the pavement. She was wearing a beret from which little strands of hair had escaped, and which she had failed to tuck back. Now she was beginning to look concerned, making movements to call her son away. The boy looked at her and then back at me.

'But it's my mother,' he said. 'It would be all right.'

Oh no, it wouldn't, I thought, especially not with a hundred eyes spying on you, from behind every curtain in every house within sighting distance, or so we thought. The sheer impossibility of the invitation made it too difficult to explain what the rules were like at our awful school, and how we were kept in a virtual cage, so that we had to be rude to nice people like him and his mother.

I am sure he thought that I was being horrible and that we would all laugh at him behind his back. Not at all, I felt utterly miserable that I had brought this upon him, and the others were furious with me, for involving them in anything so cruel. 'I'm just terribly sorry,' I said as we turned to go. But I am sure that he did not believe me. And it was to have been tea with his mother, for goodness' sake.

There was a garden at the back of Glenlea, with tennis courts and a fine lime tree, beyond which lay the green and intimidating (I say intimidating because apart from the boredom of cricket we also had to play lacrosse which resulted in several broken noses and teeth; bloody dangerous game for girls) school games pitches. This meant that we did not have to walk too far for games, but on the other hand, their very propinquity was a source of pain and danger. It was far too easy to drag us out for cricket practice before breakfast, when the prefect delegated to whip us pathetic juniors into shape hurled successive very wet and very hard balls at us that not only stung our hands but filled us with a sense of hopelessness. We knew nothing about the game except that we hated it. The prefect, Jean, struggled on grimly; she had sizzling green eyes and a sizzling green temper to match, She scared us to death.

There were only nine of us juniors so we all had to be in the team. On one of the inter-house matches the score was 135 runs for them and just nine for us. My friend Puffy dropped the bat when she had hit the ball (all of two yards) and started to run as if she was playing baseball and Phoebe knocked the stumps over with her own swing. Well, you can see that we had problems. Not one of us was capable of throwing a ball more than about five yards and usually in the wrong direction. The opposing team had to wait halfway down the space between the wickets in order to reach the ball at all, with absolutely no danger of being bowled out or stumped or whatever.

We were an ill-assorted bunch. Various senior and dependable girls, up-rooted from the conformity of other more business-like and successful houses, had been seeded into our midst, with the intention of showing us the ropes and imbuing us with a bit of team spirit. Team spirit? You only had to look at us to know that the job was a pretty futile task. I wonder what on earth induced these practical girls to quit their established and successful Houses in order to whip a bunch of stroppy colonialists into shape. It might have been pride in their loyalty to College; it might have been a reduction in school fees for their parents, who knows – but they were a tough lot, a bit like army sergeants with the latest troop of new, raw recruits.

The piteous little party from the Sanatorium formed the nub of the House, unhappy, spiritless, incompetent and inadequate as we were. Hardly the right sort of material to form the best of cornerstones for this reactivated hive of schoolgirl excellence. The majority of the other girls who, like us, had filtered back from the Umpire or from even further shores, were about as unlike and separate from the Cheltenham Ladies as the black Africans had been from the whites in Rhodesia. And we were regarded with about the same amount of disdain.

For one thing, we were all physically mature for our ages, big breasted and round-hipped. We were most certainly more socially aware. We were accustomed to wearing make-up, putting curlers in our hair (which was a bit pointless as we had either to wear it short so that it did not touch our collars, or held back in bunches or plaits), and smoked the occasional cigarette when we could coordinate possession, time and sufficient secrecy to do so. Girls who had come from the far west had different clothes; they wore bobby-sox and frightfully grown-up moccasin shoes together with long loose jumpers with the sleeves pulled up to just below the elbow. They did not look English at all, and were hugely admired and imitated by all of us – well, I say we imitated them, but it was impossible to find a shoe shop anywhere that sold moccasin-style shoes.

We had, most of us anyway, learnt to be independent, owed loyalty to no one particular place, and froze in the unaccustomed English winter weather. We were from all corners of the earth and most of us had tales to tell. There were girls from the United States, Guatemala, India, and my friend Puffy who had been dispatched to boarding school in England when she was seven, as her parents were living in India. Her father worked for the Indian Civil Service, bringing irrigation to the Punjab. But then her little English school was evacuated to Canada in 1940, before she could see her parents again. When the school was finally repatriated her parents were still in India, the only girl whose parents were not there to welcome her home. For a time she lived with the reluctant head of the school, because there was nowhere else for her to go. Like Gyll and me she had no personal possessions but for different reasons. She had not lost her things through careless abandonment but because the head of her school decided that she should not become attached to possessions so she gave away all Puffy's books – and she did not encourage her to write because she thought that the imagination was dangerous and led one astray. Her mother returned briefly from India to arrange her entry to Cheltenham and then went back to India again. Somewhere along the line it was forgotten that no special arrangements had been made for the school holidays (shades of Miss Balmforth at Liverpool), only far, far worse. For some people, sending your children away to boarding school was an excellent way of getting rid of your responsibilities. Just what would happen to us in the holidays was anyone's guess.

There we were, the genies who had escaped from the bottle and who were now being squeezed back in and the stoppers fixed firmly back in place. But they couldn't pluck away what we had already experienced and life in this stifling bottle could never be the same for us as it was for the others who had never experienced freedom. Maybe women like Miss Blandford thought they could quell our spirits (a bit like the Japs, in their prison camps, I used to think, since in my view she looked a bit like one) and then subsequently remould us to become perfect, obedient prisoners. I don't know the Japanese for '*Ja, Herr Kommandant*' but probably that is more or less what was going on. It seemed that they wanted us all to be the same – individuality was not encouraged. Perhaps Miss Blandford had a machine in her mind, turning out identical fat little pink pork sausages.

Maybe they sometimes succeeded. I know quite a lot of girls who really loved their days at College, loved the security of knowing exactly where they were, and what they were going to do next. But it seemed a pity, that the only good things we had brought from Africa, and the things that the other girls had brought with them from their experiences away from Britain, had to be snatched away and suppressed, although, always contrary, I in some ways quite wanted to be like the others, blinkered and accepting. But none of us could change the past four years.

We found that first Michaelmas term dreadfully cold. Of course there was little or no heating in Glenlea; it had been our choice to come home to the cold and the war and we were reaping the consequences. Sitting on the radiators was a frightful thing to do; utterly forbidden. It would give us piles (they said!). But it was the early mornings that were the worst, when there was ice on the inside of the dormitory windows and even the clothes that we had stashed inside the bottom of our beds when we went to bed at night (so that they would keep warm for crawling into in the mornings) were freezing. Not such a bad idea to wear two pairs of knickers at once after all, though I don't think that Daddy would have appreciated that point.

Now then, hands up anyone who loves porridge concocted the night before and allowed to burn a bit in the slow cooking over night. And oh, the lumps! Delicious. Especially as there was little sugar, but we could always add salt, which was really not too bad. Much of the eight ounces of sugar that we were rationed went early in the week, mostly for cooking, but we had two ounces of sugar and two ounces of butter, each in our own dinky little name-labelled pots, to prevent cheating. But I have forgotten to mention the scrumptious egg powder, sent by good ol' Uncle Sam, which we had made up as scrambled eggs for Sunday breakfast. The water oozed out of the eggs on the soggy toast and ran round the rim of the plate and back to the toast. Yum yum. Was there anything good?

Well, none of us was particularly thin and sometimes we had hard-boiled eggs with a bright yellow curry sauce and rice, which was, word of honour, rather tasty and different. As good as eggy bread.

Tables of ten had a top (prefects) and a bottom (juniors). It doesn't take a lot of guessing as to who got first turn with the minuscule dishes of jam laid at the top end of the table. By the time it reached ours, it was empty.

Elected by the other juniors to go and ask for more (O. Twist?) I dared to approach the twin sisters, the Misses Palsey (or was it Pawsey?), who reigned over the ancient Aga in the kitchen.

'Please, may we have some more jam?'

'Jem?' asked Number One, rather sharply.

'Yes, jam. None of us juniors have had any.'

'It's jilly, not jem, and a little goes a long way,' said Number Two.

Tell that to the prefects, I thought.

'And you should be very griteful to the Americans who have sent it to us,' squawked Number One.

It really was a circus act.

Oh yes, we already knew it was supposed to be concentrated, but like Marmite, you don't seem to use any less.

'Ungriteful' (Number One). 'You should be griteful, not griddy.'

'But I only asked—'

'Away with you. You should be more griteful to Uncle Sam for sending us anything at all.'

Miss Palsey (Number One) seized the tiny dish from my hand and plonked it loudly onto the sink ready for washing-up.

So much for lend-lease food. Oh, I know we should have been grateful, but it all had to be repaid, eventually, and with interest. The debt was finally settled in 2008.

You learnt a lot, much to do with survival, but you also learnt to appreciate vegetable (yesterday's vegetables) pie.

After that episode I even considered, very briefly, staying on at Cheltenham long enough to become a prefect so that I could have all the 'jilly'. But not for more than the two minutes that it took me to make my way back, guiltily, to our table, with empty hands.

Hairwash once a week, bath every three days. The five inches allowed in the bath could swell the height of the water according to the number of girls who got into the tub at the same time. Five of us could displace quite a volume of water.

Of course we would have been expelled at once had we been discovered, but one of us stood 'Cave' just outside, which would have given us time to scramble out. Actually, we did a bit of exam revision, testing each other on the various subjects; the books got a bit steamy and damp, but it did not seem to matter too much. We were all different: June, long, lean, brown; Jane, blonde-headed and blonde-whiskered; Diana, small and firm; Puffy with big boobs and me, dark and rather pudgy. Bodies were not anything that we were particularly curious about, but it would have made a wonderful scene in a soft porn movie, only there wasn't any porn. Maybe, though, there were members of the staff who would have had fun watching the scene. Our own main objective was to get warm and then to keep warm by getting the water up to our shoulders. It was never a question of sex. You only had pashes on older girls like the seniors who acted in the *Yeoman of the Guard*. At least, I did, but I can't remember her name.

In fact we were not very naughty, simply because we didn't have the time. Most of our so-called sins were mere accidents. I mean, who would really want to kick a hole in a wastepaper basket? Or lose her homework (pinched by one very mean girl who finally got her just deserts at the hands of the juniors)? We were all of us, from the San, in awe of the prefects and if we couldn't remember the words for the collect for the week, it was because we were stupid, not wicked.

I don't know what it is about punishment that causes the person who dishes it out never to let their victim forget it? It was not unlike Africa in that respect, but at least Gyll and I were used to it. At Glenlea, we were sent to bed on Sundays after early church. Well, bed is quite a nice place, really. It was dull, at first, not to be allowed to have books to read, but there was always the chance of secretly writing poems, a small pencil and piece of paper being a lot easier to conceal than a book. In stolen time, I wrote a very sentimental play about an extremely romantic character, who could easily have been mistaken for Shelley. The plot was just that bit familiar. I sometimes even read my stories (and real corkers they were too) to the girls after lights out, when they asked me, with the aid of a torch. But it was the achievement that was the thing. Not too easy, either, considering how time consuming was our programme for the day. We had had to get fully dressed for breakfast, tie and all, then retire to bed after church. Then get similarly dressed again for elevenses, followed by back to bed, and so the day went on, up and down, down and up and down, dressed, undressed all the day like yo-yos and forbidden to speak to anyone, also all day.

Gating (stopping us going out) was the worst, but that could only happen twice a term because we were only allowed out three times a term, and one of those was half term when, if we were lucky, we did actually get back to Fairford. In any event, very few people came to take us out. It was a long journey and lots of rationed petrol coupons required for the brief five hours that we had to smell the air of freedom. Mummy never came; Daddy did a couple of times and also my cousin John, the young naval officer on whom most of the girls had a crush.

Brazenly they would hang out of the front windows of

Glenlea, just to catch a glimpse of him, especially as he was a very handsome officer in a very handsome uniform. But sadly for them he never looked up, or if he did, it must have been a very subtle glance, because we never saw him, but one or two girls claimed that he did look, at them. Cousin John took it upon himself to inform us about the facts of life from a naval point of view, and felt that he should tell us what young girls like us should know about the sort of man who might want to take advantage of us, and how to take precautionary action should they try. Advantage? We didn't really know what that meant, but we did wonder a little if Daddy might have sent him as his representative – a quiet word in your ear dear chap – that sort of thing, and here's a fiver to take yourself and the girls out to a decent lunch. He might have added, that if he wanted to take us to the Plough, in the High Street, he could by-pass one of Coll's forbidden roads by driving in to the place from the back, where there was a car park.

The baths may have been a bit Victorian, but so were the lavvies. Marvellous they were, with names like 'The Cascade' and 'The Deluge', all made so appropriately by Messrs Thomas Crapper and Sons. The cisterns were fixed high above the pedestals, with their fine mahogany seats, and were adorned with lovely brass chains to pull, which in their turn had drop-shaped white china handles. If it had not been for the overwhelming odour of Jeyes Fluid (which reminded me of 12, Bryant Road) and the hard crackly paper (Bronco, but luckily not torn-up newspaper which left inky stains), which was kept in boxes fixed to the wall, we might have been in Paradise, since it was the only place that you were ever on your own.

Mrs Garner held court in her sitting room-cum-study just by the front door.

'Come' she would call, when we knocked before entering to say the obligatory goodnights.

She took this daily opportunity to discuss anything pertinent to the day and issued praise or punishment accordingly. The holed wastepaper basket (Puffy) or smiling at a choirboy (me — how luckly that she never heard of the tea invitation) warranted an exclusion from this ceremony until we were judged to be sufficiently repentant.

'You may come to me to say goodnight' was the signal of forgiveness. There were of course other punishments given out, but since the subject bores me I will not bore you.

I am not intending to go on too much about life at school, but I do need to include the inter-house singing competition.

Have you ever heard Handel's 'Let the Bright Seraphim in Burning Row, Their Loud uplifted Angel Trumpets Blow' from *Semele*, with words by John Milton? Well, I should advise you to give it a miss unless it is sung by a top-rank soprano. We were not top-rank sopranos. None of us nine juniors was even a fledgling soprano and only a couple of us could sing in tune, although fortunately the competition included all the senior girls in Glenlea. But there was not one single girl who took music.

'Susie,' Mrs Garner said, with a certain amount of doubt and rather reluctantly, I thought. 'As you are the only gel taking piano, you will have to do the accompaniment.'

I looked at her with disbelief, as did Gyll.

'But I can't. I can't do it.'

'Well dear, you will just have to try.' She was adamant.

I really couldn't sight read, except with agonising slowness and certainly not in tandem with singers of surpassingly awful timing. About the only time that I had practised seriously was at home, when playing, rather repetitively, Chopin's *Marche Funèbre*, just under Daddy's bedroom. He told me to shut up.

I looked at the music and played a note or two, slowly and carefully.

'We can't sing *that*,' cried Gyll, 'it's far too high.'

'Well, can any of us sing that high?'

I suppose that about twenty of us were picked by the prefects to perform our best. Each of us had a go at trying to reach a high note. We managed just about halfway, the rest was a squeak.

'Well,' said Mrs Garner, with near despair in her voice, 'you will just have to practise. Sing scales or something.'

It was fairly clear that she knew as little about singing Handel as we did.

What a useless waste of time, and which sadist in the Music Section had chosen this totally inappropriate song? It beggars belief.

Still, I feel sure that you will have guessed by now that we did not win the competition, held in the Princess Hall. In fact it was won by one of the 'good' houses, which had managed to get hold of a recording to play on the gramophone. Blatant cheating, we thought, but they also had excellent voices I suppose. Needless to say, Glenlea came bottom, but we were quite used to that by now.

'Oh well,' said Puffy, 'it's not as if we will ever have to sing it again.'

The next year there was a play in Greek. Oh well, you can't win them all.

Other things.

'Will all the gels over fourteen or who have not yet attended Doctor Griffiths's lecture, attend at the Princess Hall at five o'clock this afternoon.'

Oh goody-goody, that will let us off prep.

We duly filed into the front seats, about eighty of us, smiling a little nervously because no one had explained to us the purpose of the lecture or what was in store for us. As it turned out it was no surprise that the senior girls had sniggered at the very mention of Doctor Griffiths's name.

Behind us was a large, humming lantern-slide projector. In front of us, on the platform, was a big silver screen on a wobbly stand.

Doctor Griffiths walked in. He held a long cue for waving at the pictures which would shortly be projected on to the screen (from an assistant towards the back of the assembly) and he held a little castanet in his other hand which he could click to signal to the projectionist (who must have been staggered) when he wanted the next picture.

'Now girls,' he said, 'I am here to talk about things that you should know about. About growing up. After all, you are all growing up, are you not?'

Dr Griffiths signalled for his first diagram. It resembled the abdomen of a body; female.

'Now then,' he said pointing with his cue, 'this is your womb: you all know what that is,' he added hastily. 'And these are your ovaries,' he continued, airily indicating the general region of the tummy.

The drawings meant absolutely nothing to me.

He waffled on vaguely for about half an hour using euphemisms that would defy credulity. He did not actually say anything of any use concerning the subject of sex though he did say something about monthly periods which of course most of us had been having for at least two years.

'So you understand, there are terrible diseases you can catch if you are not very careful and clean and stay virgins. You must save yourselves for marriage.' And then he added brightly, 'And this is what it is all about.'

Up popped a final picture of two frogs, one on top of the other, stuck to the side of an aquarium, looking very bored.

'There now,' he said, 'I think that is about all. Goodbye girls,' and he swept off the platform.

We eyed each other in dismay. We had not the remotest idea what he had been talking about. It is only in retrospect that I have realised that he did not once mention the words vagina or penis, though he had said something about a maidenhead, which I had thought was a fern that Daddy had cultivated in the greenhouse at Watford.

The next day, after I had surpassed my gymnastic prowess by struggling all of two feet up from the knot at the bottom of the rope that we were supposed to climb, a skill that sadly I had never succeeded in mastering in Bulawayo despite much coaching from Mavis, I spoke to Gyll. Following the rope failure, Miss Townsend, or Tigger as we called her, a trim, tough, sadistic gym mistress not known for her sympathy towards fat, soft girls, really had it in for me.

'Do you know what Tigger made me do today? She made us sit and put our heads down between our legs and on to the floor. Mine couldn't reach so she knelt on my back. I thought I would split in half, it hurt terribly.'

'Well, what about it?'

'It's just that I wonder if I am still a virgin, you know, what Doctor Griffiths said about hymns or something. I think I've lost mine.'

'Hymen,' Gyll corrected me, looking at me with disdain. 'Don't be stupid, you have to do what the frogs did in the tank in order to be de-flowered.' She shook with laughter.

I had an instant vision of Mrs Marsh dead-heading the roses at 12, Bryant Road.

'Oh, you're so silly,' Gyll sighed. 'Don't you remember Margo's mother's book? That was what he was talking about.'

'Oh. Oh that.'

So much for the success of Doctor Griffiths and his lecture.

I wonder, I just wonder how the other girls ever got on with sex.

And another thing, just as I think of it. You can't have about nine hundred girls banged up in one place without checking on their health, their weight, their size, their figures and their frames, now can you? But who would you choose to fulfil this task? Dr Costello, of course!

Of much the same build as the dreaded Miss Blandford, Dr Costello, with her severely cropped hair, white coat and stethoscope round her neck, just seemed an ideal woman to intimately examine young ladies. Well, she certainly examined me, measuring my bust and my hips and feeling my chest as I had to breathe in and out, deeply, until I almost fainted. I trust she would have been able to catch me.

Her conclusion was that I was fit enough to endure another winter at school and that my right shoulder was lower than my left on account of having to carry my heavy sack everywhere. As this same problem occurred with many girls, she prescribed that we should carry our sacks in our right hands on Mondays and Wednesdays and Saturdays and in our left hands on the other days. So simple, thank you, Dr Costello.

The best part of the week was the two hours on a Saturday evening when we were allowed to do what we liked. And what did we like? We liked dancing!

We had a wind-up gramophone and some super records, 'A String of Pearls', 'I'll be Seeing You Again (in all the old familiar places)', 'Sentimental Journey', and 'At the Saturday Dance', of course. How we danced and how we loved it. Mind you, some of us (not me, may it be said) looked a bit incongruous with our heads wrapped up in turbans, suffering the indignity (good word under the circumstances) of having noxious and probably very environmentally and medically bad substances soaked into our hair to kill the nits, which I sometimes doubted were there at all. It was probably just Nurse wishing to pull a girl down a peg or two.

Puffy and I, who by this time had become firm friends, jitterbugged and jived and generally flung ourselves about with an abandon and energy never to be seen on the games fields.

We spent quite a lot of our school holidays together, usually in Fairford. We had walked together from Glenlea to Coll most days, since it was obligatory to find someone with whom to walk the dangerous pavements. Never alone. In which case, any girl unfortunate enough not to find a partner had to 'tag' along. This poor unwanted creature was made to walk a few paces behind the pair and not permitted to speak. Girls can be so nice to each other. Puffy and I sat next to each other at table. We were even in the same dormitory. It is a wonder that we were not separated, since girls were not allowed to become too close, unlike some members of the staff, who were usually those who were also the least kind to us. Why? For goodness' sake, whatever was wrong with a close friendship?

Towards the end of the term, Gyll and I were both summoned to Miss Popham's study.

'Whatever for? What have we done now?' Gyll asked, annoyed and puzzled.

We knocked on the door nervously.

'Come.'

Popeye was once again sitting in her delightful, friendly, winning way, on the floor, by the fire (oh yes, she had highly prized coal), with smelly Peter close to hand. Obviously she wished us to see her as being very informal and indicated that we should sit on the floor beside her. I wasn't too keen on the idea because I always got pins and needles, so I just hung there.

'Sit,' she said crisply, like a latter-day dog-trainer. So we obeyed.

'Well, you two are not doing too well at the moment.'

Ah so? This was news to me and I could see that Gyll looked bewildered as she had done rather well in her mid-term exams and was expecting praise, not criticism.

'We have been discussing your progress at College, at the staff meetings and quite frankly have found both your performances to be unsatisfactory.'

Perhaps playing bad cricket had counted against us, combined with the sheer awfulness of the Handel? My accompaniment had been dire.

'Yes well,' she continued, 'we have come to the conclusion that you are worrying about your situation at home.'

To be honest, I had given up on those thoughts long ago and all I was concerned with just now was getting through a day at college without some punishable mishap.

'So I have spoken to your father. He is indeed a very unhappy man. He has asked me, since he finds this too difficult himself, to inform you that he and your mother are divorced.'

'When?' asked Gyll in a whisper.

'Oh, it was three years ago,' she said rather casually, I

thought, as if she really did not want to say anymore. 'I am sorry.' She stood up to indicate that the interview was over and as if, having imparted her news, there would somehow be an improvement in our 'performances'. End of subject.

Oh Daddy, you BASTARD.

When Gyll and I had recovered from the blow, we decided to ask Daddy who had custody of us. In most divorce cases, I understand, the parents argue as to who is to have custody of the offspring. In our case, they had argued as to who was not to have custody.

A lot of unexplained things then fell into place. So that was why . . . The list was long and so glaringly obvious when we examined it, that we felt utter fools for not realising the true situation before. Had you?

But still, we had each other and we agreed between us to keep the whole shameful business to ourselves. We would tell no one.

15

In the spring holidays, while we were lurking on the low dry-stone wall by the bridge over the river Coln, hoping to find a 'close relationship' with the Americans, two of them, young USAF airmen, clearly at a loose end, stopped to chat with us. But we were cool and made a good show of looking indifferent, while inside our hearts were racing.

They were not especially good-looking, but they were very polite and probably rather innocent. They were certainly pretty young, maybe seventeen or eighteen, possibly having bluffed the Army Enrolment Corps about their ages. They had lovely uniforms and big smiles and one of them produced some chewing gum from a buttoned-down top pocket.

They were obviously not the boys/men of our dreams, but they were certainly better than nothing and what type of young men anyway would ask a couple of lumpy and even younger girls to go with them to see Oxford? Maybe to the movies?

'What, the cinema?'

'We'll have to ask Daddy.'

Rick and Bob came with us to see Daddy. They had evidently done their homework on the instruction book for American Servicemen in England.

'You remember that in America you like people to conduct themselves as we do, and to respect the same things. Try to do the same for the British and respect the things they treasure.'

While Daddy did not exactly treasure us, he enjoyed

playing the part of the Victorian father. He frowned when Rick and Bob came with us to the Manor Farm House and with old world gravity, shook hands with Daddy, who was not, at that moment, in the best of humours.

'Oh, all right, you may go tomorrow, but I will be at the station at six o'clock to meet you off the train. Make sure you are there.' He sounded quite menacing.

'Of course, Daddy, of course. We promise,' which would not give us a very long time to go to the movies or to see the sights, but it was better than nothing.

The next day we took an early train, which in those days meandered through Lechlade, Little Faringdon, Filkins, Alvescot, Carterton, Witney, Eynsham, Cassington Halt and I daresay a few other stops, but I forget since Dr Beeching axed the railway in the 1960s.

So we were a bit late getting to Oxford. On arrival we wasted precious moments looking for a milk bar we had heard of but which probably only existed in our imaginations. We had never been to a 'soda-fountain' before (which was what those girls who had been to America called them), but we thought it would be a very up-to-date thing to do, the sort of thing we saw happening in American films.

In the event, we had to give up the vision of us sitting on high stools against a bar sipping a milkshake through a straw, or even going to the cinema as the programmes were all showing at the wrong times, and we had to settle for something rather more sedate in the matronly tea rooms of Elliston and Cavell. It was situated opposite the Martyrs' Memorial, which was the only monument that we were to see that day. Certainly we did not see any college greens or stone spires, which are generally the main focus of a visit to Oxford. But by way of compensation, while we had tea, there was a trio of splendid ladies in floral printed frocks, who played the pre-war songs that Mummy used to hum. Mummy had a small collection of records then, which she played on her wind-up gramophone with a loud-speaker, that had the picture of the patient little white dog, ears cocked, listening in to His Master's Voice.

After tea we found a park bench and the Americans gave us some more chewing gum. Where, oh where was the soda fountain of our dreams? In Hollywood films I guess.

Rick and Bob were very mannerly but they did not have much conversation. Eventually we dragged ourselves back to the station. It was, in any case, beginning to get very cold.

After drinking so much tea, I needed to go to the Ladies' Room. I emerged, quite unconcerned, having spent a few critical moments posing and pouting in front of the waiting-room looking-glass, only to find Gyll, Rick and Bob on an empty platform. The train had chugged in and chugged out all in the twinkle of an eye, without us.

'Where have you BEEN?' Gyll shouted at me.

Calamity. Gyll burst into tears and the two airmen looked devastated. I think they were as much in awe of Daddy as we were.

'Look, look here, here's a handkerchief. Now don't cry,' just like in a film.

'Hey, young lady, dry your eyes.'

Gyll sobbed afresh. I had a vague idea of what she was planning.

'There must be another train?' Rick asked, with more than a hint of apprehension in his query.

'Hell, no,' replied Bob, 'this is England,' as if he thought England had no trains – and no heating in them to boot – though clearly the United States had more than enough.

'T-Take a taxi.' Gyll stopped crying. 'Yes, that's what

we will do.' She looked determined. I felt that I had watched this scene before.

'But we haven't got any money,' I wailed, guessing what she wanted me to say next.

'Hell yes we do, babe,' said Rick, as if he had found a plum in his pie. 'We'll pay.'

Straight into her trap.

'Oh no,' said Gyll in a sugar-wouldn't-melt-in-her-mouth sort of way. 'We couldn't possibly.'

We knew very well the saying that the Americans were over-sexed and over-paid and over here. We didn't know anything about the sex, but we both knew what over-paid meant. It meant that Rick and Bob had money, though the handbook counselled them not to throw it around. That was the bit that we liked. The money. So we did. We accepted their offer.

With the encouragement of Rick and Bob, the taxi-driver pushed on the pedals and we careered the twenty-four miles, Witney, Kingston Bagpuize, Bampton, Lechlade and the others, in what must have been record time. Surely faster than the train, with all those stops. The driver, urged on by our pleading, clearly thought we were quite batty.

It was only five minutes past six when we swerved into the station yard at Fairford. The train was there, Daddy was not.

We begged the taxi-driver to carry on to our house on the outskirts of the village. He dropped us off outside the Railway Inn, at which point Bob and Rick each parted with what must have amounted to a couple of weeks' pay, which we hoped they could afford.

All together we snailed our way up through the farm-yard. The big house was very dark and very quiet. Daddy's Rolls was parked in the garage, which in a way was encouraging.

The front door of the house was locked. We went round to the back. Locked. We thought that Margaret must be somewhere inside to hear us, but she wasn't, and nor was David's pram, which was usually kept on the back porch. All the windows were locked. We rang the bell. We banged on the door. No answer.

'He must have gone to bed?' I asked doubtfully and with mounting alarm.

'What, at six o'clock? That really is the giddy limit.'

We stood there and gazed at the shuttered grange, as we imagined heroines in a romantic novel might have done. We sighed.

'Well, babes, I guess we'd better be getting along,' said Rick, after some minutes of shifting from one leg to another.

'Guess so,' said Bob. 'Yep.'

We felt awful. I shouldn't think that they felt much differently.

When they finally sloped back down to the gate and disappeared round the corner without a backward glance, we both began to cry. It wasn't so much because we knew we would never see them again, as that we simply did not know what to do next. We banged on all the doors again and shrieked up to the closed, curtained windows. Nothing.

Eventually we went and crouched, cold and miserable, in the summer house on the front lawn.

What seemed like hours later Gyll asked, 'What's the time?'

'After half-past seven. Nearly eight.'

'I'm hungry.'

'So am I.'

At last the light came on over the porch and the front door opened slowly. Daddy was framed against the hall light.

'Come on in.'

'We are so sorry, Daddy,' Gyll cried. 'Awfully sorry. Anyway, it's all Susie's fault that we missed the train. We were at the station on time, Honest Injun, but she went to the Ladies' Room and we couldn't find her. We couldn't very well leave her there – not really. But it is all her fault.'

Judas! I looked at her and knew I would never forget such a betrayal, but I did have to admit to myself that it was just a little bit my fault. But they could have come looking for me. Where else could I have been? 'We did come in a taxi, and Rick and Bob did pay for it and we were only five minutes late.'

'I'm sorry, Daddy, we did try,' I added hopefully. I don't think he listened.

I cannot imagine what he thought we had been doing all afternoon, but it certainly wasn't sitting on a park bench in Oxford.

Where lay the blame? There was just no understanding between us. None. We were a couple of unlovable aliens from another planet and he was our wicked father.

After we had been allowed into the house Gyll dared to ask, 'Is there anything for supper?'

'No, there damn well isn't,' Daddy answered grimly. 'Margaret has gone to see Dolly, and I told Christine that she could have the evening off. I didn't think you two were coming back.'

Really?

We looked at each other uneasily. Our one hope of salvation had lain with Mrs Dalton, and here in our moment of need she had deserted us.

'You'd better go to your room,' he said with finality.

'But I'm hungry,' I whined.

'Too bad. Go,' he said coldly and with a new disdain in his voice.

Gyll said angrily, 'You don't like us. It isn't fair. You don't understand. I hate you, I wish I'd never come home.'

I started to cry and blundered past him, up the staircase. But Gyll stood defiant, arms akimbo, which for one bizarre moment reminded me of the copy of the picture of the Stag at Bay that hung in the darkened sitting room at 12, Bryant Road.

'No wonder M-M-Mummy doesn't want to come home. You're always drunk and nasty.'

I was flabbergasted. How dare she?

Daddy was momentarily put off his stride but then his hurt and anger came to the fore and he made as if to strike her. Gyll yelped and fled up the stairs after me, Daddy gave chase.

We dashed into the genteel, country-chintz-style bedroom and slammed the door shut, locking it as we did so. Gyll seized the telephone handpiece, installed on the green commode that separated the beds. She dialled the operator who, of course, knew all about what was going on in the lives of her subscribers – the people of Fairford – on account of her 'tuning-in', as Dick used to call it, to our telephone conversations which passed through her switchboard.

'What shall I say?' Gyll asked me, terrified at the noises off.

'He's mad,' I said, 'and dangerous. Call the police.'

'You think so?'

'Yes, hurry up. He's breaking the door.'

Daddy hammered in through the splintered wood just in time to hear her say, '999 please, Operator.'

Heaven only knows what the telephonist must have thought was going on. Just Mr Edmonds in one of his tempers.

With a lunge, Daddy tore the wires from the wall socket.

'You little shits,' he bellowed. I didn't know what a shit was but could surmise that it was something pretty bad, because of the way he looked at us with such malevolence.

It was all too clear that he had been goaded beyond endurance by these two horrendous daughters.

He cast an angry, baleful eye towards our trunks that lay ready packed for our return to the loathsome Ladies' College the next day for the start of the next term.

He gave a long sigh, stepping over the bits of broken door and mangled wires.

Gyll and I sat on my bed, close to each other, tears cascading down on to our necks, howling until we no longer had the will left to continue. We finally dropped asleep, still dressed in our special clothes for Rick and Bob, no longer even hungry.

We awakened to the ghastly realisation that we were due to return to school that very afternoon. How pleased Daddy would be.

We sat on our beds, facing each other, and tossed a coin into the air, ignoring the trail of destruction around us.

'Heads or tails?'

'Heads we go back to school; tails we run away.'

'It's tails.'

We looked at each other, appalled, but a bet was a bet.

I took my suitcase, packed ready for school and walked out of the bedroom, without, as they say, a backward glance.

Gyll and I – and I really don't know why we did not walk down the drive, as there was no one about to see us – swung our cases on to the garden wall and dropped, with our luggage, on to the empty road.

We concealed our things behind the Railway Inn car park and walked purposefully to the post office, which was then in the main square. We both emptied our meagre accounts, which did not add up to much.

'Going shopping then dear?' the postmistress enquired. Like the telephone operator, she knew all that went on in Fairford, because what she didn't pick up from the post office accounts and gossip over the counter, she learnt from the switchboard tuner-in, and vice versa. It was just good luck that she had not had time yet today to gossip about yesterday's strange happenings at the Manor Farm House.

'Your Daddy knows then,' she investigated further.

'Of course. He's driving us. Look, he's out there,' and Gyll pointed vaguely in the direction of the cars parked in the marketplace. One black saloon car looks much like another, from a distance.

'Have a nice time then, Miss Gyll, Miss Susie,' the post-mistress said trustingly.

Once outside we set off at a good trot towards our hidden cases.

'Phew,' I said at last, relieved, but unhappy at having told a lie. Dor-Dor, apart from discussing the ethics of telling lies, had taught us that God would most certainly know and then come to judge us.

Running away had always been an option, ever since we had left Watford in 1940, but as I said earlier, it is better when you have somewhere to run to.

'Now where?'

Gyll said briefly, 'London.'

'And then – Mummy?'

Gyll nodded her head firmly but neither of us was sure if Mummy would be too pleased to see us.

'Yes, let's get a move on.'

★   ★   ★

Paddington Station was a bit daunting. We were afraid that Daddy might have been to the Police and labelled us as 'missing'. Maybe the police might pick us up and throw us into gaol.

We decided to leave the station as quickly as possible, but we couldn't afford a hotel so we struggled with our cases towards Hyde Park. The iron railings had been taken down, as part of the war effort, to make guns and other armaments. It made it easy to get in and we soon found a shrubbery where we could hide ourselves on the damp earth underneath. We spent an absolutely miserable night, even though we clung together for a scrap of warmth. It was desperately cold.

Gyll tugged at my coat in the dullness of the grey dawn. 'I've got toothache.'

'You can't have toothache.'

'I do and it's awful.' She held her hand to the side of her face but it did not look very swollen to me, not like in the cartoons I had seen, with the white bandage tied round the chin with a neat knot on top of the head.

'We'll find a dentist when we get to Mummy's,' I suggested.

'That's just it. I don't think that I can wait that long.'

'I'm going to phone Mummy. I know she would want us to go there. There must be dentists in Scarborough.'

'Well, you phone then,' said my Leader.

We crawled back to the hostile grimness of Paddington and squeezed ourselves into a smelly telephone box.

When Mummy came to the phone she sounded harassed. 'Yes. What is it?'

It was not an auspicious beginning.

'Mummy, we're at Paddington Station. We want to come and see you.'

'What now?' she asked sharply. 'Now?'

'Um, yes.'

'It's not a very good time for me here just at the moment.' And then she asked quickly, 'Does Daddy know that you are at Paddington?'

I didn't answer. I couldn't think what to say.

'Don't tell me that you have run away?'

'Well . . .'

'Listen, sweetheart, I would help, but I can't. The most terrible things have been happening in Poland, in Warsaw, and everything is in a mess here. They need me. I can't have you here, I really can't.'

'But we need you too,' I whispered.

'I know, but you have Daddy and a home to go to. These soldiers have nothing, no one; they have lost everything and they can't go home. Anyway, it's my job to look after them, and I can't look after you two as well, I'm sorry.'

But she didn't sound all that sorry, not for us, anyway.

'Oh,' and I put down the receiver.

Gyll looked as if she had known all along what would happen. She took the telephone from me and dialled Fairford.

'Yes. Where are you, for God's sake?'

Gyll didn't answer. She breathed heavily down the mouthpiece. She waited.

'Just tell me where you are.'

'No.'

There was a long pause.

Daddy said, 'Look, I'm sure we can work something out. Only please come home.'

'Home?' She looked at me and winked. 'That's just it, we won't be coming back to "home", it will be going back to school. And in any case, that place you call "home" isn't home at all. It's horrible and you don't like us and we just want to be somewhere else.'

'Listen. Come back. Things will change, I promise. You needn't go back to that school, I promise,' he repeated, 'only come home.'

He sounded heartbroken, as if he really cared.

'Honest Injun?'

'Honest Injun.' We had to believe him. 'Honest Injun' was an unbreakable promise in our family.

Well you must have already guessed that by the time we got home his attitude had changed not a little.

'Look,' he wheedled, 'I know I said that you didn't have to go back to Cheltenham, but the fact is I've already paid the term's fees, fifty-four pounds for each of you. Up front. If you take into account the tax I pay on my income, that comes to a king's ransom.' He held up his hands to stop Gyll intervening. 'What say we get our money's worth, just for this term? After that it will be up to you,' he added persuasively.

Oh snake! How could he?

He continued, 'If it would make it any better I could telephone Mrs Garner and say that you can't come back for a week because David has measles. You're in quarantine.' Then he added seeing Gyll's expression, 'That would do wouldn't it?'

'Two.'

He sighed. That would mess up his sleeping arrangements not only with his houseguests, but also with the redoubtable Christine.

'Just for this one term,' Gyll said.

'Yes, just for this term. Do give it a try, please?'

The third term at Cheltenham was not so bad because we knew it would be the last. We hoped soon to be discussing where we would go next, but the prospectuses did not appear. I felt bad about leaving Puffy and my other friends, but I thought that perhaps Puffy's parents would change her school too. It seemed reasonable. But what did not seem reasonable was Daddy's unwillingness to talk about schools at all, not that we saw him on our first out Sunday as he said he couldn't come, so instead we went out with Jane Bowen's father, because it was her birthday and he made a bit of a party out of it for her.

When we finally did see Daddy, it became perfectly clear that he had no intention of keeping his word.

However, after a lot of recrimination and tears and shouts of liar and betrayer, he did finally offer a kind of olive branch. The promise was to give us an income each of £350 a year when we left school, providing we had finished all our necessary exams and moved on to higher education. I can't think why we actually believed him, but it was, to be fair, one of the few things he did honour. What he did not say, of course, was that he had to let us have the money anyway because it had been left to us in a trust, but lots of people do genuinely believe that the ends justify the means and, sadly, most people have their price if they really think about it. Anyway we had nowhere else to go. No one really wanted us. This is being very pragmatic and I hope you don't despise me for it. I am not going to make any more excuses. It is what happened.

Just after our frightful row with Daddy and at the time that he promised us that we would be heiresses – well, nearly! – one very significant letter, which had taken a long time, did arrive at Fairford.

Gyll read it briefly and handed it to me.

12, Bryant Road,
Bulawayo.

December 22nd 1944.

Dear Gyll and Susie,

I hope that you are both alright, and getting on well at your school. It must be very grand. I had a letter from your mother some time ago, when you were still with us here in Bulawayo. She wanted me to talk to you about what she said in her letter then, but Dor-dor and I decided that it was really up to your mother and father to tell you both about their divorce. We did not want to make you unhappy here when it was always possible that you might not be going back to England. Then you went straight from Kingsmead to Cape Town and I did not have the opportunity. By the time you get this letter you will know all about it, I am sure. I have always felt very sorry about my own part in this, in that when your mother wrote to tell me that she had met an officer on the ship on the way back to England, and had had that very brief liaison with him, I wrote to her to say how very sorry I was that he had been drowned in that naval battle very shortly afterwards. My mistake was to send the letter of condolence to the wrong address, and your father, perhaps thinking that I was writing with news of you two, opened it. I must apologise to you both for such a dreadful mistake. I just want to say now, if it is any comfort to you, because I do not suppose that there is anyone else that can talk to you about these things, that I was very sorry that your father decided to divorce your mother. I think he loved her very much but men do some silly things. Your mother had already told me that she was afraid that

278

she might not survive the sea voyage home, so I think that may have made her careless, but indeed her friend did drown, so it was not such an unlikely thing to happen.

I am writing today because it is her birthday and when you see her, will you give her my best wishes and say that I hope that she is happy. She must be very busy with all the fighting going on at the moment.

Mr Marsh and Dor-Dor (and Boots the dog, you remember?) all send our love,
Iris Marsh.

'Why didn't she ever tell us?' I asked.

'Perhaps she thought we already knew?'

'Oh no, she just didn't want to, couldn't, any more than Daddy could. But it doesn't really make much difference after all, does it? Mummy's away, and that's that'.

But that was not really all that. The universe had rolled upside down, but had ended up the right way for Mummy. She had been granted her freedom. The gilded cage doors had been opened. Not only had she joined the FANYs, but she had regained confidence in her scarred body and was able to fall in love again, which she did.

The affair had been such a difficult adventure for her. It is easy enough to fall in love, but with a scarred body like hers, almost impossible to think of undressing and making love. Eric the sailor had given her the courage to love again, the most valuable gift.

My father, with the utmost stupidity, and egged on by his brother, Stuart, who had been divorced twice by then, decided to teach her a lesson. He divorced her, believing that in doing that his honour would be satisfied, while she would be humbled and would return to him before the end of the year. He loved her, he really did. How foolish could a man in love be?

Of course she did not speak much of this to me, until years later, but I surmise, that lovers apart, this time with the Poles was the most fulfilling stage of her life.

She marvelled at their bravery, these men who had already lost so much and who had so little left to gain for themselves and their families other than revenge against the enemy and pride in their own prowess at fighting the Germans, which they did with the hunger and skill of wild beasts. I would have thought that they would have felt surprise rather than loyalty towards the British, American and Russian governments as they discovered how cruelly they had been deceived by them.

It is probable that the war had touched Poland more than most of the bombed and sacked countries, but war changes us all. It had certainly changed Mummy, but in such a different way. She discovered a new self and a new ability to show that she cared and that she loved. She cared for and loved the Poles that she looked after. She told Gyll and me how proud she was of them. I am not sure how we felt about that.

I hope that she was happy. There had to be happiness somewhere.

The war transformed the lives of many British women too. They had found their freedom, could have jobs, their own bank accounts and pride in themselves.

When we did at last return to school neither of us was certain whether we had won or lost our war with Daddy. We were both pretty busy, but our paths did cross walking to and fro from Coll. to House. We swapped school news but there was none from Fairford or Fraserburgh. Nobody wrote.

16

Meanwhile in another part of the woods.

With the total destruction of Warsaw by the Germans before they left, leaving 18,000 dead and barely a building standing, the Russians entered an empty city, which made their occupation of Poland all that much easier for them. They wanted an empty Poland. It is doubtful that even before the uprising any of Mummy's soldiers' relatives could possibly have been left alive. By 1943 one third of the population of Poland had been killed or removed to slave labour camps in Germany and all the Jews had been put to death. Those that remained owed their existence only to the fact that their conquerors needed them to work, in return for which they received a meagre ration of bread, ersatz coffee and sometimes a bowl of gruel, just, but only just enough to keep them alive.

When the Allied landings began on D-Day, in June 1944, in which the Free Polish Army participated with outstanding bravery, there was a spirit of great optimism amongst the Poles in Britain. They anticipated going home even if it was only to bury their dead, not daring to think that there might be a wife or child still living in their homeland. But the hope was there.

Then it became known that those Polish Officers and soldiers of the Secret Army who had survived the fighting and destruction of Warsaw had been either executed or sent, by the Russians, as captives, to Siberian Labour Camps. This page of the history of the war has by now conveniently been forgotten, obliterated, as it were, from history and from the guilty consciences of the 'Allies'. At the Victory Parade at the end of the war, the Poles were not even invited to march with the other soldiers and airmen beside whom they had fought the enemy (particularly the soldiers at the Falaise Gap and the airmen of Squadron 303, whose braveness and skill in the air had turned round the outcome of the Battle of Britain), because Churchill did not want to offend Stalin, to whom he had given Poland. What hypocrisy.

Wacek, Mummy's friend and probable lover, who had fled Fairford on that awful Christmas night, was one of those who had still hoped in his heart that his children might possibly be alive, even, perhaps, his wife. The impossible dilemma for him was that he was deeply in love with Mummy and at the same time, if he did return to Poland when the war was over to look for his family, he would most certainly eventually be arrested and sent to join his fellow officers in the Russian Gulag. At the time that he had met Mummy there had been no possibility that he could return to Poland. The future was still an unknown dream or nightmare. There was no choice to be made. But as the War neared its end a choice arose, an impossible one everyone knew, but it existed. He was forced to consider the possibility that when the War was over he could go home, to look for his family – even if only to face imprisonment or death. Even the most loyal father and husband would probably choose, under the circumstances, to stay in Britain. But he had also to face up to what he should do about his relationship with Mummy. He needed to make a decision. In the event it proved too difficult. By more or less mutual consent they began to back away from each other.

In any case, Mummy had already begun to feel ambivalent about the relationship since she was coming to believe that she was bad luck for the people she loved.

At last she asked Wacek to leave and I think that he saw that it was the only thing to do. It broke her heart and probably his. I don't know if he went to look for his family. I don't know his fate. I do have a photograph of him and Mummy together. She used to say, in French, '*Partir c'est mourir un peu.*' It is all so bloody sad.

She carried on with her work and inside she grew smaller and smaller and less and less capable of loving anyone.

After the fall of Warsaw, her work took her to Fraserburgh, which was a large camp to accommodate all the service-men who knew now that they could never return home while the Russians occupied their land.

Gyll and I went up there in the holidays.

The buildings were mostly Nissen Huts, hooped and ribbed (like half a gigantic pipe cut in half) and from which, at the highest point, earwigs would lose their footholds and gravity would send them cascading on to our beds. I slept with cotton wool in my ears, because even though Mummy assured me that the name did not mean they crawled in, I felt that you could never be too careful.

In the mornings Mummy would climb into and set off in an enormous truck to collect supplies for the canteen.

Gyll and I, because the weather was kind to us, would stroll down to the deserted beach, to the sand, which was a sparkling silver and to the sea, icy and clear. We would find a nicely hollowed-out sand dune and bunk down out of the brisk wind which caused the coarse grass to wave like the sea. We read our books. We also chatted about the divine Poles, this one or that one; Gyll was, of course, in love again.

Fortunately we were too lazy to stroll far, since on arrival at the beach we had failed completely to see the large red sign indicating that the shoreline was mined – not that we cared much.

When we had been in Scarborough, something had happened that had had a profound effect on us, an experience not shared by any of the girls at school, who did not know much about the War anyway.

We had just been strolling along the sea front one day. There were two parked caravans, right beside the pier, or what remained of it.

Curiosity and boredom led us up to the steps leading inside. Whoever was supposed to be in charge must have taken a few moments off. We thought, perhaps, that this was a blood donors unit, an art exhibition or a travelling library.

We had entered hell, though it took a few moments to understand what we were seeing. I couldn't understand the bones. They looked like pieces of a complicated child's game. A spillikin of bones with no flesh. Photographs of the real war.

I felt sick and jumped down the caravan steps and Gyll followed swiftly.

'What – what was that?'

'Real?'

We had never heard of concentration camps and the word Holocaust was yet to be coined as an everyday word, I think. We were nearing the end of the War and some information was coming through about the unspeakable acts of cruelty that the Hun had practised on their prisoners. Now these photographs of the dead and dying had reached a couple of caravans at the seaside in Scarborough and we had witnessed them, not fully understanding how or why. We simply accepted that life was cheap and that if you could survive with the minimum of pain, then you were lucky. We did not find ourselves to be particularly lucky, though the comparisons are ridiculous. But as I said, there is no monopoly on unhappiness.

As we chatted on the Fraserburgh beach in a desultory way, Gyll suddenly sat up, and brushing the sand from her hands, said, 'Oh crikey, that thing we saw in Scarborough, that was about something in Poland wasn't it?'

'Not Poland?'

'Yes, yes, that concentration camp. It must have been Poland. It had a funny name. Auschwitz?'

'Do you mean that the soldiers here might have had their families there?'

'What about Wacek?'

When we asked Mummy for an explanation of the desperate photographs she had said that one day, when she had more time, she would explain. But she hadn't and now, having begun to put two and two together, we buttonholed her.

'Mummy, you know those photographs in Scarborough? In the caravans?'

She frowned. 'Mm?'

'Well, were they Poles?'

'Perhaps, some.'

'But there were children.'

'Yes.'

Wacek's children? His wife? Just corpses, living and dead.

She sighed.

Poor Mummy.

Poor Wacek.

Poor Poles.

In yet another part of the woods, we were back in Fairford for Christmas. No question of Mummy coming home this time. Daddy was in an unusually ugly temper. It did not take long to find out why. He came into the kitchen while we were still having breakfast. Whether he had received a telephone call or a letter, I don't know. But bad news had arrived.

'Your mother', he said, standing in the doorway, 'your mother has made a fool of herself again.'

'What? What's happened?' Apprehension was written all over Gyll's face.

'What has happened is that she is in hospital, Bridge of Earn near Perth, I think. Anyway, she tried to kill herself.'

'Kill herself? She won't die?' – please God.

'Die? I should think not,' Daddy shrugged.

We trembled.

'But Daddy, shouldn't we go – I mean, can we go and see her?'

'No'.

'But Daddy –' Gyll insisted.

'No', and he turned away and closed the door. Gyll started to cry. We sat at the table, speechless for a minute or two, feeling, I suspect, as sorry for ourselves as for her.

'Kill herself?' I asked again, 'and why?' Gyll and I had no one to ask for help and we certainly did not have enough money to travel all the way to Perth. She was helpless and we were helpless too, continuing to sit at the table, crying.

Later, when Margaret came in to tidy up the breakfast, we tried to tell her, between our sobs, but we didn't think that she really understood.

'Dere, dere, Gylly, Susie, your Mummy loves you.' She often said that but we were not sure any longer if she really believed it. 'I tink she must be ill again, but she'll get better, you see,'

Again? Nobody had mentioned her being ill before now.

Then Daddy came back.

'I've spoken to her doctor. She has been treated for

some time now for difficult reasons. She has been dragging her left leg, a sort of thing coming from her mind. There's no particular medical reason for her limping, nothing that any doctor can find medically wrong with her. Just attention seeking, I think. Anyway, they are treating her for depression and keeping a close watch on her. Silly fool,' he added, as if anyone should be able to snap out of a depression, just like a snap of the fingers. We thought about her terrible accident, leaving us in Africa, Wazec, Warsaw, the betrayal of her Poles by Churchill and Roosevelt, her brave, brave Poles killed in battles all over Europe and north Africa, and now the end of the war soon to come. She would not be needed anymore. It was all just too much for her to bear, we decided.

So we stayed at Fairford and did not even have an address to write to her and she certainly would not write to us. We just had to wait for snippets of news from Daddy. He said that she was getting better. We were not to see her again until after the war was ended, when we went again to Scotland for another school holiday, cautious, careful and afraid. We felt that we should be looking after her rather than her looking after us.

Daddy preferred us to stay at Fairford rather than go to London and have fun, as the skies in Gloucestershire were marginally less dangerous, less likely to kill us with Hitler's latest little toy, the doodlebug. The doodlebug was a pilotless rocket/bomb. When the engine cut out it was only a few seconds until a massive explosion as it landed, mostly on populous towns. Hitler had perhaps realised that he was losing the War, and perhaps his life, and wanted to take as many of his enemies with him as possible.

One day Daddy drove us down to the Round House. It was all so beautiful with the hoar frost crystallised on the bare branches, our breath steaming in the frozen air. We stopped to open the gates at the Black Bridge and then we went across the ice-hardened fields, over the hump-backed canal bridge and into the courtyard of the cottage. It had changed.

I looked at Daddy and he gave me a half smile; rueful; wary.

He and I had arrived at a temporary cessation of hostilities, and although there was no warmth in our relationship, there was a sort of truce which we both managed to live with. I am not able to say the same for Gyll. She had been burnt deeper than me.

I watched him standing there, for once looking rather old and lost and not a little bewildered, maybe even slightly surprised to recognise, finally, what it was that he had lost. Like us, he was searching for the intangible signs of anything that we could recognise, feel or remember from those holidays before the war and I felt as desolate and sad as I had been in Africa.

I had to stop myself from crying for all the lost years, for the two little girls whose journey had started from here in 1939, and for Daddy, who waved us goodbye, so gallantly, from Watford in July 1940.

Poor Daddy, his family had become yet another casualty of beastly Herr Hitler, a family not blown away by bombs and doodlebugs but by awful partings. So many families had been flung in fragments to the far corners of the earth, places hoped to be safe from war; some not to Africa nor to America nor Canada, but perhaps only as far as the Yorkshire moors or the hills and lochs of Scotland, but nevertheless a journey too far for the separated parents and children. A million and a half children had been evacuated to live with complete strangers, while Gyll and I had been sent to an elderly aunt and her employers. I can see that we were pretty lucky with what was dished out to us.

What kind of family were we? Perhaps well enough off and perhaps aware enough to understand the secondary consequences of war; our parents would not risk death for their children at the hands of the Hun. Our family had been built on fragile pre-war building blocks of social niceties, of good manners, mutual respect and the occasional sense that God was watching out for us if we were good.

What had become of us?

We wanted back the father who had laughed while he let us ride on the bumpers of the car as he drove across the green cow-cropped fields in the summer; we wanted back the man who had so thoughtfully and gently made Martini cocktails for Mummy.

We wanted to be there where we had left off in that summer of 1939.

Poor Daddy.

He had become a stranger too.

By May 1945 Gyll had moved on to a Senior Boarding House, where the rules were marginally relaxed to give them a privilege or two over the juniors. There they worked for their Higher School Certificates and University entrance exams.

I didn't see much of Gyll at this time and Puffy had more or less replaced her as my closest confidante. At the same time I was becoming quite independent. I was even beginning to think about what I was going to do next and in view of the fact that I no longer thought of England as home any more, considered applying to go back to South Africa, to Cape Town, where Mavis was planning to train as a nurse at Groot Schur Hospital. Imagine, I had never wanted to see that place again and here I was, quite seriously thinking of going back. But I would be required to speak Afrikaans if I was to train as a nurse, and nobody in England could teach me to do that – well, that's what Daddy said.

I was in limbo land, not knowing which I disliked most, life at Fairford which was supposed to be home or life at school. Luckily we spent half our holidays with Mummy in the Polish Army camps. It wasn't the same as before because we saw these men in such a different light and felt so desperately sorry for them, but that gave us, well, Gyll anyway, the excuse of getting very close to the young, dispossessed cadet officers. At least up there we were able to escape from the sporty social life of Glos. What a contrast.

But it was at school (and by then it was not entirely unexpected) that we were told that the Germans had surrendered and that at last the War was over. It is selfish to say, but I was relieved that I was not in Scotland at that time because it would have been nearly impossible for the Poles to celebrate, even though the full horror of the Russian take-over had not yet come to light. The end of the War was only the beginning of so many more problems for Poland.

But look, we should be celebrating, dancing in the streets, hugging complete strangers, tearing down our blackout curtains and being madly happy. We should be throwing our hats into the air and shouting with joy, and laughing and crying all at once.

But oh, what did the Cheltenham Ladies' College girls do by way of celebration? Wait and I will tell you. We went to a small out-of-town cinema, I think it was called the Forum, and saw a film about a priest in China. Well, luckily that part was played by the gorgeous Gregory Peck, so something might be forgiven. And then? Well, we all stood up and sang 'Jerusalem' (a bit like the Women's Institute). Years of fear, of loss, partings, food rationing (that part was not to be over for several years), austerity, utility, sadness, bombing, telegrams from the War Office telling of the wounding or death of sons and daughters on active service, of air-raid shelters and blackout rules and shortages of almost every sort, were over and we – we celebrated by singing 'Jerusalem'. How very festive.

As we filed out of the Forum cinema, dressed in our Sunday best suits, we could hear the beginnings of the triumphal victory celebrations coming from the town centre.

Puffy and I traipsed back to Glenlea, but not before Gyll had caught my sleeve and whispered that she intended to climb out at night and go down to the Promenade to see for herself. She intended to join the revellers come hell or high water.

'But how?'

'By jumping out of the window, silly. You can come too.'

'But how can I possibly get out?' I asked pathetically.

'By using your tiny brain. Come on, you can do it.'

'Can I bring Puffy?'

'For heaven's sake no. No one must know. They'll talk.'

'Well, I don't know,' I said doubtfully. In fact, I was afraid of being caught. It was all very well for her, she had nearly finished at school, but I had years ahead.

'I tell you what to do. You go down to the basement and climb out of the games room window.'

I was horrified. The only time that I had ever done anything even remotely brave was, for a dare, to go into Mrs Garner's bedroom and take something off her dressing table, anything, just to prove to the others that I had been there. Sneaking in while Nurse was occupied bullying a girl with asthma and telling her she had better pull herself together and to stop that silly breathing, and while Mrs Garner was saying her stately goodnights, I sneaked in and seized a couple of hair pins. But that was about as brave as I ever intended to be. To climb out of a window was a challenge too far.

'Well, I'll wait for you under the lime tree. If you're not there by ten, I'll go on down by myself. Look, we went down to the cinema in Bulawayo, of course we can go down to the town here.'

I couldn't bear it. Lying there awake after lights out, with my mufti in my linen bag inside the bed, my heart beat like a ten-ton truck rumbling over a Bailey Bridge. I had put my pyjamas on over my vest, bra and pants and I had left on my socks. I forced myself to stay awake, hoping that the staff would be celebrating themselves (unlikely, if you think of it, with Nurse and her brow-beaten assistant, and the Misses Palsey and Mrs Garner all having a nice cup of tea that cheers but does not inebriate, as Dor-Dor would say), or that they might have retired early after the exertion of seeing Gregory Peck.

It was surprisingly easy to get out of the dormitory and down the corridor past Mrs Garner's bedroom and from then down the staircases to the basement. The problem was trying to get the window open. It wouldn't budge. For one awful moment I thought I might have to break the glass and looked around, feebly, for a suitable tool. But then I saw a perfectly ordinary door leading into the garden and the key was in the lock. Someone was on my side.

Gyll was waiting impatiently on the other side of the door.

'Blimey, I thought you were never going to come!'

'Well I did, so there.'

But at the last moment I couldn't. I just couldn't. I

simply didn't have the courage. Gyll looked at me while the tears rolled down my cheeks.

'Baby', she said, but not unkindly. We had been through so much together that it seemed so feeble not to go with her.

'Tell me about it,' I sniffed.

'Yes of course,' and she turned quickly from the door, down into the town with her waiting friends, and headed for the Promenade.

I could hear sounds of wild celebration, the laughter and shrieks of joy.

I wished, I just wished that we were together, but the war was really over and our lives just beginning.

That should have been something, at last, to be happy about?

A Note on the Author

SUSAN KENNAWAY was born in Watford in 1930. At the onset of the Second World War, she and her sister were evacuated to Africa. She was educated at Cheltenham Ladies' College and later at the Ruskin School of Art, Oxford. She married the writer James Kennaway, and they had four children before his death in a car accident, aged forty. Susan married Stanley Vereker on her fiftieth birthday and together they moved to the Tarn in France where Susan restores porcelain and they open their garden to the public for charity. Susan and Stanley have fourteen grandchildren and one great granddaughter. Susan Kennaway is the author of *The Kennaway Papers*; *The Yellow Duster Sisters* is her second book.

A Note on the Type

The text of this book is set in Bembo. This type was first used in 1495 by the Venetian printer Aldus Manutius for Cardinal Bembo's De Aetna, and was cut for Manutius by Francesco Griffo. It was one of the types used by Claude Garamond (1480–1561) as a model for his Romain de l'Université, and so it was the forerunner of what became standard European type for the following two centuries. Its modern form follows the original types and was designed for Monotype in 1929.